GW00864909

JULIET lives in Crete with her partner of over thirty years and two cats. She has enjoyed her travels and does inner exploration through yoga and meditation. She enjoys change and looks for the next interesting thing that life brings. The more she changes, the more still she becomes.

FLY ME TO THE MOON

FLY ME TO THE MOON

Juliet Green

ATHENA PRESS
LONDON

FLY ME TO THE MOON
Copyright © Juliet Green 2010

All Rights Reserved

No part of this book may be reproduced in any form
by photocopying or by any electronic or mechanical means,
including information storage or retrieval systems,
without permission in writing from both the copyright
owner and the publisher of this book.

ISBN 978 1 84748 566 3

Information on Astro★Carto★Graphy® and the trade name are
used with permission from Equinox Astrology.

Every effort has been made to trace the copyright holders of
works quoted within this book and obtain permission. The
publisher apologises for any omission and is happy to make
necessary changes in subsequent print runs.

Although this is a true story and depicts true events in the life of
the author, some names have been changed to protect the true
identities of persons alluded to in this text.

First published 2010 by
ATHENA PRESS
Queen's House, 2 Holly Road
Twickenham TW1 4EG
United Kingdom

Printed for Athena Press

Foreword

Juliet was born in England on the 3 July 1953 and so has a Cancer sun sign. This means she has a love of being at home, is very nurturing, is sensitive to criticism, can be moody and not able to let things go. She has an Aries moon which she has always found, alongside the Cancer in sun, a difficult combination. Juliet once expressed the fact that she only felt 'whole' in Turkish baths – a place both warm and wet. She feels at home there because her sun sign, Cancer, likes to be cool, but the sun is naturally fiery. Her moon sign, Aries, is a fire sign, but the moon likes coolness. So the hot wet environment is achieved in the baths.

In 2001 my friend Juliet told me about her idea to spend a year travelling around the world but that she wasn't sure where to go. Knowing that Juliet was interested in astrological psychology (having been on my Huber Astrology courses in Crete), I suggested she looked at Astro★Carto★Graphy® (A★C★G). This gives you a map of the different planetary influences you can experience in various parts of the world. Juliet purchased her A★C★G map and we spent a weekend investigating which planetary influences Juliet would like to experience in conjunction with what was happening psychologically in her Natal (birth) chart for the following year. From this a travel plan was put in place.

Delving deep into Juliet's Natal chart, we looked for planetary places suitable for her needs and agreed that Venus and Pluto would be appropriate planets for Juliet to experience. In Venus' influence Juliet would learn to love herself and nurture herself rather than others, which had been her previous experience. She would learn to live a life perfect for a holiday – lazy – rather than her normal busy 'doing' self. She felt that this would be the best way to start her holiday, an easy experience. Venus is about how one expresses affection and it gives a sense of self. Venus energy needs harmony, balance and unity, so doesn't like conflict. This meant that Juliet could put off decisions, especially about relationships, until things came to a head and only then would she have to confront these issues. Venus energy also evaluates experience through feelings and has a need to give value to things, people and situations, i.e. the selection process.

Juliet's Venus is in her eighth house, which is in Taurus. Taurus rules Venus which makes for an easy association. On the Ascendant her sensuality would be increased and there would be no constraints of how society might view this. This gives the reverse of Cancer being in the eighth house, which is about community and our relationship with society. The eighth house would generally require Juliet to create a good impression because the world would see and judge her according to her behaviour.

In Juliet's birth chart, Venus has only a one-way red aspect, which is to Pluto and without any blue aspects it is harder for Juliet to achieve harmony and this can lead to a feeling of irritation towards partners. Power in relationships is sought and as Pluto is masculine it can make it difficult for Juliet to get in touch with the feminine side. So there could be some conflicts for her in how she saw herself.

With Pluto, Juliet would be able to make changes she herself felt necessary and it would help her to let go of the past. This, she felt, would be a more challenging part of her travels. She made the decision to alternate between easy and difficult experiences as much as possible and this book describes her travels to just her first two major destinations, spanning a period of seven months.

Her Pluto is in the eleventh house and is about friendship based on common ideals and so there is a desire to seek like-minded people. At the same time there is a need for personal freedom and a desire to be seen as an individual. Pluto is in Leo giving enthusiasm to delve into the subconscious, bringing with it broad-mindedness.

Pluto has aspects which would provide Juliet with will power, motivation for change – even during crises – and the power to bring about transformation. In the red aspect to Venus there would be need for Juliet to have partners who were totally there for her. She would seek a perfect partner, but that could lead to a feeling of dependency in the sexual side of relationships. At another level, with a blue aspect to Neptune and Saturn, Juliet's

Pluto helps her to get the best out of her personality by helping her to look at the side she wouldn't like about herself and make transformational changes. This is helpful to Juliet's motivation in visiting Pluto.

Her journey starts with Venus, which Juliet felt would be easy and then moves to Pluto, where she thought there would be challenges and the chance to change herself for ever.

Juliet set off on her journey and kept in contact by email when she was able to. I was fascinated to hear how she actually experienced the planetary influences in the different places she visited, both on external and internal levels.

Fly Me to the Moon gives a unique perspective on travelling and I really admire Juliet for her courage to embrace all the varying experiences, good and not so good, on her journey.

Sue Parker Dip API
(Astrological Psychology Institute, Switzerland)

Introduction

The world is a well-traversed place; someone has always preceded you it seems. This is the known world. I am about to tell you of another world of exploration – a very personal one. It is available to everyone and it is accessed by Astro★Carto★Graphy, your own map of the world. This book describes how I came across this subject and my first ventures around my personal world atlas. I hope you feel encouraged to take a step into this new world to experience it for yourself. That is why I have written this book.

I was once watching an extreme sport and wondered why people engaged in it. Someone watching it too told me that, with no more world to explore, these people were exploring their own limits. Astro★Carto★Graphy lets you explore a new world without making a spectacle of yourself. Let me tell you the story.

There was a time when I was handed a gift of money and I had no idea what I wanted to do with it. As it was 'free' money, I felt I had licence to spend it how I liked. What to do? It was not enough to buy a house, too much for a car and anyway I didn't want one. Why not travel? It would get me out of the energy I was in and give me a new start.

I'll tell you, so you will understand a little history. I had the same wonderful life companion for twenty-seven years. But while we were still together as business partners, we were no longer lovers, and had not been lovers for four years. We continued to live in the same house, eat the same food and work together. We had made a successful transition, if rather bumpy at times. But I felt a bit stuck; I needed a change.

We were living an odd kind of life: seven months each year in our home in Greece and then five months in the UK. We had no home in the UK. Friends let us stay with them; we visited India (sometimes together). I realised that this was not the sort of life style that helps you to find a new partner and 'make a fresh start'. I wasn't sure I wanted a new partner yet. But I wanted something new. My father, way back, had always encouraged me to travel and that poked its head into my life. Well, there was enough money for that. After all, travel is a bit open-ended. I could go cheap (hostels) or expensive (hotels), the latter not usually so friendly – and I would be alone, not being a part of a couple on a two-week vacation.

Next came the question of where would I go? I had no urgent desire to see the Himalayas, Peru or the Pyramids; in fact, Greece is very beautiful and I love where I lived. Why go anywhere else? No – I would go. Don't let inertia get the better of you. OK, let's test out the whole idea and put a pin in the map. Ahh! The ocean. Well, what can you expect – there's a lot of it. But no, there is a small dot. The Bonin Islands (USA). South of Japan is the best way to describe their location. For only the second time in my life, I surfed the web. Now they are called Ogasawara Islands (Japan) and twenty-seven hours by ferry from Tokyo. I decided to go! My main aim on my travels was to keep warm and this was nearly tropical. And I just had to think how wet the winter is in Greece. Oh! Yes, no rain, thank you. The Cretan weather even had us scurrying to the UK each winter.

The exercise of the pin in the map I did not wish to repeat. I didn't feel it was the right way to plan a seventeen-month trip. I like a little more structure than that. Then along came my astrologist friend, Sue, and saved me further pondering. 'Astro★Carto★Graphy' was the word she whispered in my ear. Never heard of it! Well, she told me A★C★G would provide me with a way of travelling around the globe to see what it would feel like if I had been born somewhere else on the planet. A further word of explanation. You may know that, if you have a birth chart made for you, the astrologist creating it wants to know two things: when you were born and where. These are the criteria which give you your astrological data. Now if travel allowed you to experience what amounts to another birth place then this sounded exciting to me. I could experience what it would feel like to be a different person, a new me. A★C★G provides the means of knowing where to go and what it might feel like. You may have heard sometimes of couples emigrating and one person loving or hating it, or both coming back. Things just don't work out right for them when they move. Well, A★C★G provides one explanation for that: people can change by travelling.

Sue continued: 'If you travel – and stay – in another part of the world, there are different planetary influences at work there. If you go and stay for a while in another place these influences can start to manifest themselves in your life. You experience life as if you had been born somewhere else with different astrological birth data!'

'Is it like being born again?'

'Not quite, but as if you have an overlay on your original personality.' Now this sounded like travel with a difference. For me, it felt occasionally as if someone were talking over my shoulder. Hey, what is this? Did I say that? But this is getting ahead of myself.

How do you find out where all the planets were positioned when you were born and what it would be like to live where the planetary influences are different? In my case, I bought an A★C★G pack via the Internet. I supplied my date and place of birth and in return for a modest fee I received an envelope very promptly. This included a personal map of the world with a lot of lines showing all the positions of the planets at the time of my birth. In fact, each planet is shown as four separate lines, two straight and two curving. Very pretty, all in colour, with the lines intersecting each other too. I also received descriptions of what my life might be like if I took up residence in three other cities of my choice around the globe. Simple as that: armchair shopping.

The personal map showed my place and date of birth. Yes, that's me, born in Lancashire, England in July 1953. With this map, unique to me, came a general descriptive book covering what it would be like to live near the lines shown on the map. Venus on the Ascendant, moon on the Midheaven; well, they didn't mean anything to me without the little book, fortunately brief and lightweight. Everything would fit into a document folder for the travel. All I had to do was decide which lines to experience. A strange travel guide. I could travel for seventeen months! Dave, my business partner and erstwhile lover, supported the idea and I decided I would go in October 2001, the end of the Greek summer, and stay away a whole year, and more. No point in coming back to England or Greece until March 2003.

So, how come I was footloose? I think I should describe this now, otherwise the question may pop up from time to time and divert you from the plot. You may be thinking that I am an heiress or someone super-rich, and that you would be excluded from this realm of travel. Not at all! You can choose to visit a line near to where you live, or make your next choice of holiday a chance to visit a line, rather than just going to another seaside resort, skiing holiday or instead of risking your neck doing an extreme sport. But I did break my leg in four places in a traffic accident; I got knocked off my bicycle. This had actually given me the chance to stop working for a while, take up meditation and experience first-hand the healing practices I had used on other people and on myself, but never before (for me) in a situation of accident and emergency.

Three years after the accident I received a compensation package of about £32,000 for pain and suffering and 20% of the price of a new knee. Well, I will either need a whole new knee or none at all! Giving me a percentage at today's prices for something I may need in thirty years' time is just a way of closing the books on the accident. So that explains the free money. When the cheque came in the post, it felt as if the money dropped in my lap, literally. I opened the envelope and although I was expecting it, it was still a surprise and my hands, holding the cheque, dropped into my lap and I suspect for a moment I was speechless. A bit like receiving the news that a terminally ill friend has just died. The news is expected, but it's a bit of a shock all the same. The feeling of 'life isn't going to be the same any more'. I felt like that, except it was definitely all positive.

I considered my position. This could be an epic journey, alone, where I would not be known by my profession – I had no desire to work. I would be no one's partner or daughter nor a friend from the past. I might not come back! It was always understood that life changes would happen for both of us while I was away and no expectations could be made for the future.

It was now September so I still had a little time to go. I would leave home in mid-October, go to England and see my mother first. Fix things up for the travel – still to be decided. Then off!

The quest for places to visit was now on. Oh, there were some really awful astrological places 'best avoided' said the book. Maybe these were the places that caused emigrating couples to love or hate their new environments. Some of the lines sounded good, but the reality was that on my map these locations were either in the sea or coincided with cold and unattractive places. Sometimes I so wished an appetising line would go through nice places on the planet. I mean, I needed to keep warm, so going to Iceland was not on my agenda.

October came around and I travelled to England. Friends in the UK, hmmm… I had not seen for about a year… and wouldn't see them for a long time again. They must be visited! I also took a tentative travel plan to my astrologist friend, Sue. After all, she started this whole thing off. Eventually, and with further guidance from Sue, I had a plan. Sue could tell me which planetary lines I should particularly concentrate upon visiting; ones that my birth chart told her were in my life's experience this lifetime around. Yes, I believe in reincarnation. So, armed with a plan, I could now buy my round-the-world ticket.

I had decided to start in Hawaii, on the Venus on the Ascendant line, and after delays for such practicalities as tickets, money and visas I left the UK on 14 December 2001 just two days after my round-the-world ticket arrived in the post. I hadn't seen all my friends by then, but in the end you just have to go and trust that they will be understanding – and send postcards early on.

What to pack for fifteen months? Clothes for warm and wet weather, a new cagoule, less voluminous than the old one. Old clothes so that I could wear them out and buy new ones on the way. For some people holiday clothes may mean shorts and T-shirts. But I find sundresses much easier; they weigh less, dry quicker, they are easy for changing into swimwear on the beach and for that discrete pee in the countryside. And they are fun! I took 'that Lycra dress' because when I returned I would be nearly fifty and maybe 'that dress' would not feel appropriate any more. Better get some wear out of it! I also had to buy a new camera (smaller than my existing one), but the old binoculars would have to do. Then there were the twenty-four bottles of aromatherapy oils, in their wooden box, Nature Essences to use instead of antibiotics and a first aid box from my sister. Then my Reiki and Seichem notes for energy work for myself and in case I wanted to give initiations.

I had taken out a year's insurance (the time allotted to my ticket) but this didn't cover valuables above £250. Ha! Not even the camera was covered! I trusted that if this journey was meant to be then all would be well, so, against the advice of any travel guide I have ever read, I took all my jewellery. I was not sure why taking rings, etc only worn now and then was important. Maybe they would act as mementos and would give me connections to my past. Anyway, they were pretty! My mother, bless her, offered me more, but I took from her only some imitation pearls. I was not prepared to risk her valuables too.

I have hobbies too, so I took three boxes of liquid paints in glass jars and a wooden frame so that I could paint on silk. Also, of course, some silk to paint on; at least that is lighter weight than paper, and with my travel iron (!) I would be able to smooth it out. Oh, then there are the shoes and walking boots. You will have the picture: I am no lightweight traveller. I bought a suitcase with wheels – a legacy of the broken leg is an inability to carry extra weight. No backpacking for me. The only stipulation: the case had to be long enough to take the pieces of wood that make up the frame for stretching silk for painting. So the luggage would be rolling along.

I had the A★C★G information, an international hostelling card and a booklet of addresses from an organisation where women welcome women visitors, called 5W. I also packed a book on astrological signs so I could check out a new lover, should one come my way. Then the nail varnishes, little used but somehow appealing, and a box of make-up, also dusted down before packing.

I took $250 US of traveller's cheques, my MasterCard and Visa card, a couple of debit cards and off I went. My only contact with friends would be a whole year later, seeing friends in New Zealand – and that felt a long time to go!

Friends said I should contact a newspaper to sell my story over the months, sending regular bulletins, but this was to be an inner journey, finding myself after a long relationship, and I did not want the outward pressures of doing anything. It might be a vulnerable time too and, who knows, I might end up in a nasty scrape that I would not like to have to write about, knowing that people would see an unflattering angle. I needed to be unfettered. I had always tended to be a doing person – always busy, that's me. So, why add a pressure to 'do', when I could have the luxury of no work? This holiday was for being, not doing. To discover what I would be like as a person under different astrological influences and to observe very consciously those changes. The sightseeing was to be within. Hence, you may have noticed, I didn't talk of travel guides being packed. Self-consciousness for me was about observing myself in different lights, seeing what changes, which might be subtle, might occur in different astrological areas. Self-consciousness did not include having to write or think of how to write something to entertain, nor visiting the 'must see' sites.

While the planet felt well trodden by many feet before me, the A★C★G route was distinctly new territory.

I would do no work to help pay my way. This made me look carefully at my finances. I considered in the end I had about £70 a day to live on. Not a lot in Europe, probably impossible in the UK, but manageable, if I was careful. I had no idea that some places would be cheaper than others. I hadn't bought a single guidebook. All I had was my astrological text. Time to go! I can explain other things on the way.

Chapter One

GOODBYE ENGLAND. HELLO SUN AND MARS

I left Manchester Airport, saying goodbye to Dave. We were both a bit tearful and me a little fearful. Would I ever see him again? OK, we were no longer lovers, but twenty-seven years together represented most of my adult life and we have some wonderful memories and he is so supportive. A true friend.

I had been unable to set up Internet banking. I had lots of money in the bank but no fancy income or UK utility bills in my name. I was not even on the electoral register. This stopped me from changing bank and getting a new (Internet) credit card. I could grind my teeth all I might like but this is the stupidity of banking. So I had to accept that my partner would be in charge of paying my bills and, no, I did not want to have direct debit, I like to know what's on the account!

In turn, I said that if he needed any help from me in running the business, all he must do was email me and I would catch the next flight to Athens. That was it. Off I went. No time is perfect so I left, leaving behind an eighty-three-year-old mother who was not in the best of health. Would I ever see her again?

Diary 14 December 2001

Start of fifteen-month holiday. Manchester Airport, 6.30 a.m. Dave drove me here. I have the feeling of never seeing him again, but can't justify it. Slept badly – I was relaxed/excited in bouts, but my dreams revealed anxieties. My relationship with Dave feels easy but is so emotionless. I suspect I am holding something back. At one level it doesn't matter if I never see him again, but such thoughts trouble me. On my travels, I have decided to ask that the places manifest themselves safely and gently to me. But they must be obvious to me. I have been reading *Journey to Ladakh* before coming away. That describes a very spiritual journey with a

Buddhist connection. I had hoped (expected) spiritual change, and for more health techniques to manifest for me. Now I expect nothing. If I die on my journey, it doesn't matter. All will be perfect.

★

After Manchester, my first stop was London to catch the flight to San Francisco. So, heading into the unknown, San Francisco was certainly new territory for me. I felt light-headed. This was a journey into 'being' for a person who always 'did', who was always busy, always needing to finish the work before starting the pleasure, taking pleasure in a job well done. Now, I felt that I had an instruction: no work for *fifteen* months. I took little comfort in the fact that I had already managed not to work for nearly two months. After all, I had been busy with friends, family and travel logistics. A great big nothing approached. Oh!

I was not very interested in San Francisco; it was just a stop on my journey to let me buy an extra air ticket to Hawaii which was to be my first real place in this adventure. The rules of the round-the-world air tickets had changed just as I was buying my ticket. The timing was just after the 11 September attacks and so travel arrangements were altering and tightening up and Hawaii had suddenly become no longer available on the ticket, unless I chose to go there after the Caribbean. And I chose to make Hawaii my first destination, for reasons you will soon see. So, straight away, I faced an additional air fare expense that would not be covered in the £70 budget per day.

But San Francisco sounded exotic and exciting and I would not be there long. You can't go to a city like that and do nothing! I arrived in the late afternoon and tried to get a flight to Hawaii straight away, but I soon found that I needed to go into the city to visit a travel agent. This meant definitely staying overnight. Bite the bullet and book into the youth hostel.

San Francisco. I looked at my A★C★G map and saw already that I was near an unfamiliar line. In fact, two lines. Sun on the Ascendant and a little further away Mars on the Ascendant. I hadn't bothered to look at San Francisco because the A★C★G book said that you would probably need to spend some time at locations to feel their effect. But now it was worth spending a moment looking at these lines, out of curiosity. Might as well start straight away!

To précis what the book said: Mars would make me show masculine qualities of competition, sex drive, passions like jealousy and anger. I would experience feelings that change happens by fire, bridges are burned and childhood left behind. I would be clumsy (watch out!) boisterous and courageous (good). West of the line is best. (Good, I am west of the line). Of the Sun: very positive place to be, make things happen, the masculine is emphasised, and an awareness of self. I would become a radiant, self-made, joyful person building my own life and inspiring others. West is best (and again, I was west).

Really, I felt a bit flat after the flights and had no desire to do much at all, except it was Friday night and soon it would be Saturday morning when I must get to a travel agent for a flight ticket, otherwise I must wait till Monday. Time pressure already!

I *must* tell you a little about the youth hostel. I was greeted by the buzz of a security button so I could get access. No, I hadn't booked. But it seemed to be irrelevant, there was space. I couldn't take my eyes off the man at the desk, and it was not necessary to be shy. Staring seemed to flatter a man wearing black eyeliner, sporting a long, waxed, Salvador Dali moustache, black nail varnish (chipped), with black slicked-back hair, black T-shirt and trousers to match. And with a very pale skin, oh my! So this is California.

I went to the dorm, it was quite small, and unpacked what I needed. A tiny locker and a large suitcase – hmm… It felt a very quiet moment after all the transportation. Then Sara came in. In her early twenties (I was forty-eight), she was from the north of England, like me. She had been travelling for fourteen months and was to return to Warrington, England for the family Christmas. She would leave in two days, and she still had one full day and wanted to spend it sightseeing in San Francisco. She mentioned several places she wanted to see. I felt a bit over-whelmed, because I had no plans and no street map or any idea of what lay outside the door, waiting to be seen. OK, could I tag along with her? Yes!

But the best thing was, she had travelled for fourteen months and was still sane and lucid, and if she could do it – so could I! I felt she was my gateway to the world. I had just travelled from Burnley, my birthplace, about twenty miles from her parental home. So, in turn, I was her gateway to England. I took enormous comfort in this and it was emphasised by us walking over the Golden Gate Bridge together. So, I became bigger and bolder from my contact with Sara. I gained the courage I needed. Oh-ho! So was this the astrology stuff kicking in already? Maybe my bridges got burned, but nothing deleterious happened to the Golden Gate from my visit.

Photos of the day show us having lunch in a street café with me wearing a bright red pullover, and scarlet nail varnish, drinking tomato juice. Thinking of the astrology, well, to be big and bold and sun-like and masculine I would wear red, wouldn't I? Everything around us was bright and colourful and the hills really are like roller coasters. When the top of a hill arrives you just see sky until, oh, you're over and the ground way below you comes into view vertiginously. Doesn't do much for your lunch.

Sara led me around and I agreed to all her suggestions. It all sounded good: a look at the docks from where you could see Alcatraz, the prison island so near to the city that the inmates would hear city life. A ride on a street car, food in the Italian quarter and of course the walk over the Bridge. The weather was sunny and chilly, which kept us moving. But the sunshine reminded me constantly that I was near the Sun line.

I also bought my air ticket. It was a return ticket of fixed duration, three months, flying into Big Island, Hawaii. I would travel early on Sunday morning to Oakland airport for the flight, travelling by Barts, the underground rail service.

Sara asked me if I wanted to do a dummy run of the first part of the journey, walking from the youth hostel to Barts. No, I felt it had been adequately described by the travel agent and I had a map with a line on it from the hostel to the station. No need for more. Strangely, our doorman at the youth hostel said in consternation, 'You will walk to Barts? But it will be dark!' As if there could be a problem with darkness in the morning more so than at night. Why should I take on his fears!

Diary 15 December 2001

Yesterday I travelled to San Francisco, got up at 3.45 a.m. in Burnley on the fourteenth and really slept until 7 a.m. this morning, the fifteenth, except for changing planes and briefly unpacking and meeting Sara.

I arrived with one hell of a headache; OK when I lie down, bad when I get up. So I lay down.

Did my yoga practice and a meditation to Venus. I did as Sue had suggested: I stood in the centre of my astrological chart and rolled out my imaginary carpet in the direction of Venus. My guide was a little girl, all ringlets and pretty frock. The planet Venus appeared like soft pink candyfloss. Venus wanted more attention and for me to be more attractive and attentive to myself and my female side. This all seems in keeping with the A★C★G book. I saw my nail varnishes and chose red. Now to go out with Sara and buy the air ticket and experience San Francisco for real!

★

Sunday morning I rose early and left the hostel in the timescale I intended, rolling my suitcase along. It was dark still, no problem for me. You walk around in the dark at night, so why not in the morning? Well, I was immediately buttonholed by a man who gave me a long story about his car breaking down, his need for money and difficulty with insensitive police. It all seemed so incongruous because he was well dressed and well spoken, and his tale had the ring of truth. But, really, he was begging. I felt exasperated because I needed to keep going, so I gave him $10 and he looked downcast. So I had not fulfilled his expectations and I left him feeling very uneasy. Had I been duped, should I have given him nothing, should I have given him more? No one seemed to have won in the deal.

I found my way to Barts, now later than I wanted to be. Or was it Barts? There was what appeared to be an underground entrance, but a gate closed it off. The map wasn't clear enough to show just what it would look like. Leaving my heavy suitcase at the top of the steps unattended while lots of difficult-looking people shuffled in the street, I ran down the steps. Well, yes it was all closed but I was not sure whether this was Barts or something else. If it wasn't, then where was Barts? I felt breathless and anxiety began to set in. Quick, back to the suitcase! I asked in a café and at a kiosk, but no one spoke English or showed more than a tired face to me. Oh, and time was passing! Someone told me maybe there was a bus to the airport and described the start of a long journey which I did not remember. My head was in a spin. So, I just walked in the direction they first pointed. How could I possibly get to the airport in time – on foot?

Then I saw a hotel and called in. No, on Sunday Barts doesn't open till 8 a.m. – the screw of anxiety tightened. Yes, they would try to get me a taxi, but at this time of day… I sat in the foyer and recovered a little of my composure. Where was my resolve to understand that things work out just as they should and not to get anxious? I paced the lounge. Then, after many calls, the taxi was on its way. Time was passing. I tipped the night deskman well and he told me the taxi would be $50 dollars. Bang went any cheapness of flight attained by going from Oakland Airport! Off I went, still in the night air. Now it was a bit touch-and-go for catching the flight. Oh, this is not how I wanted it all to start!

At the airport my cab driver asked for $55. No, I could only give him $52, all I had. The rest had gone on the 'beggar' and on the tip at the hotel. So, the taxi driver complained bitterly. Someone else I left dissatisfied!

I still felt jangled by the morning. What a way to be before even reaching my first proposed destination! I searched the airport bookshop for a book on Hawaii, but all they had were books on San Francisco. How self-centred it felt – and this in the departure lounge. But I caught the flight. Excitement and sleep suffused me by turn. The moment of lift-off on the Aloha jet felt incredibly momentous; then, I slept. Later, I was to paint the episode on a silk scarf that I made my visual diary. I showed it as a dark, almost black area with a shining plane rising out into a pink sky.

Chapter Two

HAWAII – VENUS ON THE ASCENDANT LINE

Hawaii. Home for me of the Venus on the Ascendant line. The only area on the planet where the line passed through land, except for one of the Aleutian Islands and Antarctica, and there were other influences there – and cold weather! So, what had Venus to offer, and why was it so necessary for me to go there first?

To précis the book, this Venus line would cause me to love myself, find myself beautiful and seek and ultimately find a useless life of laziness and leisure. What could be a better way to start the holiday? The downside was that I would show vanity, liking anything pink and bubbly with Hollywood-type glamour. Material things would take on an importance – clothing, etc. – and I would be superficial and my laziness would make me prone to needing others to lead me.

The part that appealed for the start of a holiday was the useless life – and self-loving. Oh, how nice this might feel, setting the tone maybe for the rest of the holiday. To experience a useless life and loving myself for it sounded perfect!

In San Francisco in just one day very near to Mars and Sun influences I had seen myself become courageous: I had felt myself bracing my chest like a warrior, and brightly clothed – scarlet! With such changes from Mars and the Sun influences in just a one-day visit, how would three months' stay be in Hawaii?

On the flight to Hawaii I sat by a couple who were going on holiday and I just felt love flow around me – a promising start. I arrived at Kona Airport in Big Island. My travel companions had booked accommodation and knew their holiday destination. Oh! I never thought of anything like that! The A★C★G book didn't list hotels! But there I was in the most relaxed and open-air airport I had ever seen. Even nicer than Chania Airport in Crete, which I had always rated highly.

At Kona Airport I found a tourist information point and confidently approached it and received extremely courteous assistance, just as I expected. The Sun influence seemed to have travelled with me from California. Somehow it just all started to feel right. I found that there were hostels to stay in. Yes, and they would pick me up at the airport too! Just a few minutes' wait in the lovely warm sunshine. Off to a place called Kailua-Kona.

The hostel was in a residential area of town and I immediately felt at home. No glitz of tourism. I settled into the dorm. Then I stripped my nails of their bright red polish, despite the fact that it was still pristine, and put on bright pink. I just couldn't wait to get rid of the red. How unusual!

Less than an hour after arriving I headed for the beach. But I needed a beach bag. No problem, Kona is blessed with little shops for gifts and swimwear and an easy life.

Now, I would normally buy a black beach bag with jungle pattern and parrots on it. Nice and practical. No, I headed for a turquoise shiny plastic one with a floral pattern, held it up, and heard myself ask the assistant, 'Have you got this in pink?' No. Oh dear! OK, turquoise is pretty and I have turquoise clothes that will match.

That was the start of a new 'me' where pink and girly things appealed, the pink nail varnish had to be fixed every day, and glamour took off.

I made friends with a young woman, Elle, also staying in the dorm. One wet morning we went shopping together. Now, I don't normally shop and so I was very surprised to find myself drawn to buying things. Me on a budget! And what things! Anything pink, fluffy, frilly took my eye. I bought two ankle bracelets. Some women do these things, but not me. I was acutely aware of someone seeming to stand behind me dictating my taste. Kona's frivolous little shops suited me.

Diary 16 December 2001

First day in Hawaii. Beach in Kona small, I will look for somewhere better another day. Sea a bit cool, that's a disappointment. Went to a free concert in Princess Bernice's palace gardens. Hula dancing and choral singing. Father Christmas in a grass skirt! I feel lazy and at ease in this place given over to the pleasure of tourists, yet still having an old culture that local people take pride in. Couldn't wait to get the red nail varnish off. It was a strange relief to move into pink. On all nails, feet too!

★

Every day I took account of how much I spent, so in my diary is a daily list of what I bought and the cost. I did this to know how the money was going. It felt a bit excessive but it was methodical and a good habit to get into, I believed. It also helped me make my diary entries because it was another way of remembering the days.

Patey's Place, the hostel, was not very salubrious. There were mice in the kitchen but the general ambience was nice with an inner courtyard with picnic tables where I could paint on silk without fear of the consequences of spilling the paints. The telly was a problem. It was outside the women's dorm and was left on whether people watched or not. I just switched it off as often as possible. I have never lived in a house with a television, so I am something of a throwback.

Diary 17 December 2001

My old masculine-style black washbag won't do. Spent ages poring over new ones but they are all dark dismal colours. Oh for a little floral waterproof bag, just big enough for everything. Today I enjoyed a little swim and then tucked myself up in bed and slept in the late afternoon. Just listening to people talking outside the dorm I have the feeling that I never have anything important to say now! I am quite content! What a lazy life.

Diary 18 December 2001

What a strange day! Two people staying at the hostel said they would give me a lift in their rented, convertible Mustang. They messed around for a long time at the hostel and I had to come to terms with that. What does time matter after all?

They dropped me off at the Sadie Seymour Gardens, just outside Kona, just where I wanted to be. The gardens were filled with wonderful tropical and Mediterranean plants collected and exhibited by geographical zones flowing down a series of terraces between beautiful flat green lawns striped with the shadows of trees, mainly palms. Oh, how the Mediterranean plants made me feel at home! My heart leapt and pressed against my chest hard enough to burst.

The surprise was on the way back through the gardens, where there is a large house. The place was full of old people inside sitting down, perhaps for a late meal. No. I was accosted and asked if I could play bridge. They were short of one to make up tables. The woman asking me put on a winning smile. I was asked: would I join them? Oh, this is a bit sudden, but why not! I played awfully. They are really quite sharp and I haven't played for ages. What cards have gone? Oh dear. I tried not to be embarrassed because they had asked me to make up numbers and, without me, three people could not have played. So, OK, I missed the beach, but it would have felt mean to have declined. Anyway, how do you add colour to a holiday if you don't take advantage of what flows to you?

In the evening and back in Kona, I gave a massage to Guy, one of the hostel workers, and cooked pasta for second day running. Yum. Doing things I like.

New health techniques: in the massage I asked Guy to visualise energy in his solar plexus and to move some of it freely to his heart and back to create a two-way highway, waterfall or whatever. He immediately found a blockage. It was dispelled by purple light (his choice). When the highway was complete I asked him to visualise light in his heart and send it to his throat chakra to look for blockages. No blockages. Good. Asked him to visualise a colour of energy that would keep it open so he could speak his truth and be kindly to himself.

Can't bear my old washbag, nor my trekking clothes.

Diary 19 December 2001

During the night I visualised for myself white light (from a torch) at my ground chakra. I asked for all negativities to be burned in the light. I moved the torch to my feet chakras and looked at them. When they were clear I made a link of light back to the ground chakra. I continued this practice up my body finding blockages and negativity and burning them away. Sometimes a candle was necessary and like moths the negativity was attracted to the flame. Where I found fog a wind blew the fog away and the candle healed and dispersed the fogginess. I did this for the seven major chakras and the spleen and eyes. Eyes full of judgemental fog. Maybe I will see more clearly now (I am short-sighted, with astigmatism). I felt the chakras above my head lighted by the torch and reaching out to God. Then I took the energy down to the ground. All my body went warm and my toes have gone all soft and effortlessly wiggle more freely.

★

The bus service in Big Island is very limited, so I decided to rent a car. No luck. I tried day after day and I came to realise that they were all sold out to fly-drive packages over the whole of the Christmas period. Tourism was at a low ebb due to the 11 September attacks and the excess rent cars had been shipped to the US mainland. What to do? While I had no real desire to sightsee, nonetheless I must do something! Seeking and ultimately finding a useless life, how do I do that? What does it mean? If my life is useless then if that is my aim it can't be useless! If laziness is the goal, how can it be both lazy and meet an objective? It is a puzzle.

I decided that if cars were not available and buses were only local, in order to spread my wings I must hitchhike.

Off I went – the start of an adventure. A twenty-minute wait in bright sunshine and blue sky sunk my heart. Then I realised I could see the sea. So what's so bad about a wait if I am warm and have a view? Two short lifts saw me out of Kona and along the road to Waipio Valley, a beauty spot, the leaflet had said. Then a further lift. Yes, he would take me very near.

We got talking. What's his name? Jerry. Same age and height as me. Oh, at Waimea, a town on the way, it started to rain hard and to go cold. Me, in just a little silk dress having no idea it could rain here. In Waimea, we made a short stop for Jerry to visit the 'rest room'. I watched him walk away from the car and realised he looked like the male equivalent of me! Same cast of shoulders, slightly built, but hips as narrow as mine are wide. Oh, he is quite nice! He was visiting his son in Honokaa just beyond Waipio. Yes, he decided to detour and take me all the way to Waipio. I knew he was coming back to Kona that evening so, opportunistically, I said if he would drive me back too, I would get him dinner. Anything to avoid having to hitch a ride back in the cold and wet in a soggy silk dress. No big response to the proposal of dinner. So maybe I would be left at wet Waipio thumbing a lift back home, shivering with sprays of water from traffic for company! So as we travelled the arrangement unfolded. He would take me to Waipio; then we would visit his son. Then drive back together. Great!

Waipio Lookout was very foggy and a touch disappointing and very quick. Out of the car, photo shoot, brrr, back in car… off again, too blustery and damp for more. At Honokaa Jerry's son was out, so he asked me if there was anything else I would like to see. By contrast to Waipio, the little town of Honokaa looked nice in bright fresh sunshine so it encouraged me to say I would like to see Umauma Falls. Oh, what a long way down the coast road they were! I felt embarrassed to have taken Jerry so far out of his way.

Eventually we got to the falls and they were *so* lovely – a three-tier fall. I turned to Jerry and asked if he would like a kiss! Sure, he said. So, we kissed and hugged for ages. The moment felt so romantic and I felt all the joys of being sixteen years old with all the experience of being forty-eight, a potent combination. The earth didn't move; the world just felt as if it had stopped. Oh, I could have stayed for ever! There was something a bit strange too. It was rather like kissing the beauty of myself – maybe like looking in the mirror and having the surprise of seeing your reflection in a dazzling new way, and being impulsively drawn to it. Superglue! A deep breath, this is hot stuff! Time to move on before we roast.

Looking in the text of the A★C★G book sometime later, I began to feel I understood what had been meant by the phrase regarding Venus (previously totally opaque to me), 'You are rather possessive here and the integration of others' personalities into your own seems to give you the right to play prima donna.' The integration, hmm… I had been taken by the similarity in appearance at the car park and now wanted to merge with him. I had never experienced a longing like that before. And in reality, being half-Japanese and half-Philippino, he didn't look like me at all. I'm tall and blonde with sharp features including a big nose with a bump in it.

Back to Umauma: I drove the car, Jerry had a beer. Oh, my first time driving an automatic car. Back through the rain to sunny Kona and dinner for two, but Jerry says he must pay. OK, well it looks as if we are now boyfriend and girlfriend. Ate out in a restaurant in a suburban mall and then kissed like crazy... oooh. The mall had seating ideal for the job.

I was in a mood for more so we visited his place, in reality his nephew's house. But Jerry was ill at ease, feeling he would not set a good example to his younger relations if I stayed. So, he came to see me next day and evening and we started to plan Christmas. I told him that his family and arrangements, already in place, must come first. I am only here for now; his family is for ever. He wanted to slow the pace a bit. He was certainly uncomfortable to be in a relationship without the prospect of a future. Now, before you put this book down, thinking it will be a romp through sexual encounters, it is not. Just a frank account of me and the astro stuff.

Diary 21 December 2001

Slept like a log and knew something had happened. I had decided to respect Jerry's position of taking things slowly and to be more passively feminine and to stop myself swamping Jerry with overt sexual behaviour. I asked for help from Sai Baba and knew I had received it.

I have started a silk painting which is in the form of a diary. I painted my diary entries with Umauma Falls and Jerry. Then I went off scuba diving near the Cook memorial – Captain Cook got killed here. Spent £106 pounds on the afternoon trip. Never mind, most days have been inexpensive. Got a lift back and was told that the fish were more plentiful at Kahaluu Bay and that it is easy to snorkel there. Great! It's on the bus route too.

Met Jerry in the evening for dinner. I was so cool I hardly showed any emotion. I told him I was in no hurry and respected his position. The effect was almost instant and we made love in his car looking out over the lava flows to the sea.

I realised that I had felt as though I had been holding my breath till we made love. A desire that caused me so much tension! As if a bead of water lay spilt on a cloth, the surface tension causing the drop to stay there against the force of gravity, the meniscus aching to be released and the drop to seep into the cloth. Suddenly, the bead is no more. The tension gone, surrendered. But, in my case, I felt as if I had dissolved into myself, Jerry as another manifestation of me. The need to be unified with myself in Jerry goes far deeper than the physical; it is a state of impossibility.

★

Elle, my dorm-mate, wanted to travel. We decided to travel together. This gave Jerry his family Christmas, although I had by now met his livewire daughter who lived in Los Angeles, and quieter family members, including son Jason of Honokaa. Everyone was gathering for the family festivities.

Travel with Elle during the daytime meant using an old car with a chauffeur who lived in the hostel. The chauffeur, Tammie, filled supermarket shelves by night and drove people around by day. Tammie was big and had a slow, lazy drawl, courtesy of Texas. Somehow I always felt as if I was talking to a huge pink slug, slithering slowly along in a swimsuit, drifting from one subject to another, but she got us around so we could sample the beaches in Elle's travel guide. Just as in San Francisco, I was quite happy to tag along, particularly if I didn't have to organise anything.

But by now I had a guidebook: *Hawaii: The Big Island Revealed.* It was the most thorough guidebook I had ever seen. It tells you what is down every road instead of pinpointing attractions. You decide what may be attractive with the help of great photographs. If you find yourself in Hawaii, get this series! I realised I had come to Hawaii not even knowing there were volcanoes.

Elle and I decided to go to Volcano National Park and, again, I found myself on the verge of commenting that we were late making our getaway but I found myself saying that it didn't matter. Where is the lazy useless life, after all, if you can't bear being late?

Now I have explained a few of days in Hawaii I will speed along a bit, because otherwise it will be a tale of 'what I did on my holidays', an outward journey instead of the inner one. I hope I feel my way to the right balance for you.

Considering how important these astrological lines are in my travel, you might have thought that I would be more precise. When I arrived in Big Island I thought I must travel to Honolulu to be right on the line. Honolulu was the only place I remembered as marked on the A★C★G map. So, I knew I must aim to go there soon! But one day I looked at the A★C★G map and realised the Hawaiian Islands are shown quite clearly: there's Big Island where I am. And the line, oh where did it fall? It passed directly through the Umauma Falls! I would have kissed a toad there! My head felt light and dizzy with this observation. No wonder I felt so fond of Jerry. But, would I feel fond of him anywhere else in the world?

So, I had no need now to go to Honolulu. I was pleased I had not looked at the map before, because I might have started to project things on my travel, making interpretations appropriate for the Venus line, but consciously. Now I knew. So, this was how I could see myself as beautiful. I identified with beauty and saw it in Jerry. I saw him as me despite my being fair and blue-eyed and him being dark-haired and brown-eyed. He has oriental features yet for me we were the same. This would also explain why he found my desire for him overwhelming.

But that would not explain the sexy stuff, just the romance. To be perfectly honest with you, when I was young, between eighteen and twenty-one, I had many lovers. In those days it was called promiscuity. I had some trouble leaving this behind when I had met Dave. But I had been largely faithful to Dave and felt pleased that I had left that phase behind. But here it was again: a desire to short-circuit the normal courtship processes and go headlong at top speed into bed. At forty-eight now, not eighteen! But I was travelling and if I were going to experience full relationships I couldn't wait months. This was a bit of a dilemma. Oh, too much to sort out right away! But I was aware that I have a lot of masculine energy and as Venus's romance is only an overlay I was bound to find the mixture of potent romance and male sexual desires a heady combination. But, go with the flow; see where it leads. And that is what I did.

Just a few Hawaiian highlights: Elle and I travelled to the Volcano National Park, booking in at Holo Holo youth hostel, which is wonderful. I have a photo of the kitchen where orchids stand in vases on the table, a gift from a visitor. Outside, the large-leaved jungle plants (this is rainforest) press so near the window they look like a blown-up photo pasted on to a kitchen wall rather than the real thing.

Elle and I went to the Park and hitchhiked to the lookout point where you could see lava flowing into the sea as dusk was approaching. Even at some distance (the black lava is impossible to walk on in the dark without a torch) you could see the flaming red-hot lava flowing down the hillside and the steam as it hit the sea below. Oh! What wonderful energy!

Now, Elle and I were without a chauffeur to go further (supermarket shelves call too), but all was well as we met a fellow traveller (with a car) on our first night and so we then travelled together next day. First we went to the National Park again to see the things we had missed the day before: sulphur banks, bright yellow and steaming and lava tubes so big you could walk through them, like tunnels. A word of explanation: lava tubes are caused by lava flows under the surface, rather like water forming caves in limestone areas.

Elle described, to my amusement, the many crater floors we saw as looking like giant cow pats, brownish black and ropy-looking. It took a while for me to understand why one big volcano, covering 600 square miles, could have so many craters, but in this area of volcanic activity eruptions take place wherever there is a weakness and enough pressure. It doesn't all come out of the top spewing down from one point. Although it can, and the Gold Coast, north of Kona where I spent many days testifies to that. There, huge black lava flows from the summit of Mauna Loa run right down to the sea. Oh, how I loved that black landscape! The Gold Coast is the tourist resort area with wonderful gold sandy beaches and only ten inches of rain a year, so it is almost a desert and hardly anything has grown on the lava flows even though the flow dates from the 1800s. Just black congested and contorted lava for miles and miles. It does something to my insides.

Back to the National Park. Tomorrow would be Christmas Day! Stu, our driver/companion had to head back to Kona for his flight home. He was a private detective from San Francisco. Never knowingly have I met one of those before. Except in crime novels. We missed out on some of the things I wanted to see because of the needs of our car-driving companion. That's the problem of working with other people's schedules. No time to see the black beach or green sand beach or most southerly point of the United States. Never mind, back to Kona and Jerry.

Together with Elle and Stu, I stayed over Christmas Eve night at a small hotel in the south part of the island. There was no breakfast. What a Christmas! Everywhere was closed on Christmas Day. No presents to open, no tree, no family phone calls and no breakfast and little likelihood of lunch. Everything felt dead and a bit anticlimactic. We ate nasty fast food at a roadside shack, standing up.

Then, on to Magic Disappearing Sands for a swim. Now that was nice! I learnt, however, what the warning signs meant which show people tipping upside down in the sea. Yes, I tried to follow a wave into the shore and was hurled head first down into the sand, driving the side of my head smartly into the sand, rather like my head doing an emergency stop, still with my body in motion. I felt as if my neck would snap! I lay on the beach and took stock.

Diary 26 December 2001

Back to Kona, to Patey's Place. Still no rent cars to see the parts of Big Island I had missed: Pahoa, Hilo, Mauna Kea. I sat on the wall of the bay in Kona and idled the day. I love being here – everything is a joy!

Diary 28 December 2001

Have met up with Jerry again. He tells me he is going to live in Los Angeles for a year because he has lost his driving licence. He says he feels lost. I feel helpless, just an observer. I may as well be a piece of stone for all the advice I can muster!

Jerry is bad at showing up. We have been agreeing to meet, then he doesn't show up. We agree I will ring so he can join me at a beach (he is driving at the moment!). I ring; he doesn't come. He turns up in the mornings and apologises. Disappointment tends to spoil things for me and I notice I get a bit moody when I am let down. One thing about travelling alone and not having the diversions of work or company: you learn your moods. Yesterday, he gave me a lei of tuberose flowers. Oh, the smell is divine! I kept the garland overnight by the bed and it is sweet still, in the morning. I can even smell its scent on my neck from the night before.

★

Then the bombshell came. One morning Jerry came to the hostel and made his apologies for not having met me the evening before. I instantly knew just at the moment he told me: he is an alcoholic. Now, if anyone had said they were courting an alcoholic I would have counselled them against it: no good could come of it. But he might just as well have said he was going to get his hair cut for all it deterred me. I felt I could offer him nothing. I looked through my head for the something appropriate to say and found a complete void. The cupboard was bare. But it did make me realise that he was a vulnerable person and that I should take care with him. But, for me, this could only mean to kiss him and cuddle him more – here comes Venus again!

I was puzzled by my lack of reaction to Jerry's alcohol problem – and the problem became most marked. All our outings were to bars, often with his family, and at some point he would move off beer and into the fog of spirits. My only reaction was to decide not to drink alcohol in his presence.

I emailed my astrologer friend, Sue. She advised me that Venus on the Ascendant is about my needs only. If it was Venus on the Descendant I might be able to help him, but on the Ascendant it would not be possible. Ah! So that is why I could be no more than a piece of alabaster when faced with his problem! My needs for romance not only outweighed his difficulties: they could make me ride roughshod over him! How careful I would have to be!

Diary 30 December 2001

Jerry comes to see me. It is all over. He cannot bear the short-term nature of our relationship or the demands I place on him. We have only made love once. He doesn't want to see me again. The bottom has dropped out of my world and I don't know what I shall do without anyone to kiss and cuddle. I feel like half a person. Also, wasn't I supposed to be the one who said goodbye – I am the traveller.

Elle and I are thinking of going to Maui and maybe other islands for a while. That's good. I don't think I can cope with being so near to the Venus line. My emotions are just too sharp, too keen and overwhelming. I need a break to come to terms with myself here. Today it is raining. Elle and I do the girlie thing and shop. Pink things, always pink things, I really must get away!

So, my plan is: travel to Maui, then Molokai, then Kawai and to Oahu for 17 March, my flight back to California. But Big Island remains the best place for the Venus line and maybe with Jerry gone I can explore both the island and the line some more. I haven't come all this way just to avoid the line.

★

Elle and I had been 'doing' the beaches of the Gold Coast, with the assistance of Tammie, the chauffeur, and some hitch-hiking. We would set off and maybe visit four beaches in the same day. One day we visited a beach so beautiful I painted it on my diary scarf. As I wrote the place names on the scarf too I became aware that I had lost track of this beach's name. Elle looked at my picture and said it was Kua Bay. It was such a fine beach: pale gold sand fringed with palms and no hotel to mar its beauty. You know – paradise! But with so many beaches a day, a blur can set in.

Strangely, much later, I visited Kua Bay and realised I had misnamed the beach on the scarf. When I arrived, thinking I was revisiting it, I realised that I had never been to this Kua Bay before and I never again found the bay I had painted.

Diary 30 December 2001 (continued)

Elle and I met two people who were planning to drive up to the observatories on the volcano, Mauna Kea. We went with them last night. Unusually, it rained and rained. The observatories are located there partly because of the high number of clear nights. We stopped at 9,000 feet, the highest you can go to at night. The professional observatories are at 13,000 feet. Through the heavy fine rain and in the shivering cold the moon was full. Only one star was visible. But something else happened, far far more wonderful than a starlit night with telescopes and a crick in the neck. The light from the moon was refracted through the rain and produced a moonbow. It being night-time, our eyes could not see colour, so we saw a rainbow without colour. It was just an arc of white light across the sky. It needs very clear conditions to see this and of course a rainy night and full moon. We had the lot! It was so magical and my heart pumped hard against my chest wall. It hurt to breathe for the pleasure of the moment.

★

My A★C★G book told me that a move away of about 200 miles would significantly dilute the effect of a line. So, on 1 January Elle and I made to go to Maui. I wasn't sure how far that would be from the line, but at least it would be some distance. But Venus was more tenacious than that. A new factor, Elle's boyfriend, of whom I had heard a great deal, not all good, had come into our lives. He was a pilot, working up his number of flying hours to get his full qualification. So on 31 December he took Elle and me in a four-seater all around Big Island, just on a jaunt.

Generally, we followed the coast. We saw the lava entering the sea at Volcano National Park and the waterfalls between Hilo and Waipio; the rainforest and desert and beaches. As we flew up the coast from Hilo to Waipio I was overcome with a desire to see Jerry again. I ached all over for him and could barely see anything out of the window I was so overwhelmed. I resolved to see him again, that night, New Year's Eve!

Then, as we flew inland, over Mauna Kea volcano, the feeling diluted itself. I could see the snow on Mauna Kea and the moment had passed. All of a sudden, I realised we had flown directly along the Venus line. Oh Venus! How powerful you can be! And, yes, I did see Jerry that night. Seeing in the New Year with his family and watching him get drunk – and nasty. The homey firework displays I remember well. In the residential side roads people place their fireworks in the middle of the road, right on the white line between the carriage ways. There they go off, often quite dangerously for passing cars and children running in the road. Watching their antics, I tried to recall what to do with burns from my first aid course. So this is New Year, Hawaiian-style.

Diary 1 January 2002

It is 1 January and I'm still harping on about Jerry. I am completely fascinated that his alcoholism can mean so little to me. I should feel relieved that it is all over, but I am not. So it feels good to be leaving and to get a bit of respite. I have, however, resolved to return to Venus, once I have cooled down, come to terms with my feelings and hopefully be on the way to recovering from an unsuccessful love relationship, which, after all, is finished. I just have to get over it. I have spent a whole day in bed. A healing time, licking my wounds. I have learnt just how different life can be living on or near an astrological line, and now I just need a break! What will Maui bring?

Chapter Three

HAWAII AND AWAY FROM THE LINE

Elle, Tim and I went to Maui, again flying in a four-seater. I had flown in small planes before, but somehow this had a real buzz to it. Fancy, staying in a youth hostel and flying in a private plane. Venusian vanity was raising its head. Off we went. Thank goodness for general aviation, and what a sham all this post-11 September security is in the commercial sector! Here we were – I had only just met Tim, the pilot, and we all passed through the airport gates to the light aircraft, no identification needed, no questions asked, no search of bags, or asking how long the pilot and passengers had known each other. Tim could easily have been carrying me, a terrorist for all he knew, with the aim of flying into the high-rise blocks of Honolulu!

Maui Island. No waiting for carousels for luggage, just straight out from general aviation (what a common name for such a luxury!) head held high and away to the rent car office. I ordered an economy car and yes, yes, they did have a car. Never on Big Island, but here, straight away. Aha! A change in energy! I walked to the car lot expecting to find a tub but, no, a silver Pontiac Grand Am stood there. Venus took over and I felt all pleased with the choice. That's vanity and materialism for you.

Elle and I toured one half of Maui the next day, Tim flying back to Big Island. The Grand Am was fun, with automatic lights as well as power steering and all electronic gadgets. Pity I couldn't even work out how to centrally lock it. I bought a dress – well, it is still Venus influence – but I managed to choose floral silk, without a vestige of pink. I was no longer wearing lipstick and my nail varnish was chipped and I didn't care! Jerry was receding and I could move on. So easy! I felt more open to considering how I could have behaved differently and better, and been more sensitive to his needs. Again, it reflected a move away from the

Venus line that I could be more circumspect. It began to feel a nice compromise: some Venus effects, but not the full blast.

Elle was full of headaches, so the trip around the east of the island was not so good for her. We hoped to go to a red sand beach, but the walk proved too treacherous for our footwear. My camera lens had decided to stop opening properly and so I lost a film's worth of photos, including some frivolous giggly ones of Elle and me in grass skirts and leis on the beach in Big Island. Elle was also having difficulty with her mobile phone. She wanted to keep contact with Tim but reception was terrible. Sometimes I was surprised at how much she felt for him because he did not seem always to treat her well. However, am I one to talk! On our trip around I bought a piece of Chinese fluorite, green and purple, not pink. Don't ask me why, because it just sat in the bottom of my bag.

Elle was the source of information on Maui. I just steered the car in the direction she said. I was happy to be led around. So, next day it was beaches: Big Beach, lots of soft, bright gold sand, Little Beach with nudes and whales. Elle and I passed comments on the sizes of men's genitalia and agreed that it's better to know what men have before you fall in love; otherwise you could be so disappointed. No wonder men usually wear clothes!

Whenever we returned to the car I found myself looking to see if I had the best car in the park. Oh yes, it would do! Now, in England, Dave and I used to pride ourselves on driving old cheap cars till they wouldn't pass the test. Venus again! How strange to feel such pride over material goods.

Ah, just two days with Elle and she decided to fly away to Oahu to be with Tim. Oh, what a good friend she had been.

So, I was alone in Maui and I did not like where we had been staying. It was a hostel with too much telly, and outside at night it could feel like a ghost town. No tourists in sight, just a few aimless, maybe homeless, people without all their wits. Unusually for me, the night-time felt quite threatening. It was a strange contrast to Big Island and the pretty tourist paradise of Kona. The roads on Maui were bigger and faster. There were flat areas and it felt more featureless. It felt more American. Big and Little Beaches are distant from the town I was in, too, so I was always driving around.

Diary 4 January 2002

Elle left today. But I have the car for a whole week, so I shall stay. I sit and watch the big waves at the little town of Paia. I like Paia. It has wholefood shops and quirky little features. I see an advert for a surf hostel and take note. Trying out a Bikram yoga class tonight! Paia, known for its alternative culture.

Diary 5 January 2002

Bikram was hot work with heaters blasting out temperatures to make you sweat till thirsty with it! I thought to go again, but my inner self says no. This is supposed to be a lazy, useless life. I still don't feel to have achieved that. Jerry rather turned my focus from that. I feel his move to Los Angeles will be good and maybe I will visit him there when I return to California. Checked out the alternative scene here in Paia: massage and therapy available in downtown-type malls. Books on the occult and everything for cults – and more asparagus! Yes, I have taken to eating asparagus every day, with red wine to wash it down.

I went for a drive up Haleakala, the volcano here, and watched my petrol gauge fall. Oh, what a gas guzzler I have! 10,000 feet, brrr. I wanted to see the sun go down from the summit, but it was too cold for me. Way above the clouds, it felt like being in an aeroplane. You could see the observatories over on Big Island, silver-white, glowing in the sun. Who would think that you could see so far! That's clear air for you. I wore a diamond ring today and realised that another feature of the clear air is how the stones sparkle at altitude. Now, I would never have known that had I followed the guidebooks and left my rings at home. I'll be wearing them again; they do look good.

Diary 6 January 2002

Back to Paia to the surf hostel, Rainbow House, and move in. Mixed dorms! This is a first, but I am the only woman in the dorm so it doesn't feel so mixed; more as if I am an honorary male. No one snores, that's a blessing.

There are mice in the kitchen. They seem to be a standard hostel feature. I find myself eating asparagus and butter every day, regardless of cost. Nine dollars for a bunch, one time!

Washed down with a tumbler (no wine glasses here) of red wine.

Met Jason in the hostel and we went to the beach together: Big Beach. Then we separated as he went his way. He's in his twenties and gay and can't stand the macho quality of the surfers of Paia but he seems quite happy to be travelling around with me in the Grand Am. I lay in the sun and later opened my eyes to a young smiling face, Tristram. He introduced himself to me and invited me to Little Beach. Now, where did he spring from?

It was Sunday and there was drumming music at Little Beach! Now, nudism is fun with drums and dancing. Everybody celebrating their bodies with none of the serious naturism that Elle and I had seen here before. There was body painting. Tristram persuaded me to have a flower painted on my arm. As I walked away with a small rubbery-looking flower painted on me, the man behind me in the queue asked if the body painter would paint his foreskin. Sure she would, she said enthusiastically! I paused to listen as the man then asked how to get it off. Just rub, came the answer. I smiled.

At sunset, the sun went down over the sea and everyone cheered and jumped around. I found Jason again and we went home to the hostel deciding that tomorrow we would walk the volcano together.

★

And we did just that! The walk in his guidebook began at 10,000 feet, the summit, and you walked down to 7,000 feet through wonderful lava flows and moonscapes. The shapes of the lava flows form the shape of the landscape and each flow has a different rich colour. It's a symphony of colour and curving, flowing lines. The movement that created all this feels to be so palpable you feel that if you stood still you would see the lava still flowing, sliding and forming in front of your eyes. I was so glad we did it together. It was lonely and often in cloud, but so beautiful and clear at other times and the colours of the lava ran from orange to black and my diamond ring just sparkled!

What I didn't know was that the walk actually fell to about

5,500 feet, so we had to climb up and out of the volcano. By late afternoon it was completely misty so you could never see the extent of the task. You could see just to the next corner of the narrow hillside path that is really a series of climbing hairpins. It felt like a chapter out of a fantasy book, a journey where you could only live in the present and could only see the land just around you. Maybe it was moving as we did, all floating in the ether. Maybe if we stood still it would continue to move. It felt quite eerie in the fog and I got tired. A legacy (excuse the pun) of my leg injury is that when I am tired I don't lift my right leg so well, so I kept stubbing my big toe on the knobs of lava that were our path. Oh, how many times did I do that!

The car was due to be returned and I decided I felt strong enough to leave Maui and see what Venus would offer me next.

Chapter Four

BACK ON THE LINE

Diary 10 January 2002, back in Kona

My calf muscles have been sore ever since the walk. It was so memorable: sometimes cloud above and sometimes below us with such dramatic sunshine too, making the clouds look like white waterfalls pouring down the sheer sides left by the lava flows. Rainbows came and went and sometimes they were entirely in the ground area. We passed one small crater and the rainbow ran around the rim, never breaking into the sky at all. At one time when we were approaching a big mist it looked so dark I felt we were travelling in time, walking towards nightfall.

But before the cloud, on the high, clear parts, bathed in sunshine, were the silverswords! Now, I tend to break the word up as 'silvers words', which somehow added an endearing touch of humour to these wonderful plants. Growing only on Maui, they say, they grow singly and directly out of the ashy lava. The silver leaf blades curve inwards and the plant presents a round, ball-like cluster of scimitars. How do they grow in such harsh conditions, so arid and bare? Bless them in their struggle. How I love them.

Phoned Jerry (despite all) and he agreed to meet me at Kona Airport. At 6.23 p.m. I was there, but not he. Then he was. Oh, how I would like it if someone were there in time to lift my luggage off the carousel for me.

We had dinner together and it felt quiet and gentle and not so intense. We decided to go camping together. He is drinking less, he tells me, but has not stopped. So this morning I went with Jerry doing odd jobs and seeing his workmates. He was saying goodbye to them, preparing for his move to Los Angeles. He would live with his daughter there – the only family member I have met who I think might stop him drinking. He said he couldn't stay in Kona because he couldn't drive but that would not matter in the city because there were buses.

Then we took the roughest road I have ever been on, keeping in our sights one tree on the horizon. Across the black lava to the sea! We parked by the tree, behind a beach of black lava rocks and white coral. This time we were in a pick-up truck. Interesting camping: we let the tail gate down to level, rolled out a futon and lay in the open air. Oh, this was the style! No little beasties ran over us, no draughts chilled us, just a view of the stars and the sound of the sea. Our time together was intense and special, but something held me back for a while, like a little cloud, stopping me from feeling absolute pleasure. Regarding my sexual desires, I learnt in that moment to say, 'I love and respect you,' and, piff, I saw the cloud leave. The night was just bright and exquisite and we were like little wide-eyed children, lying there innocently in the night air. I realise that the expression 'I love and respect you' is one that I am also addressing to myself. Another aspect of Venus.

★

The following day we revisited the Waipio area for me to take a walk and for Jerry to play golf with his son, but the weather didn't allow either. One of the great things in Big Island is that you can choose the weather. The west coast is wet, maybe 170 inches a year, but the Gold Coast has just ten inches and miles of sunny beaches. So we went to the beach.

Jerry was going on the Tuesday to Los Angeles and I was cooling the relationship down. Maybe fortunately, the weather was too unsettled to go camping again.

I felt a bit bereft: Elle had gone, Jerry was going and I was feeling as if my holiday stretched a long way ahead of me. However, an email came from Mary telling me that she had a friend, Mike, visiting Maui soon and asking if I would like to meet him. He was fifty-two, spiritual, a man of colour, with a great sense of humour and young for his age! I was not sure, so I asked Mary for his email address. So maybe I now had new plans and a future. In the meantime, I expected to leave Kona when Jerry left and go to Hilo, the other main town on the island – and tantalisingly close to the line. Go for it!

That night I met Kirsten at the hostel and chatted about life.

Diary 11 January 2002

Feeling a bit at sea. Got a lift with Kirsten. Went snorkelling at Kahaluu again and then went to see petroglyphs with Kirsten. She's good company. Jerry on answerphone. Everything feels temporary and without substance. The lazy life hits in now and then, but it's difficult to maintain. I realise it's there, and it's gone! Elusive. Ate potatoes for dinner to bring me back to this planet.

I am reading a Caroline Myss book and each time I open it I seem to read the same page and it says the same thing about having sex to avoid intimacy. But I am struggling to make sense of this; it just seems a hypnotic phrase. It must be for me.

I consider the matter: I avoid intimacy via sex. I have sex, then I avoid intimacy (getting to know someone better) for fear of being hurt or deciding I have slept with someone who is not kind/loving, whatever. Hurt means that I am not as self-sufficient as I thought. Hurt means feeling alone and blue. Hurt indicates that my ego is still playing a big part.

Jerry was supposed to come for me at 9 a.m. I wait till 11 a.m. at the hostel. It gives me chance to think. I feel:

(a) pissed off (ego)

(b) understanding, because he is leaving and has lots to do (intellectual)

(c) anxious in case he is drinking (fear) or doesn't want to see me (ego).

I feel it is God's plan that I go through all this and Jerry's not showing up gives me the time to process all of this. I am also frightened of my reaction to his lateness (ego), knowing it will make me fed up and put me in complaints mode when he does show (emotional victim). This is not how I want the romance to end!

In my navel gazing this morning I looked at what I find difficult to let go of and found little phrases to help me:

I desire to be admired; I am enough without the acknowledgement of others.

I desire to remain youthful; I grow old gracefully.

I desire to control others; I have no fear of loneliness.

I desire to be superior; I am not, I learn from others and they learn from me.

I desire to work and be busy; reflection is growth.

I desire to be part of things, included; I am enough, I create myself without the need of others.

★

My relationship with Jerry gives me a focus; it helps fill my day and gives my life a structure. So much for my life view of not requiring others! But then, Venus talks of being led and I am not used to that. I also see the relationship as temporary, going on until we have no messages left to give to each other.

Time passed, and after all these thoughts I still hoped Jerry would show up, but no. Then when I phoned him later he was mean with me and later still I learnt that he had gone camping with his family and went on a bender! I gave myself permission to cry and lay down on the bed. I loved our camping trip so much – how could he go without me?

Well, while I was in this state of horizontality, into the dorm walked Hannah and Flo. And into my life walked my next long-term girl friend, Hannah. Doors definitely close and open here. I went swimming with them and to dinner and gave Hannah a massage. My life felt changed, cleansed by my tears and renewed. So what had changed? I had new company and had been able to talk of my experience and make light of it; and giving a massage had felt 'worthwhile'. Hmmm… not sure this is part of the lazy uselessness! I felt pleased to have had the opportunity to explore myself via Jerry and Venus and to chat about it. Hannah and Flo had sympathetic ears.

Next day I went with Hannah to Pineapple hostel down the coast near the Captain Cook memorial. She settled in for camping there and we walked together, hitching a lift to the beach. We agreed to meet the next day. I asked Sai Baba to take my mind off playing old records about Jerry, of how it might have been.

Then we went to the Place of Refuge. The Place of Refuge is historically a place to swim to in order to avoid death at the hands of priests for indiscretions as minor as letting your shadow fall in the wrong place. Such was fear on this volcanic island, with tsunamis, earth tremors and eruptions. And it still is. Respect for the old ways still makes sacred places out of bounds: *kapu*. I felt this was *my* place of refuge, but an emotional refuge. It had great peace and dignity.

Diary 14 January 2002

Because I don't see Jerry, I feel I have unfinished business (crazy really, because it was supposed to be all over when I went to Maui, but somehow has resurrected itself). To help get him out of my system I want to try writing him a letter telling him how upset I am that we don't meet now, even when we arrange to do so. How disappointed I am. An opportunity to have an indulgent grouse! But…

Dear Jerry

I sincerely enjoyed our times at the waterfalls, camping, being at the beach together, going dancing and receiving the gift of a lei and sarong and enjoying the New Year party with your family. These are beautiful, memorable occasions. On the downside I have got really fed up with you for not showing up, and for shouting at me on 1 January after midnight telling me that you don't need help with your alcoholism. Telling me you went camping without me, not meeting me and then being distant on the phone as if I was the one who had stood you up was more than I could bear. You said you needed time because you were tired, but I called by your house and it was empty. I've never seen you again. I had hoped to break the link with you gracefully, inevitably as you went to Los Angeles.

I do want you to know that you have been very special to me. However, the unpredictable nature of our friendship – except the certainty that through alcoholism it will go wrong – has wrecked the dream of a beautiful relationship. Maybe not long-lasting, but it could have been good while it lasted.

> Let me thank you for giving me the statement 'I love and respect you', including myself.

That's all there was to say.

★

I didn't send the letter, of course, but I was made calm by writing it. It came from the heart – at least in part – and not the spleen.

The next day Jerry left, without seeing me. I had no forwarding address. But I did phone him to say goodbye so my own need to tidy things up was done. I felt sad and felt it was reasonable to be sad. How could he just go when we had kissed such sweet kisses?

I had seen him just twice since I had returned from Maui. I had originally left for Maui on 1 January and that felt OK but now it was 15 January, Jerry was out of my life and I felt gutted. How is it possible to feel calm and collected one time and so upset the next when nothing has changed?

After that, I went snorkelling at Kahaluu bay in the morning and, as it gets overcast in the afternoon south of Kona, I did my usual trick of heading up to the Gold Coast for the afternoon. This was the occasion I visited Kua Bay and found a different place from the beach I had expected to find. There were two other people on the beach and they consented to take my photo so I could send a copy to Mike, in preparation for my second visit to Maui.

The photo showed me startlingly brown. From Kua Bay I could see Maui. I felt the move away from Venus would help, again.

From Kua Bay I hitched back to Kona and so met Charles, whom I took out for dinner, a gift for the lift. After dinner I gave his shoulder some healing work, for the first time calling into being an aromatherapy oil I didn't actually have with me. I felt he needed a specific oil and asked the universe to place it on my hand. The delivery system worked, I felt it arrive, so I could apply it. Charles told me that he travelled by being at home and did not have to go places physically. Interesting.

The next day I had planned to move only to Hilo, the wettest town on the island and near the line. Hannah and I intended to go together, but no rent cars were available so we had booked Tammie again to drive us there. Hannah wanted to camp. I love camping but had no equipment.

So to Hilo, where we would meet Hannah's cousin. On the way to Hilo we stopped at Honokaa and enjoyed the fruits of a wonderful bakery there, in sunshine. Honokaa was growing on me and formed a connection with Jerry, being the home of his son. At Hilo we went to an art shop, Island Supplies, owned by Hannah's cousin Eva. Oh! Now that *was* a treat! She actually had silk painting goods on special offer and I indulged, feeling that this was a great way of showing my appreciation of her letting us stay in her house. I had also been to the sister shop in Kona because when I arrived in Hawaii I realised I had left my paint-brushes behind on my mother's kitchen windowsill, in England. The connection to my trip to the art shop in Kona also felt good.

I usually feel that money spent on art materials is an extravagance. This reflects my doing and working self – and my mother's 'money doesn't grow on trees'. Here I was unfettered; the more I bought, the better I felt. I bought some silk too, and later hand-sewed a sheet sleeping bag with it. What luxury I knew that would be! Then Eva handed over her car keys to Hannah and gave both Hannah and me directions and we drove back out of Hilo to Eva's house, which she shared with Carl. It was a wooden house built on stilts, as I would say. It felt so good to be living in a house again instead of a dorm, even if we did sleep on the floor.

I was looking forward to my return to Maui with the prospect of making a new friend. Just a week to go. Mike and I were in regular email contact, preparing for our visit to Maui. I had seen his photo and he looked good. But then he was a tennis pro. Mary had said he was a man of colour, but his photo just showed a suntanned smile.

Diary 17 January 2002

Felt much better. Happy all day despite the weather: raining and cool. Went to Hilo shopping. Hannah had Eva's car again, so we took in Rainbow Falls (no rainbow, just rain) then to Boiling Pots, low in water when we saw them. Too wet for Peepee Falls.

All these falls are on the same river, just above Hilo. Lazy day, ah, and no rent cars! How can this still be? Never mind, something will happen.

Diary 18 January 2002

In the night, an earth tremor! The house danced on its stilts and then settled back to sleep for the night. That's a first for me. Hannah and I have decided to stay another night. I have promised to do the cooking and give Eva a massage. I stay around the house; it feels lazy and good to be at home. Most of the time I just sit. Hannah is in Hilo helping Eva at the shop. Pleased with everything. This is the life of leisure, fleeting and beautiful.

*

Hannah and I discussed future plans. We decided to go to a hostel, with camping, near Pahoa, where she might be able to get work. For a fee, the owner of the hostel-cum-campsite would come to Hilo and pick us up. We bought loads of food for the stay and so had a cardboard box to add to the camping gear of Hannah's and my roll-along case. Far too much to carry! Our chauffeur and landlord-to-be took his trip to Hilo as a chance to stop and shop hither and thither, so we did not get to the hostel till late afternoon.

Oh dear! I have never had such a thought before or since, but the phrase went through my head: this place needs torching. It appeared that the owner had wanted to sell it and had not been able to and so had decided to reopen it. Well, everything was damp. Mattresses were tired, the cooker looked too rusted through to bear a saucepan's weight and all was grimy. Hannah said her allergies would not stand it and we could not stay. Our man rang around and found us a room in a guest house. He drove us there.

The guest house was in the countryside. On the way there we had totally lost our bearings. Our new host was unfriendly and unhelpful. The options offered to us were that we could stay in a damp caravan where we would have to stay a minimum of two nights, or we could stay in the house (more than we could afford)

51

and could only stay one night because he had another booking. The steam vent in the garden saved the day. Hannah and I decided to stay in the room and headed off in the rain for a steam bath. We massaged each other, in the nude, squatting on planks of wood in a rocky niche with our sarongs covering the steam vent entrance thereby conserving the wonderful natural heat. It felt a very Venusian experience! Smiled all the way through it.

In the evening we cooked and ate sumptuously on the fare we had brought with us. Wonderfully, our host gave us the use of a kitchen. The following morning it was raining still. We went in the grey mist to the steam vent and meditated. We took a journey to Pele, the goddess of the volcano. My guide for the journey was so tall – he was like a big spume of lava. Pele was a woman, manifesting as heat from the steam vent. She wanted to give and receive from me warmth, joie de vivre, love and energy. In the meditation I was given a golden amulet to wear on my left arm. This is to help me to stop substituting sexual love for intimacy. I will receive energy from the turquoise stone set in the amulet.

We went back to the room to find a terse note that said we must vacate by 11 a.m. I phoned for rent cars and Hannah enquired for a taxi. No joy. Hannah asked our man if he would drive us into Pahoa so we could find lodgings there. No.

So, we sat and had a wonderful breakfast of our food, realising that we had food enough to last us for about ten days and certainly still leaving us with more luggage than we could possibly carry. What to do? The answer was to sit and chat in the lounge, keeping our sangfroid. Neither Hannah nor I panicked, we just sat chatting, relaxed on the sofa as if there was not a care in the world.

Time approached 11 a.m. We sat, completely without excitement or stress at the contretemps that was soon to happen. The minutes ticked by. Hannah had left the room when a large car drove up outside. Now, when we had been beach travelling around Kona and Captain Cook, I found that Hannah couldn't hitch-hike and stick her thumb out. That was my job. But what she could do was to run up to people as they were leaving the beach and ask them if they would give us a lift. That I could not do.

So the solution had turned up just in time. Hannah and I smiled quietly at each other, feeling the bond of friendship born out of going with the flow. Both of us tacitly knew that we had maintained our sangfroid against all the odds.

When Hannah returned to the lounge, I asked her if she would ask the car driver if we could have a lift. I asked her very tentatively, knowing I was asking for something that I could not do myself. But of course, yes she would! Two minutes later we found ourselves in a large car (big enough for all our luggage too) with two German women on their way to Volcano. They had just come to the guest house to enquire about the possibility of staying there the next year. It was ten to eleven.

I was a bit sorry to find myself going again to Volcano when I wanted to stay and explore Pahoa. But our rescue party asked if we would mind stopping to see a few attractions in the area before going to Volcano. Oh-ho! How you can fall on your feet! So, in the falling rain we went around the Pahoa market, a wonderful craft affair with great food too (more food, when we already had a box full). Then to see nearby lava trees, where lava had engulfed trees which had then left tall columns of lava behind. On to the Red Route, a beautiful tree-lined road, shaded to darkness, but with brick red lava lining the road edges. So bright in the rain! So we got to see the area, albeit briefly, after all.

Then to Volcano, returning to Holo Holo youth hostel. Our German friends were staying in the National Park hotel. The hostel was closed till 4 p.m. so Hannah and I hid all our things under a tarpaulin in the heavy rain and hit Volcano village high life: the café with Internet. Two machines, her on one, me on the other. Lava Rock Café.

I still felt to have been pretty much swept away from Pahoa. Once again we had no transport and Hannah no work or camping. We were back at the hostel for opening time, everything dripping wet except for our luggage, cosily stowed under the tarp and undisturbed. We met Bob, fresh from Hilo with bunches of orchids for the kitchen table. We all ate evening dinner in the kitchen. Then Linde walked in. She was hungry and by then the Thai restaurant in the village would be closed. Well, we had bags of food, so please, we will cook for you!

You can guess the outcome. Next day we were at the Volcano National Park doing the sights: craters, tubes, sulphur beds courtesy of Linde's car. This time I took a walk on my own across one of the biggest craters to rendezvous with Linde and Hannah on the far side. I took time to meditate with Pele and felt that she and Venus were now working together. The walk was desolate, miles of black lava to traverse, like Elle's cow pats, with a smell of sulphur in the air, steam rising here and there. Warning signs abounded for people with respiratory problems or pregnancy.

Linde was glad of our company and navigation skills and we were glad to be getting around. Everyone won out of the arrangement. This time I did get to see the black beach of Punaluu. And it was lovely: a crescent curve of black sand, sloping gently up from the sea to a fringe of palm trees, then the land dropping away to a marsh. The sea was blue, the swamp was green and verdant. It was popular: some people had beach loungers facing the sea, others the marsh – both equally beautiful. The black sand seemed to really give life to all the colours around: sea, sky and beach-going paraphernalia.

Hannah and Linde were both in their twenties. They went off swimming and exploring. Maybe age gets the better of you, so I just lay and sunbathed on the gritty black lava beach. I felt forty-eight. But it was not to last and off we went to the South Point, the most southerly point of the USA, where the water pounds the cliff base and goes all the way to the Antarctic. It felt like it. Photos show us braced against the wind before heading off to the Green Sand Beach. What a long walk that was – only to arrive with the light falling, no appetite for swimming and only a hint of the colour the sand is famed as having.

I had had it in mind to follow the *Hawaii: Big Island Revealed* guidebook and go for a trek to Puu Oo, the name of the vent that was erupting at that time. That was the lava flow Elle and I had seen at dusk on the first visit I made to Volcano National Park. Ironically, the vent was outside of the National Park, and then the lava went through lava tubes, entering the National Park and emerged still hot and fiery just as it hit the sea. The trek is not recommended by the Park people. The guidebook gives the walk, but has many cautionary notes: getting lost, tracks unmaintained, wild pig tracks to confuse you, not having enough time, needing rainproof clothing for the rainforest, noting where you leave the rainforest so you can re-enter and not falling into the crater!

After our Green Sand Beach trek I was tired, so the next day when we left Holo Holo hostel I just noted where the Puu Oo track started for future reference. Then we headed back to the Pahoa area, Linde, Hannah and me.

So, again, I saw the Red Route and the lava trees but this time we also went to the hot springs pool by the sea. In the rain and under cover of a very grey sky we swam in warm water, heated by Pele's bountifulness. Oh, what an experience: a cosy outdoor swim in the rain. I noted in my diary: Hawaii is for me!

Linde was keen to see many things and it was raining so we headed out of the area and towards Hilo. Again, I saw Rainbow Falls, Boiling Pots, added Peepee Falls and then north of Hilo to Akaka Falls with a 420-foot drop and nearby Kahuna Falls. Feeling somewhat blessed with the surfeit of falls, we headed to a village and I bought a lovely rope of pearls. I didn't ask why they were cheaper than the rest in the shop but they were well selected and looked pretty on my neck. Ha, that's back to the Venus line for you!

The evening found Hannah and me back at Eva's and cooking dinner. We had said our sweet goodbyes to Linde. Next day, Hannah helped Eva in the shop and I stayed home, idling my time away. In the afternoon I went to Onomea Falls and the Hawaiian Botanic Gardens. That was interesting. But the house dog, a big cream Labrador, would go with me! No, no, I said you must go home. But the company was reassuring as I crossed private agricultural land and old sugarcane plantations to get to the main highway. Eventually, I got to the road. Go home! I told the dog. No avail. Eva's dog had absolutely no road sense and had the traffic on the highway swerving and practising emergency stops while car occupants glared at me and I shrugged. Eventually the dog sat by a lamp post on Eva's side of the road and after a brief visit to a shop I returned to find the dog gone. At first I was relieved but then spent the rest of my trip just slightly anxious in case it was not at home when I returned.

The afternoon was delightful with lots of photos that I could turn into silk pictures. The plants and wild setting of waterfalls tumbling and hissing down and over boulders was just beautiful. It was made the more enchanting because the path was easy to traverse and so I could give my eyes up to the foliage without risk of taking a tumble. There was a little gift shop so I bought a T-shirt for Dave. It later became a favourite one.

The late afternoon light had come into the Botanic Gardens in dramatic shafts, threading its way through fronds and leaves of the exotic, luxuriant vegetation. But as I walked home the Hilo heavens opened. I was not far from home and had chosen the road this time for my travel, not the sugar fields. I have never seen such bouncy rain! It came so fast and furious that in a moment it was above the level of my sandal soles and just rushing between the soles of my feet and my sandals. I was forced to find shelter.

I looked around and quickly a house with an open garage came into view. I took shelter in the open garage; the occupants were seemingly out. I felt a bit like a burglar as I stood there next to their car watching the road turn into a river. Of course, I was already wet through, so I started to get cold. I decided that I must head on with the water still pouring in and out of my squelching sandals. But the driving force of the rain got the better of me. I stopped again and, this time, I learned Hannah's trick and asked a couple who were getting into their car for a lift. Yes, they would take me all the way.

Tomorrow would be Maui, and Mike. Everything felt to have such a perfect fit. I would fly from Hilo and Eva would even take me to the airport on her way to work. Who needs a rent car!

In writing this, it always seems as though I was constantly on the move and doing things. A frenetic travelogue, rather than the search for the lazy useless life of leisure. Why didn't I just stay in bed all day? Surely that would have made the lazy life happen. But rather like seeking sleep, it has to come to you, you can't force yourself to sleep. At least my days were frittered away with this and that, all of little consequence. And maybe that was just the point of it all – even though it might exasperate you, the reader. Maybe my inability just to laze in bed, but at the same time to engage in little more than what beach to go to, reflects the inner wrangle of a usually busy, focused person, exploring the new arena of Venus. The fusion of my normal Uranus in the Midheaven of my birthplace – a place of personal power and battle for ideas – with this newfound Venus could bring this about.

Chapter Five

AWAY FROM THE LINE AGAIN

Diary 24 January 2002

Out to the airport and to Oahu first and then the connecting flight to Maui. At each stage my bags were totally unpacked – I had to take my shoes off, etc. Security you know, for your own good, you know, ma'am. How different from general aviation.

I have told Mike I would wear a lei around my hair. I think they are so becoming, even with artificial flowers – yes really! I sat on the wall outside the airport and very soon a car came by with a set of teeth between the stretched lips of a big smile. Ah, yes this is him! My friend Mary had said what a wonderful help Mike had been to her and her partner at the time when her partner was terminally ill. He looks nice.

★

We drove off around the west side of Maui, an area I had not been to before. Mike asked me if I was hungry. I said a bit, but could wait, no immediate urgency. The land became broken and wild; the weather looked stormy and turbulent. We saw the reddest cliffs and brightest tomato red puddles. Quite startling! Then to a garden open to the public where Mike tried to beat the owner down on the admission fee. I felt a touch uneasy; I don't do that. We sat next to each other on a seat in the garden; maybe a bit too close. It felt so strange meeting someone for a holiday like this purely on a friend's recommendation. How would it all work out?

We drove on, looking for a beach where Mike said he had nearly drowned many years ago. By now I am famished, but Mike seemed to have forgotten that I had said hunger would need to be assuaged sometime. But a change took place on the journey.

Ambivalence turned to a feeling of tenderness, particularly when I thought of how he had helped Mary.

Now, Mike had the use of a friend's condo in Kihei so we eventually wound up there. Nice place, bed settee as well as bedroom, no pressure. Except for my own, and with Mike's delightful smile I found myself in his arms and then in the bedroom just six hours after meeting. He had a charming love-making manner so it was all good fun. What about intimacy and sex? Never gave it a thought!

I wrote in my diary that looking back over that first day, every time I inspected my feelings, they had changed. Sometimes I felt appraising and possibly judgemental – did I like his teeth, for example. Where would all this lead? What expectations did he have? I suppose we just got to know each other better as we went on, and became more relaxed and in holiday romance mood.

Next day the weather changed and was largely grey for the rest of the week. We spent time doing things that Mike's friend had recommended and wound up at a retreat, Shangri-la, which I really liked. Could I somehow incorporate this place into my business in Crete: West Crete Holidays, some kind of link? I didn't find one, but took a leaflet in case inspiration got the better of me, later, when I was not looking for a lazy life.

The day after we went to the beach in the morning, and then Mike left, as he had told me he would, to take a boat trip with a friend in the afternoon. I felt a bit downcast, but painted all afternoon as a diversion from my disappointment. If it's a private party, I can hardly gatecrash!

However, when Mike returned I realised it had been a public whale-watching boat trip. Yes, he had met his friend, a woman whom he said he had had to keep at arm's length. I cooked dinner and pondered on the afternoon. To feel at ease I gave Mike a massage, glad to get out from my little cloud and into the neutrality of my professional role.

Then I discovered that while Mike had invited me to come to Maui on Thursday, he had actually been there since the Tuesday and the condo would not then be available after Monday! This began to feel like a long weekend, not a week's holiday. I told Mike I knew of a surfers' hostel (with private rooms as well as dorm) so we could stay on. There was a confusion in my mind over Mike's flight and whether it was on a fixed day or not and I began to feel more uneasy. Not worth making a fuss; I need never see him again, so why create a row?

Sunday came round and we went to Big Beach, then Little Beach for the drumming music. Lots of people, but none of the people I had seen before were there. However, it was great fun, dancing till the sun went down in a gold and blue sky. Even the rain that day hadn't deterred us. In fact, it became a bit of a game. We kept considering leaving the beach and each time we packed up to leave the rain would stop. In the end we decided to leave only if it was still raining when we got to a particular point between the beach and the car. Ah! Each time it stopped and we returned to the beach.

Mike makes friends wherever he goes. He is a networker. I find it almost hard going. I think my holiday alone has caused me to need my own company at least some of the time and to be quiet. But at least Mike readily accepts my regular need to give him kisses and cuddles. That feels uncomplicated.

Monday was pack-up day at the condo and Rainbow House hostel was fully booked. But I was told of Steve's Place in Paia. Never say goodbye on the telephone without another lead! Steve's Place is a house in the centre of Paia and our room was lovely, off a communal sitting area, and there is a kitchen for feeding. Mike immediately made friends with the other people in nearby rooms, all leading directly off the kitchen and living room.

I thought on price we would go fifty–fifty, but I paid and that seemed to be the end of the matter. Hmmm. I'm not good at sorting this type of negotiation so I decided just to feel a bit uneasy. This was not the first time money had been an issue between us. Not worthy of a discussion and possible estrangement just two days before we separate. So, we started to talk of meeting in California when I returned in March.

Mike managed to upset me again before we parted. The next and last day we went shopping for a little food in Hilo Hatties (I had the nibbles for my much-loved macadamia nuts) and I found Mike in a different area of the shop where he started to pick my brains over which earrings he should buy as holiday gifts for his tennis clients. This took hours. I began to feel I might like a pair too, but I was not a tennis client, just a lover. I felt a bit cool.

I don't know what caused it but twice in the last two days I had laughed till I cried. Once over a comic book and once at a tale Mike told me. My emotions seemed to be running high. At one moment I felt glad Mike and I were parting. It had not been such an easy time. Then again, I would soon be on my own, without yet another person I had come to know on this holiday. People kept leaving me!

Then tears again in Mike's arms, a feeling of being left behind. Mike went to the airport, with the car, and that was that. It rained hard all day so I sat home and was quiet. I decided to stay on for a few more days to give myself a chance to come to terms with such a lovely five-day relationship, even if it had had some difficult moments. He had been beautiful and we released each other nicely on the last day, gently saying our goodbyes. Then, there was the possibility of seeing him in California. I had an unease about this because I had already thought to see Jerry's son and ask him for Jerry's address in Los Angeles so I could visit him too. What sort of an emotional tangle would that leave me in! An exciting one, I decided.

While it rained I read the hostel's copy of *Lonely Planet* and realised that I could visit Lanai and Molokai on day trips from Maui. Lahaina, on the other side of Maui, was the place for the ferry boats. I took a walk out and changed my flight. Steve, my landlord, then took an interest in me, wanting to give me a massage. I had noticed he had a treatment table. I agreed to give him a massage instead, in exchange for his taking me to the ferry terminal. But why was it that I attract so many men? I'm no great looker and forty-eight years old! Is this another aspect of Venus?

When Elle and I had been together on Maui we often gave lifts to hitchhikers and now with no Mike or car I resumed my life as a hitchhiker, finding it so easy. Women particularly picked me up, maybe fearing their husbands might do so if they didn't. The more feminine I looked on my travels the more women helped me. This was helped by a day of Venusian shopping, spending $245 on clothes in Paia, oh all so feminine: a skirt of chiffon, a shiny off-the-shoulder top and a silk dress – more like an underslip really – in peach. I could have bought lots more – all this was so unlike me! On a more normal note, I had a lovely time visiting birdwatching areas, walking beaches and then going to Lanai and to Molokai.

First to Lanai: this was a great trip. The island is largely grass-land and the city, in reality a small village, is in the centre, quite elevated and isolated, reached by a long avenue of Norfolk Island Pines. They look so incongruous standing in line like sentries in the otherwise rolling grassy plain. Not yet tall enough to be majestic, but still obtrusive as the eye follows them.

I felt Lanai City would make a delightful home and mused on this idea, exploring all around the one-storey buildings, prettily painted, and drinking tea in the café. Uh-uh! The clouds suddenly descended, the City was shrouded in a thick dark mist and it was raining. My attitude towards the City changed instantly. How could they build in such a godforsaken place of mist!

I escaped to the coast, passing through the doors of the fine Manuele Beach Hotel to get to a beautiful beach. The hotel is part of a bygone age and quite self-consciously kept so. A haven for potted palms and aspidistra, with carpets depicting flowers and fish of Hawaii, all realistically represented. Oh, how wonderful to stay there. The atmosphere is relaxed and the energy so peaceful. I took time to make a photograph; and the hotel staff are so gracious, they didn't rush me along.

The storm of the other day (when Mike left) had left the hotel's golf course flooded and the beach damaged, but it was still lovely. A woman asked me to swim with her as she was not confident on her own. I enjoyed the company but needed to go off exploring and so met four American women, all about my age and all very different from each other and all setting up camp together, with suitcases. I love my photo of them and I saw myself in all of them. Oh, to go camping on Lanai! One of them had lots of bracelets and a straw hat and town clothes; another was more tomboy like. I smile as I think of them anticipating their camping holiday – they were as excited as children. But, oh, what a lot of luggage they had!

On the boat back, I admired a lei of plumeria, only to find its owner took it off and gave it to me. This gave me the opportunity of giving it away, in turn, to thank a woman who gave me a lift back to Paia. Back to a dinner of asparagus; yes, that again!

Diary 1 February 2002

Back to smiling all over. I love life! Had a lift today from two drunken men in a truck, both wearing sunglasses. Now, I never know who people are in sunglasses, but I could hardly ask them to take them off so I could judge whether they were trustworthy companions for me. I sat just behind them, in the back where there was no door (i.e. no escape). They would have to get out to let me out. Oh, I prayed and trusted my life to Sai Baba – and all was well.

I feel every lift is an opportunity for me to give someone a message or for that person to give me one. So, I am not waiting for a lift any more, just waiting for the person I must exchange information with. This takes away any possible impatience, but with on average every second car to pass picking me up I don't have time for that! More birdwatching too. Maui is nice.

Molokai will be an early start. The boat leaves before dawn. I stay overnight at the Maui branch of Patey's Place, but it is a hot, sweaty dorm and I am glad to leave in the early hours.

A room-mate tells me of whale research that she is doing and says they don't know why the whales breach the surface or flap their fins. (I had seen whales on my boat trips.) Well, I went in a reverie and met whales and asked them. Simple, they enjoy it and it allows them to experience a different pressure than they have in the sea. They fin flap to stretch their flippers. Nothing more elaborate than that! Well, that's what I got, anyway!

★

I took food and clothing to Molokai with a view to staying, but no. It was not for me. You need a car. I got lifts, but there's no traffic so it was slow going. The condos are on one coast, next to a derelict golf course; the town on another coast and the beaches supposedly on a third side. I didn't get that far. I found two people driving around who couldn't navigate so I managed to guide them and so saw quite a lot of the island, trying to stop them from bickering about which way to go at the little junctions. I served them well. Then I waited for the boat back at 2.30 p.m. I was there in good time, idling my time away by the jetty, waiting for the boat.

I arrived back in Steve's Place and he had moved my room. That was fine with me. My new room was brighter and I could paint more easily. The silk scarf diary was coming on well even though it was a stretchy crepe silk which I had discovered was really hard to paint. The paint on the silk spreads too easily and so my little pictures were made difficult and blurred.

So, with Lanai and Molokai under my belt I could leave Maui. My trip to Maui had taken me via Oahu and I decided Oahu was not a place for me. I had been woken on the flight (I often sleep on flights) to the sound of the air steward saying welcome to Oahu, and I looked out of the window. In a moment of confusion I thought she had said Ohio and panicked that I had boarded the wrong flight! We were over Honolulu and, as the steward soothingly continued, it stretched twenty-five miles up the coast. High rise blocks, city life – not for me. I decided I didn't need to visit this island. OK, Honolulu is only one part, but for me it would taint the whole island with its energy. I felt I now had only Kawai to visit. But this is the furthest island from the Venus line, and surely that was the point of my trip to Hawaii.

The day after my trip to Molokai (Sunday), Juqua rang me. She had picked me up while I was hitch-hiking and we had agreed to go together to Little Beach. We agreed to go that afternoon. A new face! I spent the morning painting my neglected diary. At last, the paintings showed that I was on Maui.

I was still mulling over where to go next: spend more time on Maui, exploring bits I had not seen, go to Big Island, which I had largely seen, go to pastures new on Kawai. But Kawai could wait. That was because I believed at the time I was due to fly back to California from there. I had got muddled because of the many different flights the agent had looked at for me in San Francisco. The flight was 17 March, a long time off, so it was more important to continue exploring Venus. Where on Big Island might I like to be? Well, Kona I had seen plenty of, and Hilo is so wet.

There is a hostel in Hilo, Arnott's, which sounded nice, with lots of trips out arranged by them. But I had got used to a single room here in Maui. A dorm? I don't think so! I felt that Honokaa could be the best place to stay. But the absence of beach at Honokaa might be a problem – I am used to swimming easily in Crete and also in Hawaii, so, while I like Honokaa, even as I made up my mind to go there, I questioned my decision.

Diary 4 February 2002

Steve, my landlord and would-be suitor, took me to a New Age church in Haiku today. It's Sunday and Haiku is a small garden 'city'. The service was warm-hearted as Steve said it would be, with readings and songs, and was actually held in a private house. The room was bedecked with pictures of saintly people, but I didn't spy one of Sai Baba. Then home with Steve and I gave him a chakra balance. Difficult to pull bad energy away from him, it seems to cling hold. But I learnt that if I asked it to come with love, I could get it away. It helped. There is still no way I would let him treat me, he is like a bag of nerves.

I went in the afternoon to Little Beach with Juqua. The weather has improved, in fact it's been a mini heatwave, so a beach trip was nice. Sunday at Little Beach again with nudes and dancing. I gained another potential boyfriend: a man just introducing himself in the waves, but I am just not ready for that. But I did learn something from him however, about how to surf. The sun went down as the drums grew louder and we all cheered as it disappeared.

With Juqua I had a change in lifestyle and we went to Starbucks for coffee, then a fast food place for dinner. Back home, we walked around Paia and found a clothes shop which had cushions scattered on the floor. Chanting of sacred songs relating to Sai Baba was about to commence. I took a place with alacrity, sitting on the floor with rails of merchandise all around! Juqua had pain in her base chakra so I did some work on that then stayed up late packing. Tomorrow I leave; I have a ticket back to Big Island and so out of inertia I shall go.

Diary 5 February 2002

I slept badly on the coffee and woke to a busy day. I have learnt a trick when moving: I try to get all my photos developed and printed and out in the post to my mother so I have less to carry and the films get less exposure to airport X-ray machines. Anything else that needs posting out must go too, just to keep down the luggage weight. So I like to travel mid-week, time to get photographs in and back then posted out, without the impediment of Sunday down time. Still rushing around I got home to Steve's and he asked me if I would like a free night's stay. Oh! Yes, that would be nice. The rush evaporated, I changed my flight by a day and slept the afternoon away. This is perhaps the lazy useless life I seek. It is still a dilemma: how can it be lazy and useless if that is the aim? Goals are usually the result of doing things and are achievements. How does this fit with 'lazy and useless'. How will I know when it is achieved?

I tried to phone Jerry, just to check he has left Hawaii. Ah, it seems so; his number no longer works.

I suddenly felt very fond of Maui. Maybe it's the familiarity, the health food shops and Sai Baba shop. Also beaches, Paia, birdwatching and Steve's Place. Back at Big Island I would have hostel dorms – even at Honokaa I heard that there was a dorm. Then again, the lure of Pele, goddess of volcanoes and those black lava flows – oh! Maybe it was a rush of nostalgia as my flight is tomorrow.

★

But life changes, as I packed again to leave Steve's Place, Kath arrived, taking up the next room to me. She had a car and so we went together exploring the local beaches that I had somehow not concerned myself with before. I had the impression that they were just surfing beaches, but no. At the end of Baldwin beach, just across the road from Paia was a baby pool where the waves break on a reef and leave a lake of calm water, just perfect for swimming. Kath and I talked like old friends about relationships. No intimacy was spared. I think we were both surprised that our candid conversation seemed to flow, uninhibited by our usual social ways. Our short, sweet relationship had a beautiful closure: she had to return the rent car to the airport and I needed to go there for my flight. This probably represented my most delightful day before a flight – no sense of clock watching. Finding that beautiful beach, I was tempted to stay. But no, I had spoken to Kurman, a friend of landlord Steve, and had decided to stay with him. Kurman's place was near to Pahoa and so put me back in easy reach of the active volcano on Big Island. Kurman also wanted to go on the walk to the volcano's erupting vent, Puu Oo, so I could take his measure and decide if it felt right. You may remember, I said that the guidebook said it was difficult and lengthy and I had certainly not felt like doing it alone. Kurman's was also near the Hot Pool that I had only sampled once, so that would be wonderful. Kurman's place – Papaya Plantation – was a retreat where they ran workshops, but not in the following week. So, it was easy for me to stay and for him to do the walk. I would touch base with Hannah too, to see if she had managed to get into permaculture and camping.

Chapter Six

BACK ON THE LINE

I left Maui feeling very excited and happy, but somehow sad to be leaving the Maui that I now so dearly loved. I saw such advantages in staying there: the newly found beach, Steve's Place, the good shops nearby. What more could you want? Well, to be closer to the Venus line answers that one! Although I was heading for Kurman's place, I stopped off in Hilo and took up residence at Arnott's, a very well-known and respected hostel, advertising in-house tours and walks. It was still a few days before Kurman's place would have a vacancy.

I slept badly in the dorm and found security very low (please remember I was travelling with thirty-eight diamonds set in rings and other nice pieces too so lockers were useful). Here, the dorms did not even have doors, let alone locks.

The next morning, over breakfast, I met a group of young, English women: Becca, Sam and Kirsty. We decided we would join the Arnott tour of the day: a walk to see the eruption of lava. The lava flows from a vent, goes underground (lava is like water and finds its easiest way), then comes out on the surface near the sea. However, my new friends thought the tour timetable was too short, so to give us longer we would go in Kirsty's car and make our own way back, after the group had left.

The plan was delightful because our guide, Ian, was a fast walker (and Kirsty was not). Very macho too. He was such a turn-off! Never mind, at least we were able to stay on and not go back with the group. He literally had people running across the lava and told us we must hurry. He was anxious because he was not sure where he would find the hot lava. It had moved and was no longer issuing out by the sea. To give him his due, he did find the place where you could see it. Halfway up the hillside, there it was. A red and black tongue of molten lava, slithering at quite a low speed, but relentlessly and somehow unpredictably, finding the easiest route across a landscape already swollen with previous flows. This flow was obviously new and making a new stream, crossing the older lava, this way and that. There was an incredible sense of power. Nothing would stop it as it crackled away like an angry fire spitting at the cold of the lava it crossed. All this black, shiny lava for miles and then suddenly this red!

One man in the group had brought a lei, like a wreath of green leaves, and threw it on to the lava. I wished I had thought to do that. Then the group left, leaving us four women behind. We sat down and held a meditation, right by the lava flow. It was not the most relaxing environment. I kept a vigilant eye on the ever-present lava tongue as I led my three new friends on a guided meditation to Pele, the goddess of the volcano. I joined in too at the stage in the meditation of seeing what Pele wanted from us, whether she was getting it and whether she had a gift for us. I remember a tremendous sense of love and power, a feeling of contentment – extraordinary!

We then made our adieus to the flow and to Pele and headed back to the car. Except that we split up: Becca with Kirsty, me with Sam. This was, I felt, a mistake as time went by. With the sea on one side of us and the hillside on the other it had originally felt an easy walk. But there is no path, just hard, black lava every-where. It actually comes and goes in ridges so sometimes you can see a distance and then you get lost in the ravines where there are no distant views. At one time Sam and I saw the other two way over in the distance, near the sea. Although we had lots of time before dusk, after walking for three hours I let anxiety creep in. I had to work really hard not to panic at the sheer immensity of the black landscape. It occurred to me that we could overshoot the small car park, not even noticing it, by being too near the sea and walking beneath it. Sam, like the others, was in her twenties and so I did not want her to be influenced by my fears, I just kept breathing and getting on with walking and hoping! Eventually, on the skyline, I could see people – through my binoculars – and they looked as small as ants. So far still to go. As it dropped dusk we made our way off the lava and were reunited with Kirsty and Becca who had, in the end, beaten us back.

As it happened the wardens at the car park had been tipped off to watch for us by our Arnott's guide and they had kept us in binocular sight. We were known as the four who included a woman in a bright pink dress. That's me, who else! I realised at that point just how safe it was to wear idiosyncratic clothes for walking. Where would we have been if we had all been wearing grey shorts and blue T-shirts? Before leaving we looked back in the darkness and could see two newly formed streams of lava down the hillside, where we had been. Just like two lines of fire.

Soon I was due to leave Arnott's and go to Kurman's place near Pahoa. How was I to get there? There's no public transport and I didn't want a rent car because I only needed transport to get out there, not after I had arrived. As I mused on this a little miracle came along. Actually a big miracle in the form of Tammie, my previous and ample chauffeur. Great: women were helping me out again! Into Arnott's she slid, just visiting, she told me, and so effortlessly I arranged transport with her for the move. Just a few days left in Hilo so I agreed to cook for Eva and Carl on Saturday, took films in to be processed and generally made my ever-present pink nail varnish respectable again after the lava walk.

Before leaving Arnott's I went to Mauna Kea, the biggest volcano in Big Island, now quiet and bearing about thirteen observatories at 13,000 feet. The trip had a nice guide this time, Darrell, who I kept thanking for the little things he did to make the trip good. We were to go to 9,000 feet where there is an information room – where I had seen the moonbow. Darrell had telescopes for stargazing. We picked up constellations and although we got very cold it was informative. As with all things you are told in adverse weather, the information didn't stick, but it was fun at the time! We did see Jupiter with four moons and Saturn with two rings of dust and many, many moons, but Venus, he said, is the morning star and so not visible at dusk – ha!

The following morning Sam and I did a walk together and she confided in me that she didn't get on well with Kirsty. Sam and Becca were old friends but Becca was on a more lengthy holiday than Sam. They had only recently met Kirsty. But she was able to tell Becca lots of things about travel and they were arranging to meet up again in Australasia. Sam felt this was good for her friend and so had held her tongue. But she was piqued – and unhappy about her feelings. So, that was why we had split into two groups on the lava walk! I found myself offering counselling advice. I have never felt myself to be good at this, but it just seemed to flow. Part of being loving, I suppose. I certainly have a much greater affinity for women than I used to. My counselling was just to keep asking her why she felt the way she did after everything she told me. Fancy, I can't do a thing for a lover with a drink problem but can empathise and freely offer support to a woman. That's Venus for you, and the fact that there's no need for me to pit intimacy against sexual tensions with women.

While it rained on and off all day (this is Hilo of 170 inches per year) the sun shone for Sam and me the whole while as we sat on the grass looking at the sea and her problems. But the weather was cold and I now had winter clothes on and dark red nails.

Back at the ranch I gave a healing to take away pain, with the condition that the man, Mike, would give up his views that science was all and that spirituality was nonsense. It did the trick: the pain went and so he had to believe. I noted in my diary: Sai Baba at his best!

Then off to central Hilo to meet Eva and shop for our evening meal together. I had been hitch-hiking quite a lot and again felt that I was not waiting for a lift but to meet someone for whom I had a message, or they had one for me. This took all the frustration out of a wait. Although I rarely do wait long! As it happened my lift this time took me right to Eva's shop, where my driver got out too because she recognised a car parked outside the shop as belonging to a friend of hers. I felt I had caused an impromptu rendezvous!

The evening was not all I had hoped it might be as a thank you to Eva. She had to make another engagement, Hannah was ill and so Carl and I were the main partakers of the food and wine. Oh and thereby hangs a tale.

Mike, Mary's friend, whom I had travelled to Maui to see, had kept in touch with me by email. We had been arranging to meet in California after my visit to Hawaii was over (18 March). That morning I had received an email to say, 'When you come to San

Diego, where will you stay?' Somewhat puzzled and incensed, I replied, 'With you, where do you think I would stay?' Now, you may remember Mike and I had had a bit of a rocky time, but it had not seemed worthwhile making a fuss.

After the meal I stayed over with Eva and Carl and in the night I woke and felt really sore about this email. What a cheek, where would I stay! The whole episode of the minor grievances of the holiday took on a more urgent turn. I really needed to kick the table over.

As I lay in bed, I observed myself getting hotter and crosser, and at the same time thinking, I haven't felt like this for such a long time! I came to realise that the wine not only poisoned my body (organic, too) but my mind as well.

In the morning I used Carl's computer to look at my mail – and discovered I had actually misread Mike's email. He had asked where I would stay in San Francisco, not San Diego! So, I had spent all night feeling sore about something that wasn't even accurate. I felt so deflated having prepared an indignant response along the lines of, 'Do I ever want to see you again?' Only to find it was not necessary. I had spent a night seething over nothing. At that moment I decided that was the last time I would drink alcohol – unless I chose to do so, of course. Leave the door open, Juliet! Never say never!

The 10 February had arrived, and off I went with Tammie to Kurman's Place at Pahoa. Well, actually some miles away in the countryside: Papaya Plantation. I had no idea how I would get around, but then I wanted to spend some time painting my diary.

I was the only guest at Papaya Plantation. Apart from Kurman there was an Italian woman, Veronica, and her young Canadian boyfriend, Nigel. Veronica was working there. The place seemed very disorganised and its poor attendance reminded me of some weeks of our own holiday venture in Greece. Hmm… On our first evening together, we all watched the film *A Fish Called Wanda*. Afterwards, they all seemed to think it had enriched their lives. Mine wasn't. But I had had little option but to watch it given that the building is open-plan. So open-plan that I woke in the morning to noisy lovemaking between Veronica and Nigel, in the loft area. It was not my idea of a quiet retreat, as advertised.

But I did some painting so it obviously was not too chaotic for me.

It was cold and so I was in winter clothes again and sorted out why I was wearing red nail varnish – Pele! I mused on the useless life because of my proximity to the Venus line and asked Archangel Michael to protect me as I felt that my thoughts could take me into a different place, disturbing to me: somehow, beyond the beyond. Would it be a useless life if I stopped painting, writing my diary, sending emails, cooking and shopping? What does a useless life mean, and if it is sought, can it then be one, when it happens? I'd got no further with this one, whatever words I used.

Perhaps I had achieved some elements of uselessness and leisure because, although my diaries read like constant action, I did not feel that I was achieving anything very much. I just needed more laziness maybe.

Diary 12 February 2002

So, on the tenth, I wrote a list of things to do while in Pahoa. Then I decided that nothing was pressing and so all could wait at least two days. I would stay put and see if this helped the lazy life. So for two days I sit all day in the chair on the veranda and look towards the sea. I feel I am somehow waiting for something to come from the sea, almost as if I am on a passive patrol. Just watching the horizon. Two whole days. The view is lovely: nearby coconut palms frame the view of plantations and old lava flows. Beyond is the sea, seen in the far distance, a thin silver line. I can see I may get a little lonely here. Maybe that will change as I get to know people better. Except I have little interest in getting to know the people here.

So for two days I have sat in the chair, sat in the hammock, always an eye on that silver line that marks the sea and the horizon. In the afternoons I have gone to bed.

Then on the twelfth I had a watsu session with my Italian host, Veronica. What a woman: she constantly screeches at Kurman (her boss) and makes scenes. Not at all conducive to peace and quiet. Never mind, she has offered me a free taster of watsu (more on that later) at a nearby health retreat: Kalani. We go together and in the shoulder-height, thermal water she cradles me and lets my body flow this way and that as she pulls me through the warm water, turning me around as we go. Ooh! That's a bit sore on my lower back, but it felt really supportive and kindly – as long as I didn't breathe in the smell of her nicotine-scented skin. Despite this drawback, I decided on a full-length watsu session with her, in the outdoor Hot Pool. I have always loved Turkish baths because it suits the sun sign in me, which is Cancer, and the moon sign in me, which is Aries: water and fire together make me feel whole. Fire and water will both be present at the Hot Pool. Maybe this too will help the laziness. It is becoming a preoccupation.

Diary 13 February 2002

Got up, had a coconut, sat in the chair till noon, went to bed till 3 p.m. Cooked i.e. made a stuffed pepper with some cooked rice and nutty trail mix and placed it in the microwave, adding a slice of cheese at the end. Now, for me to use a microwave and make something so simple needs to be noted! I have never, ever bought a ready meal or looked towards convenience foods.

Everyone is out and then Shana arrives, expecting to be welcomed in as a new guest. I take over this role and show her the only unused room. She is bemused at the casual way no one is here to meet her. She has a car and so we go together into Pahoa so she can get provisions – and for me too, and we go to the Internet café. Then we decide to eat at Godmothers, recommended in some guidebook she has. It's a good day and a diversion from doing nothing. I feel something stirring deep down as if coming out from hibernation. Shana is bubbly and full of fun, with lots of energy, not like the rather serious and spineless Kurman or the frenetic, angry loudness of Veronica or the aloofness of her young boyfriend. I explain to Shana what the folk are like. I liken Veronica to something from a Fellini film – a little wizened witch with skinny legs and an overlarge head, masses of frizzy grey hair and a cackling laugh that shatters glass.

With the spare room gone to Shana, I am due to start sharing my open-plan bed space with Ashaman. Ah! He has such beautiful long hair. He's another visitor, recently arrived and Shana's arrival has kept him from using the spare room.

★

And so the days went by, sometimes contemplating the uselessness, other times going out with Shana, an antidote to my rather
serious self-study. We went to the Hot Pool and to the Puna area
at dusk where we could see the lava flow in the distance and
throw a lei in its direction. Then we had a magic moment. It was
almost dark and we had ventured a way out over the lava (we had
torches) to see the glowing light from the lava flows, miles away
up the coast. There was a thin sliver of moon and one cloud in
the sky. The sky itself was just turning from teal blue to the dark
of full night. There was one single cloud in the sky. It was
positioned over the hillside and its underside was bright red. I
realised that it was directly over the erupting vent, Puu Oo. So,
the red was a reflection in the sky of the erupting vent! It was
really beautiful. We gaped for some time and then in the darkness
wove our way carefully over the black, uneven, glassy-looking
lava back to the car.

So what had happened to my idea of going to the erupting
vent on foot with Kurman, my reason, in part, for moving to
Pahoa and Papaya Plantation? Well, I wouldn't have trusted
Kurman in an emergency or even to have the common sense to
notice one. He seemed very spineless with Veronica, and for the
walk I would need someone at least as mentally strong as me and
to have a good pair of ears and eyes and a nose for danger. So, I
had abandoned the idea and pacified myself with the fact that it
was not part of a lazy useless life to go on an ill-defined trek
where there would be pressure to get back before nightfall. All of
a sudden Shana's constant chatter had started to weary me.

Diary 14 February 2002

Valentine's Day. There never seems to be a man in my life at this
time, or at least not one who rises to the occasion! Shana and I go
to visit some steam vents and I realise we are next door to the
house where Hannah and I stayed in together, remember? When
we were rescued by two German women. So it was called
Volcano Ranch – we never even knew that much about it! Shana
and I sit in a steam vent together and discuss our hosts at Papaya

Plantation with much laughter and take photos of our nakedness being a little coy so they aren't overly revealing. The car is useful so we go to a more distant and smaller hot pool, taking in some shrines on the way, decorated with little plastic windmills with angels' faces on them, flipping around in the breeze. In the pool, I gave Shana a little watsu – as much as I could remember from Veronica's work on me – then some boys came and we apologised for our nudity. They left and then a family arrived and we left. They were very prudish and even wore towels to get changed so they couldn't see each other in the buff.

★

Then, following Shana's guidebook we went to the Green Pool. I tell you, no stone was left unturned in the area. The Green Pool was strange and not immediately good for swimming. We left the car at the roadside and walked through recently mown fields and gardens and a crowd of, for want of a better word, hippies all chanting in a circle and banging their fists on the ground. Who owned this maintained place? What were the hippies doing there, and what were we doing there? Were we intruders? The Green Pool is a lake in a crater-like setting, with steep, wooded sides. Shana and I took photos of each other hanging Tarzan-like from a tree and then we dropped down to the lake, but it was in shadow and forbidding, particularly given the air of mystery that was hanging over the place. We had even walked by a state-of-the-art greenhouse, empty save for a state-of-the-art tractor/mower standing in it. Now this is a part of the world where you don't look around too hard, where there are aerial patrols to uncover marijuana production and guns are commonplace. Back to the car.

Shana had met a man, Joel, the night before, so we poked around, driving hither and thither – and found his place. A well-appointed shack, but with no electricity. Bed at dusk. It seemed in this subculture area such places were the norm: shacks hidden away up lanes in the heavy woodland.

Shana and I got our glad rags on and went to the Thai restaurant in town. These were moments when I became very girly and chattered about relationships with men, clothes, etc., the way other women do. All giggles and light-hearted fun. This had now happened, for me, with both Kath and Shana. In both cases we talked of ménage à trois, something that we had all done! Mike sent me a great email Valentine's card. That's nice, but not the same as a hug on the day.

Next day, Shana left. She took with her a friend of Joel's, and Ashaman, who infuriated me by making everyone hours late. Oh, my liking for punctuality is difficult to break, even when it's not me who is being inconvenienced. Come on useless life – help me out.

Better weather had arrived. So Nigel was out in the nude. With people gone I started to think about my life here. I felt guided to stay on another month on Big Island with just a quick trip to Kawai to catch my flight 18 March. My thoughts moved beyond and I started to plan my time in California. I had thoughts to stay with Jerry, with Mike and with friend, Maggie, whom I had met on a Findhorn workshop back in 1997. A phone call to the airline showed that I could make a change to my round-the-world ticket – for $75. So, my journey could be: fly to Oakland (my return ticket from Hawaii) then instead of flying from San Francisco to Miami, I could go down the Californian coast by train and fly from San Diego to Miami. And I would be back on route again. So, between Oakland and San Diego, I could take in Jerry in Los Angles and Mike near San Diego, finishing with Maggie in San Diego itself. Nice and easy, it felt good except I was not sure how my psyche would stand reopening and then closing two relationships with sexual bonds. All in ten days!

I had taken to hitch-hiking up and down from Papaya Plantation to the town, Pahoa. This seemed very easy. In a community where electricity was not commonplace, helping with transport was. Ashaman had told me he just wished that he had a little pink frock like mine that brought the first or second car to a halt. I learnt all the roads in the area, going this way and that around a rough triangle.

I had become the only guest again and took once more to surveying the ocean and coconut groves from the veranda seat. Settling my next leg of the journey had a pacifying effect on me. I felt as if I had a future.

I then planned the next few days: A trip to Hilo to get more macadamia nuts, my staple food (Tammie had given me a whole carrier bag full, but they had now gone). I had been eating about a pound weight of mac-nuts (as they are called in Hawaii) every day, since finding them early on, way back in Kona. I did not know how I would live without them! During these days I also got photos printed and scanned for the Internet. People kept asking me for images of the boyfriends that they heard about so regularly.

A decision: sometime, I would go to stay in Honokaa where Jason, Jerry's son lived and where the sun had always shone for me.

Kurman and Veronica had some huge noisy arguments. I suggested to Kurman that Hannah came to take her place because her emails had shown that she was still footloose. But he was torn because he did not want to lose his watsu therapist.

I visited the Hot Pool regularly and got to know local people who were also frequenters: Mark, who scoured the Pool for lost treasures, little bracelets, etc., and a woman who taught me a better way to do butterfly stroke and, yes, it worked better, less tiring, and more distance moved per stroke. Mark, I felt, could easily become another sexual partner, not because I fancied him but to keep away the loneliness I felt at Kurman's place, where I just did not fit in. I hoped that would not happen.

Diary 18 February 2002

I have slipped into a sense of inertia where my plans to move are stalled by my unwillingness to initiate change. Here I am, not terribly happy (lonely) and yet not moving on. I observe it for the useless life.

I am reading a book about watsu and how to teach it. It suggests that if you have sexual feelings towards the client that you raise these feelings to the heart and they change. Now, besides the client/therapist relationship that's a good one for me: to stop me maybe going to bed with someone too fast or for wrong reasons. So, if I get sexual feelings that I don't wish to consummate, this could be the answer, raise the feelings to my heart. I am reminded, too, of the statement I made with Jerry, when he was not happy to have a sexual relationship with me: 'I love and respect you.'

I slept in the afternoon and had a strange dream of wanting to get away. The only way I could do that was to put on a uniform and join a military procession. I was second (number two) in the processional line, but then as we entered an auditorium full of rows of seats the first person motioned to me to lead the procession. I did this, but when I turned around the procession had all gone the other way. I was alone on stage and with just another crowd of people all sitting in the auditorium, looking at me. I felt stupid, afraid and abandoned in my military uniform, so I took off my hat. I would have stripped all the uniform off, but I had to go, to leave where I was. Strange. I woke a little perturbed. My dream book was of little help in interpretation, but I supposed the dream to mean that I had been comfortable as part of a uniformed group, but then the time had come (I was number two in the procession) to peel off and become an individual. As an individual, my uniform felt ridiculous. And the newness of my individuality was not easy either as I had awoken feeling disturbed.

Diary 21 February 2002

At last I have decided to go to Hilo, stay at Arnott's again and from there arrange my trip to Honokaa. I contacted Tammie, and, yes, she will meet me and drive me to Hilo. Before she was due to come, I went to Kehena Beach, where there is nude bathing and black sand. It's also the place where rumour has it a young man fell and injured himself very badly after a drugs session. He is the owner of the Green Pool estate: the hippy area. He is rich but now incarcerated in a wheelchair and requiring constant help. So, that's a story to tell Shana – a mystery solved!

Diary 22 February 2002

Yesterday a strange thing happened. I waited for Tammie, with all my bags packed, ready to go. Unbelievably, she didn't show. The phone number I had for her was on answerphone – good, she's on her way. Other people who knew her had wondered at her steadfastness. I just put this down to a prejudice against slow fat people and told people that she would not be employed by a supermarket chain as a shelf-filler if she were not reliable. But here I was sitting waiting. Kurman, Veronica, Nigel all looked in at me and found me still there, but I was totally unperturbed by the wait and their concern for me. What will be, will be. So, I just stayed another night.

As the evening had worn on, without Tammie coming for me, I phoned Hannah. She is staying with Eva, in Hilo, but she has her sister and friend over too, from California. However, they will come down, Hannah, her sister, Summer, and friend Katlan, to rescue me and bring a picnic lunch with them. We eat the picnic, naked and with muddy feet, between midday nude swims in the Green Pool. Hannah's beautiful figure again! At midday, and with the mystery solved, the Green Pool looks all inviting. There's even a raft floating off shore to swim to. Somehow it has the cast of a film set. Idyllic and lazy. I show them other local sights. So, a woman to the rescue! What a good friend Hannah is!

★

In Hilo I got active. Towns can have that effect on me. Catching up with emails, buying provisions, a weekend ticket to a Tahitian dance festival, Friday eve through to Sunday. I was late to the Friday show, but the festival all started late anyway. At Arnott's hostel I stayed in the dormitory and my only companion there was a Japanese woman, Yasuko, who had come to Hilo to see the dancing too. So, on Saturday I had a companion. Company at last, such a contrast to Kurman's place! We both hired bicycles from Arnott's to make the trip into town easy for the festival. I caught sight of myself in a shop window: black and white tight pedal pushers, a clingy bright red top, black helmet, red nail varnish and gold shoes. Oh, don't I look nice. Ha! There's the Venus vanity for you!

Friday night of the festival had been pretty solo dances. It turned out the festival (held in a tennis arena) was actually a competition. There were different categories with everyone going through their sequences before a panel of judges. Saturday was hot and I wondered at the logic of being indoors for such a day. The whole competition was late running and very small-townish. It was sweet, but a bit infuriating to the slick city mind. There was even a fashion parade and Mr and Miss Hilo beauty competitions thrown in for good measure.

Next day the weather was totally the opposite. The heavens were well and truly open and it was cold. A friend from Patey's Place in Kona, Rex, had come down to Arnott's and so all three of us went to the festival. I asked after Tammie, but didn't find out much about why she had missed picking me up from Pahoa. The weather furiously beat through the open-ended building and I got really cold sitting on the hard metal bleacher seating. I had a floral dress on with matching jacket that just skimmed my waist. Not enough! At 5 p.m. we left, with me shivering. I mused on how different the sexy hip-wriggling Tahitian dancing was compared with the very symbolic storytelling hula dancing.

Yasuko and I ate together to eat up my stock of food. It was time for me to move on. I had asked around for a lift to Honokaa and, yes, to my surprise someone was going to Kona Airport; they would drop me off on their way. Ooh, a very early start – 6.15 a.m.

I felt the need to paint, my diary was behind again. But, no, the weather was too wet for painting. In cold, wet weather the paint takes a while to dry and I haven't the patience for that, so I tend to smudge things. So, I wrote a short email to Mike in San Diego telling him, inexplicably, to break it to me very gently if he ever tired of me, rather than giving me the cold shoulder brush-off.

Diary 25 February 2002

Oh dear! Arrive in Honokaa, not sure where I am staying, except it's called the Paniola Club Hotel, but I don't recall seeing that name when I passed through town before. The weather is wet, windy, grey and cold all the way from Hilo. And it's always been sunny in Honokaa before for me.

The car driver and other passenger unload my bags promptly on to the Honokaa pavement – the wet weather has made the journey a little slow from Arnott's – they might miss their flight out of Kona. In unpacking the car, all I had to do was to get a small plastic bag from the seat next to me and put it on the pavement while I said thank you and goodbye. That was the theory! In reality I put down the bag, winced in pain and couldn't stand up. I said goodbye to them more as if I were bowing to them. They looked so concerned that they couldn't do more for me as the airport beckoned them. At least they dropped me under an awning and I shambled to a bench shivering and gasping with pain. 7 a.m.

★

I left my bags by the kerb. I could see my wallet sitting atop, and so would anyone else, but I couldn't bend down further to remove it from its obvious position, nor could I stand up straight. What was this, a lack of support, not knowing where I was going to stay? Leaving friends behind, off on my own? I left my bags and wallet and shuffled in the teeming rain and wind squalls to the nearby hotel. The erratically swinging wind-blown sign said Hotel Honokaa Club. Thank God for that: I knew the hotel has both names. The steps to the door required a valiant effort, but in I went with teeth gritted against cold, wind, rain and pain. What a sorry sight!

The manager met me and, yes, there was a dorm, so this was the right place. I was so relieved I felt well enough to say I would fetch my own bags. Slowly but surely I dragged my bags up to the door. The manager, Kath, told me I couldn't go into the dorm at this time of day because other people were sleeping, but she got me breakfast, as well as for others who were early birds (on their way to work). She sat down with us all for breakfast. It reminds me of how we are in Greece; sitting down with the guests is always the way to say that you have time for them.

As soon as was possible I went to bed, saying I would stay there all day. You bet! A little later in the morning I tried to get out of bed and the pain was so acute I felt faint. Everything went grey and I was paralysed by the pain and couldn't even put my head between my knees to counteract the faintness or lie back on the bed. Then I sweated and became nauseous. Recovering, I inched across the bed, cursing every slight give of the mattress. Then, holding my breath I stood up. To the bathroom, shuffling laboriously, inching my way on shaking legs. Every step felt like a step into the unknown, not knowing whether I would get away with it or land in paralysing pain, not knowing how to go on. My lower back felt as if it had parted company with my sacrum. No strength or support whatsoever. Even breathing was painful if it hit into my abdomen.

The second trip to the bathroom, I crawled there. My legs felt totally unable to support me. My feet and legs felt perpetually cold. Evening came and Kath came to see me. I said I felt a bit better, the truth at that moment. Nightfall eventually came and a door started to bang annoyingly, waking me. I decided to investigate and make a last journey into the unknown (i.e. walk to the bathroom) before settling down for the night. Ah! I could not even get out of bed. The pain was too severe when I came to move. The dormitory was in the basement and I hadn't heard anyone else on that level nor was there any light coming under the door. I was just lying there in the dark. But I knew that one other person was sleeping on that floor, so I would just have to wait. What was I waiting for? I didn't know, but I felt I must tell someone of my predicament. I heard myself scream in pain and that made for more pain. Eventually, I heard the man next door arrive. I called out and he heard me. But I had locked the dormitory door. He went to get Kath.

They both entered the dorm together. Kath sat on my bed and fortunately she was lightweight and so did not rock the mattress. They both saw the agony I was now in. Kath said she had no bedpan, but there was no way I could get on to a bedpan anyway! But pain can be kind, so the desire to go to the toilet just evaporated. Kath said she had some anti-inflammatory and muscle-relaxant tablets on prescription and so she would give me the two. She was reluctant about this but compassion was the greater spirit than legality. The next thing, how could I take them? Well, she got a glass of water and a straw and actually placed the tablets on my outstretched tongue and held the glass so I could drink from the straw. Had I been through this with a friend I would have said afterwards that I could not have managed without them, but I had no friend! After the tablets, I slept till 5 a.m., when I took the second dose that Kath had left for me, all by myself. I lay down and slept the rest of the night through.

Next day, new activities. Because of the medication I was able to walk upstairs to the phone. I contacted a chiropractor who had kinesiology skills, perfect! But she was flooded in at Waimea (I told you that there was a lot of rain) and so couldn't see me that day. Oh dear! Never mind, tomorrow she would come to Honokaa and see me at the hotel.

I arranged a massage for later in the day and got an appointment at the orthodox medical clinic. If I had to wait a whole day for the chiropractor, I had better have some drugs. One can scream at home, but not all night in a hotel.

The Hawaiian massage is very caring and I realised that I needed to confide in the masseuse about how Dave and I split up. How in the end he had told me he couldn't keep trying at the relationship, it was making him ill. From which I deduced: I was making him ill. I still felt his words like the sting of a lash from a whip. This then explained my email to Mike, asking him to be kindly if we should part at his behest. I was frightened of a recurrence of that rejection. It held me back.

The medical doctor looked at me and prescribed exactly the same formula as I had been taking from Kath. From then on though, I would take them as a vibration, without the chemical. I had a piece of paper that allowed me to duplicate the beneficial part of the medicine, without the side effects caused by the chemicals. It is known as a Sanjeevini. The paper shows two circles with a line joining them together. You place the tablet or other chemical for duplication in one circle, and place a glass of water in the second circle and make a fifteen-second-long prayer of your choice. This duplicates the vibration of the medicine into the water. So then you take the water and leave the tablet for next time, doing the same process endlessly. For me, this means I heal faster because my body is not full of chemicals and adverse reactions. The label on one of the tablets said not to drive or use machinery because of drowsiness, but I never felt any tiredness, but I did know that the same tablet from Kath had knocked me clean out!

The weather was atrocious with cold squalls of rain. So, if I had to spend a quiet day at least it did not feel as if I were missing anything. I spent the time thinking of why I had a bad back. Yes, I know, sitting in a draught in the stadium in Hilo watching dancing with a howling gale blowing rain through the stadium and me wearing a waist skimming jacket, bending forward on metal bleacher seating. A chill to the back. But I also noted that I felt unsupported, and that could cause lower back pain. I had set off from Hilo not knowing the people I was travelling with, the weather had been awful with squalls of rain sweeping waterfalls across the road and I had not known where the hotel was located in Honokaa or whether they would have space for me. That could be enough on top of the Hilo chill.

Two people at the hotel invited me to go to the cinema with them to see *A Beautiful Mind* that night. I was well enough to sit without fidgeting through the two-and-a-half-hour film! What a recovery, thanks to the massage and the Sanjeevini method of taking tablets. I was even able to walk home easily, enjoying the full moon. I enjoyed the film too, finding it rich and varied with some real moments of beauty. It would give me something to think about when I lay resting beyond the need for sleep.

When I got back to the hotel I found that Mike had phoned me, having sleuthed me out by phoning Arnott's. I was overjoyed and let my reserve of the past few days drop away, and I really enjoyed talking to him. I felt that my feelings for him eclipsed those for Jerry and made me query my desire to see Jerry when I returned to the States. However, my inner self said that I should get the address, or at least ask after Jerry, via his son. I was living with such strange impulsive and mixed feelings, as if I were on a see-saw and a merry-go-round all at once. Just observe, I told myself!

Diary 27 February 2002

The Sanjeevinis are working well. No big pain now and no side effects. Slept through the night without waking for a 5 a.m. dose.

I even had a quiet meander through town, finding the wonderful bakery there. I rang the chiropractor and got an appointment for the next morning and smiled secretly because the orthodox doctor had advised against a chiropractic correction – enough to make me have one even if I had not been as convinced (as I was) that this was just what I needed. In the evening I met

Trevor, another single traveller who has come to stay at the hotel, and we had dinner together. That was nice. But then a bombshell! I rang Mike as we had agreed and he told me he had a 'significant other' who had given an ultimatum: monogamy or nothing! He is to make up his mind today! So, which pair of earrings did she get out of the ones we selected, me guiding Mike's choice?

★

I phoned again the next evening, held my breath, and bang went my trip to see Mike in California! Yet despite all this, I went to bed and slept right through the night without intense back pain. Sanjeevinis worked well!

Diary 28 February 2002

Didn't take even Sanjeevini, wishing myself to be 'clean' for the chiropractor. Went out round the little town, looking at shops, idling the time away before my appointment. Honokaa is a quaint place with cavernous antique shops, junk emporia and one-off stores. There's been no outside investment. Being closed is normal here. There are signs on shops indicating 'Back Soon', 'Opening Hours When Achievable: 9 a.m. to 5 p.m.'. Even the police station was closed all that day. One shop stank of old wet gabardine. Rents must be low to allow the slack trade to take place. One shop had a sign on the door saying 'Closed for lunch, open 2.30 p.m.', but the owner and his wife were just sitting on chairs idly outside the shop and it was noon!

★

The chiropractor, Dr Willey, came to the hotel. She was small and strong with masses of curly dark hair. If mischievous smiles could cure you then no one would ever be ill. She did a load of adjustments on my back and then told me the problem with my back was that I hold anxiety about sexual relations there! I told her of my travel plan and she deduced that when I reach Cape Town I would meet someone who would be associated with this problem. We would see! I loved her so much, she was such a hoot!

She loaned me an ice pack, but the only good it did was to make me lie down. I mused on the lazy useless life that should come my way.

After Dr Willey's visit I felt much better and walked out to Jason's (Jerry's son's) house. Down the long hill towards the sea. The ocean looked beautiful and the day was fine and sunny. It was a long way on foot and I started to regret my boldness in taking such strenuous exercise. What if he was not in and I could not rest before returning? However, in he was, with girlfriend Sunni and their new baby, born a little prematurely, but thriving well. I gave them a money gift for the baby and cooed to it and held it. Sunni was a very able but quiet mother and did not talk to her baby as she fed it, unlike me who never stopped chatting while I held the child. But then, I had noticed she was always very quiet. Maybe a feature of Hawaiians is that they don't talk much, because it seems fairly typical of Jerry's family too.

The news from Jason was that Jerry was back in Kona. The reason: Jerry's father had died so he returned for the funeral and Los Angeles had proved too cold for him. 'He couldn't hack it,' Jason said. Jerry was now living with his daughter, Amy, in Kona. I got his mobile phone number. Jason then kindly gave me a lift back into town, for which I was deeply indebted.

I walked the main street and went to a youth centre which I had noticed had Internet. But it was full of children. I was advised to come back in the morning, when it would be quiet. But they did not advertise a morning opening time, only afternoons – 'in case it encourages business' I was told quietly. What a town!

Sorry to give such lengthy detail about the town, but it fascinated me. It probably suited my vision, narrowed as it was by illness. I found a photocopy shop with a dusty, endless drawing office with two old drawing boards, no computer and nothing really happening there. But, hey, that's Honokaa. What business would the town generate? The supermarket advertised photo processing but couldn't tell me when the prints would be back! In the post office one day, I was their only customer, until others filed in behind me, but to no avail. All attention was on placing Easter bunny decorations on all the shelves, before the staff dusted themselves down and turned to serve me. I was even asked whether I thought the bunnies looked cute. One thing I could not do with my painful back was stand up for any duration. It took some patience. I tried to smile and nod, despite a slight tension in my jaw. I am not a lover of cute fluffy toys and never have been. Even on the Venus line…

Diary 28 February 2002 (continued)

So, everything about Honokaa has shrunk in size. The earlier importance of the town has disappeared and trading is now on a different scale. It mirrors my own life with the back injury. All premises are large and those filled with junk and antiques have a quaint, sleepy, dusty look. Hawaii time in a big way.

I contemplate how I feel about receiving the news that Mike and I will be no more and I shed a tear. Then I consider Jerry, to decide whether to make contact with him again, now he is back in Kona. Aha! The news that there will be no Mike and no Jerry in California affects how long I will want to stay there!

★

That was actually good, because I was aware that I had not originally scheduled travel time for California and realised it could affect time in other places if I were to be in mainland USA for perhaps three weeks.

Where was Venus in all this? I felt that the email I had sent to Mike carried a prediction. I had asked him to tell me gently if he wanted to finish the relationship, and finish it he had! But Venus protected me from feeling alone and provided me with a diversion. Mike was gone but Jerry was back in Hawaii and coming back into focus once more. My life felt like a door turning, one out, one in. A disturbance ran through me, but I was in too much physical pain to analyse it, or rather I did not wish to think about my life right then.

I slept, ate a snack, got rid of ants from the dorm and took the Sanjeevini. I was tired and sore from my visit to Jason. I had overdone it.

I gave Trevor my washing for the laundrette, knickers and all. How kind he was! I lay in bed resting, and I looked at a cute little surfing angel which would make a suitable gift for a friend in England. Chrissie runs angel workshops, so please don't think I had been persuaded by the Easter bunnies. I decided I must post it. I must carry nothing more than I need to.

Diary 1 March 2002

Email time in Honokaa – thirty-one messages! A bit upset to find that one person who had received my carefully and expensively sent photographs complained to me that it had taken too long to download them and how costly in time and money this had been for him. I felt my eyes prick with tears. Shows I am not quite myself.

Next I spend time phoning about rent cars. My horizons are expanding and there is no public transport. There appear to be two scales of charges: if you phone from outside of Hawaii they are cheaper than if you have already arrived. Ha! I get a price of $30 a day for a basic car. I am advised to take out further insurance because of the high cost to me if I incur an accident. Oh, this is too much, I just want to order a car, not an accident. I arrange to collect it at 11 a.m. from Kona Airport. I have no idea how I will get there, but never mind. I phone and arrange to meet Jerry in the afternoon. Felt a bit lonely. Preparing to leave can do that and I have seen enough of Honokaa now.

★

Next day I awoke to breakfast and asked around to see if anyone was going to the airport. There were not many people staying, but, I would ask anyway, and yes! A couple of people were going to the airport and needed to be there at the precise time I had agreed to pick up the car. Eleven o'clock found me in a rent car. No, I would not pay for a better rate of insurance, I was renting a car, not an accident. The basic insurance, not included in the $30 rental, had already pressed me on my budget. The car was basic, oh so different from the Grand Am of Maui. I even had to wind the windows myself! This was an irony given that I used to drive old bangers in the UK – the simpler the better, less to go wrong! Part of the vanity of Venus. I smiled.

I rented it for eight days. I had it in mind to travel to Kawai after that but a series of phone calls indicated that all flights were full (maybe Mother's Day was the problem) or expensive. I felt moody. Perhaps my back pain coloured my view, causing me to feel that I was being victimised and so I was being offered the worst deals.

I headed to Kona to see Jerry. The day was bright and beautiful – and I was mobile! I had shaken off the inability to rent cars – Big Island was mine! But of course I had been to most places. As I said, I had had it in mind to go to Kawai, but with a bad back I just felt like staying put, in reality. The thought of heaving luggage from a baggage reclaim carousel sobered me and I recalled that I was there to witness the Venus line, not to go bagging another Hawaiian island, the most distant from the line.

I found Jerry's new home and Jerry was at home. The house was on the ground floor of a low-rise block of economy housing where children's toys were strewn around outside and the sound of televisions came out to greet you. Somehow it looked flimsy and thin-walled. The windows were hardly set in, being almost flush with the knobbly concrete-panelled walls.

Jerry seemed neutral, but then there was no reason why he should have been overjoyed to see me. Really, I was pursuing him. He was neutral and drinking. So we talked of this and that and stayed at arm's length. The television was blaring; the indoor temperature was stifling and the air dense with smoke. The room was heavily occupied and the people in the room seemed dull and mulish. They seemed to be watching the same video over and over again, while they snacked, none of them talking. Just munching mechanically from brightly coloured, cellophane bags.

It made me feel as if I were booming loudly, competing with the telly, when I was just trying to hold a personal, if rather awkward conversation. With this sort of welcome committee I decided it was time to go, pretty soon.

I was undecided about where to go to next, but I thought again that a change of area might do me good. Honokaa was a little out of the way. There were no beaches and the weather there is uncertain. So many days to go with the rent car and nothing really to do.

I went to look at a little hotel that had been recommended as quaint and interesting. The journey there took me down the coast to Captain Cook. The Manago Hotel was an old wayside hotel on the dusty road edge and traded on its stylish, if a little run-down, original features, with sepia prints of the old days – showing what seemed to be exactly the same as now. But it was not at all for me. There were no dormitory accommodations – not that I thought for a moment I could have managed to climb into a bunk bed. But the room I saw was small and bleak, probably as basic as it had been 100 years before. OK for then, but not for now, and not for me in my pink Venus-inspired mood! Mushroom and brown-painted walls, bare floorboards. Loneliness crept over me. I started to query why I was on this journey, why had I chosen to go alone, but who would have come with me? The bleakness of the room had infected me. Or was it mirroring me? What was that disturbance I had felt earlier that I had cared not to look at? Not now.

Well, my mood inspired a sleep on the beach at Kahaluu Bay. It was cool and a bit windy when I arrived, but when I woke it was sunny and warm. That's unusual there. Usually the afternoon mist on the hillside coffee plantations (so good for the coffee!) cools the beach.

I took a trip into Kona to look at my emails. Nothing from Mike. That was it, I supposed. Monogamy had won and I felt defeated.

Back to Honokaa – and a restaurant that closed while I ate. I held out as long as I could as the chairs went up on to the tables, clack clack. It was 7.50 p.m. Home and to bed.

Diary 3 March 2002

Last night I asked for Sai Baba to fill all my chakras with his energy and I now use this energy to overcome the muscle spasms in my back. I seem to be moving a little easier in bed, but walking to the bathroom is still a hell of a chore. Honokaa feels a lonely place: no dorm companions, just a few regular residents who work in the area and a very few passers-by, usually taken up with their own preoccupations and plans. Anyway, I don't feel up to being encouraging and entertaining. I would only feel happy to join in with other single travellers, such as those I have met at hostels. No Elle, no Hannah, here it is just me. Since leaving Arnott's Lodge, after Maui, I have really been on my own. Looking back to Pahoa I was lonely with just two couples who were into each other, even though it was supposed to be a retreat centre; a brief respite with Yasuko and Rex at Arnott's and now loneliness washing over me again. I would love to stay in a house again so that at least I would feel at home, but although I might be able to set something up in Hilo with Eva, I just don't want to be in the wet climate zone.

Diary 4 March 2002

I bought a pretty dress yesterday. It's the most wonderful shocking pink with a white pattern of racing cars on it! It's got a full skirt which flows beautifully when I walk and has a boned, ruched bodice with no straps. I look like a glamour model out of the 1930s. I suspect the dress was originally made in the fifties. I have never had a dress like this before. Honokaa has its moments!

In the night I talked to Venus. The lonely times are for me to love myself, not be deflected by others. And no, I should not leave Big Island, it would be too far from the line. One week here in Honokaa and then the last week of my stay somewhere else – maybe I'll meet the socially high bit of my stay! After all, so far I seem to have enjoyed all aspects of the Venus line, except for two things: the elusive useless life and even more the socially upmarket company, which I have never really touched upon. And I shan't find the latter in Honokaa. But with a rent car to pay for, I could do with a sugar daddy.

Maybe Pele, the volcano goddess, may add an extra twist too, if I stay in Big Island.

★

It was raining hard that day in Honokaa. Kath told me Trevor had asked after me. I went to see him and we went together to 69 Beach where I wrote my diary in the sunshine of the Gold Coast. Black Gold, I always think, given the endless lava.

The beach was truly delightful with no facilities, just sea and sand – and the warmest sea I had experienced on Hawaii (outside of the Warm Pool). There were fallen, but still living, trees gracing the beach and providing shade almost up to the water's edge. My back was not a problem when I swam and the sea was only five steps from the safety of my beach mat.

I now had beach, food (as long as I was not too late) and hotel. I would certainly stay another week or two!

Trevor left me to continue his journey. I took him to what we presumed was the bus stop and I went back to Honokaa, in time for *Pupus*, the name of a buffet where everyone contributes. This was to celebrate Gerald's leaving. He was the guy who called Kath for me on my first night in Honokaa, when I couldn't get out of bed. And now he was leaving for Australia. Going home, hmm...

Then in walked Chris, joining the celebratory *Pupus*. He gave me a deliberate glad eye. In fact, he didn't take his eyes off me. He peeled my clothes on and off with his eyes every few minutes. He was cycling the Island, but had developed a bad knee, so was grounded. I recommended the masseuse, Susan. We sat around, but I didn't want to suggest that I did any healing on him. I was not well enough. Bed early.

My back was still causing a lot of pain and kept prompting me to ask why it was so. I rang Dave, my ex-partner, and enjoyed that very much, but really I just fancied a chat with someone I knew. He gave me the news that Fiona, a friend from Sheffield (although Canadian by birth) had surfaced again after a long absence. Her sister had told Dave that she would be married on 9 March and was living in California – near San Francisco. He had her email address for me. Now that was a surprise; and a new reason to go to mainland America.

I told Dave, too, that maybe I feared growing old. My eyesight sometimes felt awful and my painful back was curved and made it difficult to stand upright. It made me think of my mother, registered blind and bent badly by osteoporosis. My back so mirrored hers, even to the point of the tilt of the pelvis lifting my left foot off the ground. But she was thirty-five years older than me.

Next day it rained in Honokaa. I had a massage and read my emails. I agreed to take Chris to the beach. My rent car gave him mobility too. Beach 69, of course with its lovely fallen trees. The name comes from the number marked on the telegraph pole where you turn off the highway, except that it's now another number. Maybe they have changed the numbers...

On the beach I told Chris that I hadn't laughed very much recently, with being ill. However, he had me in fits of merriment. So, I fell to kissing him until he feigned complaint and fended me off. I learned he was a Taurus; I could see that by the focused way he had continued his cycling tour despite his knee. A little rigidity in the face too, which caused me to ruffle up his combed back hair and thus made him look twenty years younger – to match his firm cyclist's body. The focus on other things caused my back to feel much better. How much I feel I let pain dominate me! So, maybe I substituted sexual arousal for pain.

We had a nice evening meal together at a small Italian-style restaurant by the harbour on the way home. At the hotel we both had single occupancy of a dorm and so took advantage of this for the early part of the night, moving apart to prevent any embarrassment for a possible late arrival into the men's dorm. Somehow such practicalities seemed to be about as romantic as having sex with this man felt. It didn't feel romantic, just a diversion from pain. Too soon in our relationship also, but what to do? And next day he was gone. How can one develop a long-term relationship, letting it gently take shape, when life feels so fleeting? He was gone without much of a glance, just the focus of the bicycle.

Diary 5 March 2002

So, the end of Chris! One man is for a few weeks, one for five days and another for one night. Venus, oh Venus!

I had arranged to go to Onomea (near the Botanic Gardens) near Hilo, to pick up Hannah. I smiled at the delight of helping her out with transport. I met her sister, Summer, and Katlan again. We reminisced about the Green Pool picnic and swim, when they rescued me from Papaya Plantation. When I got to Eva's house, Carl said I was welcome to come any time. That felt so warm, particularly as I had always found him a bit reserved.

From the house, I made some calls to rent-car offices in Hilo to see if I could get a cheaper deal for my final week, but no. And I must be in Honolulu by the eighteenth for my flight (that's fixed). Maybe I should go to Honolulu early, but no. That would take me away from the line. Plus Honolulu is city life and even though the rest of the island of Oahu may be nice, I feel the city will dominate it, giving a certain taint. But I need to get out of Honokaa – always wet and closes early!

Hannah and I take our leave of her family and head north to Honokaa and on to Kona. There Hannah is meeting her boyfriend. I take her to his house and take the opportunity to get X-rays of my back taken. The X-ray machine is set up to take three pictures all at the same time of the total spine – except that my back is so far off the normal scale of curvature that the centre portion misses and I have to have another picture taken, manually. At least I now have the base line pictures now that Dr Willey advised me to get. How different from public medicine in England where only your own doctor has the ability to arrange X rays, unless you go privately. Terribly expensive in the UK, but cheap here. They cost me just $100.

Hannah is most concerned for my health and offered me a massage – an offer I take up with alacrity. After the hospital visit, I returned and Hannah gave me a massage, but part of the time I had to lie in the yoga pose known as child pose with my back curled into the foetal position in order to be comfortable. The spectre of my mother's back reappeared but Hannah was reassuring and her newly learnt Lomilomi massage was fabulous. Later I sat and watched the Kona sunset, sitting on the wall between the pavement and the sea, with the green ray as the sun finally went. So many nights in Kona the sunsets are thus.

I found a shop selling locally made Volcano moisturiser and perfume. Oh, it smelt so delicious! I had never felt so sensually stimulated by a perfume. I loved myself. I also bought a CD of Hapa, Hawaiian music that I heard playing in the shop.

Life certainly seems to be lazy and often useless – although nothing ever feels completely useless. Laziness and leisure I can understand and have achieved. But useless… Maybe living at Honokaa was useless when I could be somewhere more lively, closer to the sea, etc. But somehow even then it doesn't gel for me. How can one achieve uselessness? Maybe I'm trying too hard.

Got a parking ticket this morning! Coming back with Chris last night from the harbour restaurant it had been so very wet, raining so hard. I had parked outside the hotel. Chris told me in the morning that he had informed me that I was parking in the wrong place. I either hadn't heard him or had misunderstood him but parking laws must be different from what I am used to. The slip of paper was so wet it was disintegrating and nothing could be read of it. But nonetheless, Kath advised me that I should not ignore it.

I have decided not to get anxious about jumping into bed with men. After all, they don't get anxious about it, do they? When I am ready, it will change. Just don't resist it or apply force – just let the change happen when it is ready – and observe it. Forget it and do what feels right/good/fun. Life is not so serious.

★

Being on the Venus line meant getting dressed up to go to the police station on the following day. The pink dress! After all, I couldn't read the soaking wet charge sheet and had decided to make the most of attempting to find out, politely, and then hopefully be let off the charge. The thought of batting an eyelash to help this felt quite natural on the Venus line. So unusual for the 'normal', more combative me. The local police in Honokaa referred me to the police at Waimea. I had to go to Waimea anyway, to see Dr Willey so she could see my X-rays and check me for any readjustments. But she wasn't in (she was in Honokaa that day) and at the police station I couldn't find the piece of paper that they had left on my windscreen. Is this the useless life?

So, I set out for Mauna Kea Beach Resort for some swimming. I had not been there before. As I had done a day trip with Elle covering nearly all the beaches up the Gold Coast I was never sure whether I would find I had been there or not!

The beach had some shade but was heavily overlooked by the hotel. Too much manicured lawn and not enough nature for my taste. But there was easy swimming. Two cyclists who had stayed at the Honokaa Club/Paniola Hotel were there. I asked after Chris and, yes, they had seen him, further back, near

Hawi. I felt that that was the last contact I would ever have with him.

On the beach I started to read: Trevor had given me a copy of *Lolita*, the fifties scandalous book of child love. A new take on love given to me by Venus, no doubt. The book feels hateful with its cover proclaiming it to be the true love story of the twentieth century. Set against later paedophile cases it feels very difficult. The lingering detail is designed to be erotic and is successful sometimes even though I wish it were not so. It caused me to muse on the sexuality of children and reminded me that even as children we are sexual beings. I felt it was Venus-inspired to find myself reading this fifties book about child love. But I found the book itself completely uninspired by Venus.

I pulled myself away from the beach so I could return to Waimea and see if the doctor was in. No. Never mind, I chose to take a route through to Hawi, rather than going straight home to Honokaa. Route 250, an old road known for its scenery which I had never travelled before. I picked up a hitchhiker, the third that day (not the useless life) and he told me of a place to stay in Kapaau. It's an out-of-the-way spot near the coast, beyond Hawi and nearly at the end of the road as the terrain becomes too precipitous for the coastal road to continue. I always like places where nature forces road builders to stay their hands.

I went to Kapaau and found the adventure centre. It was too expensive for me, but I halved the price by bargaining so I could afford it. I never do that! It had been a quiet year for tourism following 11 September. I had to stay a minimum of two nights. That was OK, Kapaau would get me out of the heavy rain and put me a little closer to the beaches. I would stay in the games room annex, next to the house. Just what I wanted: to stay in a house, with a garden too. I thought I might have seen Chris on the road. His knee must be difficult if he had stopped as early as Hawi, but not enough to deter his travels.

I still hadn't sorted out a car for the final week.

Diary 6 March 2002

When my hitch-hiker told me of Kapaau I went directly there and did something quite bold. I bargained down the price of a room by fifty per cent, and then said I'd pay a little more. No point in making my landlady feel put upon should I overstep the mark of hospitality while sharing her kitchen. I will be sleeping in the games room, built rather like a large garage with a metal roof broken by light panels. The kitchen and bathroom are in the main house. I have a little use of the kitchen, but not sure how much, hence me paying a little more than the bargain basement price. So, the rooms are about $100 in the house and I have the games room for $30 a night. This puts it in the top edge of my budget which stands at roughly $70 to $100 a day. So with the rent car and food, it's my tops! Here, on the north-east coast, however, I am going to find better weather and it will be less far to travel to the south Kohala beaches for my 'gold coast' Beach 69 experience! However, for it to be a success it does rely on my continued rental of a car, something I haven't nailed down yet! I have the car now till Saturday – what will happen if I can't keep it? How will my back be by then?

I muse on Venus and Pele and both seem happy with my move, so I assume it will work out. I could do with an expensive lover to look after my finances and give me the part of the Venus line analysis I have not felt a whiff of yet: moving in high social circles. Maybe because I stay in youth hostels and cheap places I don't reach the high social life, but the trips I make to the resort beaches would surely give rise to a lover with money, if that were to happen. But the beach resorts only have couples – and mainly much older than me too.

★

To make a change I ate at the Waimea Mexican, but it was very average. So, I went home to Honokaa where everything was very quiet. I was possibly the only guest. Cliff and Gerald, who lived downstairs near me, must both have gone. Nothing to do except to make plans for the future. Pack tonight and go to Waimea tomorrow, then off to Kapaau for my new start. I noted that the toenail I damaged stubbing my toe during the Haleakala volcano walk on Maui was now breaking away. Like everything else that has been a health problem for me, it was on the right side of my body.

The next day I took my leave of Honokaa, leaving behind a gift for my landlady, Kath, for her kindness, and the medications I did not want and a Sanjeevini card, so she could duplicate the medicines. I went to the computer centre to say goodbye to Judy who worked there. But once more the computer crashed so I couldn't send the mails. Off then for a last trip along the old and narrow highway to Waimea with its avenue of trees so tall that the straight road was made gloomy. Many potholes to avoid. After the trees, came rolling pastures and wonderful sightings of lava tubes in the cuttings the road made through the lush meadows of the Parker cattle ranch. I had never been well enough to stop and explore them. Then the road passed small ashy lava flows and into Waimea. I knew the route like the back of my hand.

That day I was carrying a hitchhiker who worked at the Chinese Medicine School. I got an offer of a cheap treatment; I noted it but somehow didn't ever do it. Going to the chiropractor seemed enough.

I went to the courthouse and this time I had the paper, now dry and stiff and, yes, I could write a letter to explain how I did not know it was against the law to park my car as I had. I was asked to leave my credit card number in case my appeal failed! I then met Dr Willey in a car park and she held the X-rays up to the sky and pointed out that my L5 vertebra was tilted and not fully formed and that I had an extra vertebra too: L6. However my sacrum was straight so that was helpful. She gave me two tennis balls to sit on while I drove the car to make the pain easier – and it did work! Looked funny when leaving the car, making sure the tennis balls didn't bounce out with me.

In the afternoon I arrived at Kapaau. No one was in except a young man called Darren, so I took him with me to the beach. We went to Mauna Kea Resort but he then showed me a little beach instead of the resort beach. This was Mauumae Beach. It had a lovely private feel to it – away from the more crowded hotel beach.

Back at Kapaau I met Bobi and got dispatched to the games room. Darren was interested in learning massage so he could make a living, so I agreed to teach him with Bobi as the model. All this should help with the goodwill I had hoped to engender having beaten her down on price. Then I went off to try Aunty's for dinner. This proved a great place, chairs around the bar, no smoking and food produced with love. An elderly man, Ronald, took me off to his house to show me photos of his visit to Puerto Rico (I had told him that I was going there) and of the lava flows on Big Island at their most spectacular. We agreed he would take me on a trip out the following Tuesday. I crossed my fingers that he wasn't hoping for any romance, otherwise I would certainly have to tell him no thank you! In the end the trip did not happen – maybe just as well.

Diary 8 March 2002

On a whim, I rang Hannah at her boyfriend's house in Kona to see if she would like to go for a drive to a part of Hawaii I had not been to before and where I thought we might be able to take some photographs of me in my various outfits I had bought while on Big Island and Maui. Sure. She jumped at the chance having had a difficult patch with the boyfriend and glad of something different to do.

We made a rendezvous for 11.30 a.m. and I had all the new clothes I had bought in Hawaii and a couple of rolls of film. The route we took was the Kopala Drive above Kona and it was as scenic and winding as my bible, *Big Island Revealed*, suggested, with lush vegetation hugging the road. At the top you come out into a lava flow, grey with lichen growth, the first vegetation to be established. The whole scene seemed grey with mists creeping around the small, sparse, lichen-covered trees. We stopped by the gates to a telecommunication mast. The end of the road. Out of the car, off with the clothes. One outfit after another photographed carefully by Hannah. This position and that, with the car and without. Pity it was not the flash Grand Am from Maui! Never mind.

At one moment we were both standing by the car with no clothes on, as Hannah wanted some photos of her outfits too. Oh, how lovely she looked, a body to die for. I am about twice her age, but I never looked like that! Her breasts were pearlescent and beautifully held; their weight had not dragged them down to make even the merest crease. Mine, by contrast, I describe as rose buds that got nipped in the frost and never came to very much. Frank Zappa once said that more than a mouthful is a waste, and I have not much going to waste!

I looked around and smiled at the surreal presence of two nudes either side of a car, just draped in mists. After the show was over we got in the car. It immediately came to rain and another car drove up and parked. We sat and ate sandwiches and laughed at the story lines we could have put together if our (male) visitor had arrived but a moment sooner. What fun it was.

★

Back in Kona, I dropped Hannah off to go for a job interview – she was trying to live in Hawaii permanently. And then I met up with Dante. Dante was the hitchhiker who had told me of the place at Kapaau where I now lived. I had given him a lift into Kona that morning so he could shop. I also took the opportunity to buy more macadamia nuts. These had become a stock item since day one in Hawaii. I could not imagine life without them. Is Venus a part of that? Everywhere else in the world they would be frightfully expensive, and I just could not stop munching them! At one time Tammie gave me a whole carrier bag full, but I ate nearly a pound weight each day so they went quickly.

Dante and I went together to the airport beach, but I didn't care for it. It seemed rather soulless maybe because of the nearby regular comings and goings of planes – a constant change of energy. So we went to a new resort, Hualalai, and tried out their beach. Full of turtles and lots of fish. But the current was a little strong for my back. I could swim well in calm water, but if the waves hit me and turned my body awkwardly (something I had never noticed till then) it gave me a lot of pain. So, after a brief dip I got out and dipped into *Lolita* instead. Dante (a young good-looking Romanian) disappeared for a walk along the rocks, getting back rather late and so jeopardising my appointment with Bobi and Darren for the massage and tuition. I felt a bit vexed with him. I do like to teach punctuality in treating clients and suspected that this would be a terribly important lesson for Darren! Never mind, we headed for home.

No one noticed that I was a little late, so I was able to show Darren how I set up the 'salon' and how I prepare myself, quietly calming. Darren had difficulty with my rigorous approach to teaching. I showed him quite meticulously how the strokes are done, just as I was taught, and expected him to follow, rather than fall into a free-form style. However, Bobi enjoyed the massage, even though the room was a bit cold – and this was Hawaii!

So many things in Hawaii have two names – towns, hotels and now the place I was staying in at Kapaau. I found out I was staying at the Kohala Adventure Centre. They had Internet, so I used that as something of a favour. That was nice. The garden between the house and my home in the games room was pretty and my eyes both rested and feasted on it. I used the kitchen and bathroom in the house, waiting sometimes for Bobi to finish first. It was all very informal and intimate. You know – her bathroom floor was sprinkled with water from her shower earlier and I added to it. Then off to eat at Aunty's – again good love food and perfect for my budget. I expected to make a habit of eating there. After trying unsuccessfully to eat satisfactorily around Honokaa this was paradise! And they did not close too early.

So, the weekend had come and I drove to the airport and bit the bullet, renting the car for the rest of my stay. My flight from Oahu to Oakland was 18 March, still nine days away. Altogether it had cost me $700 for sixteen days. While travelling down to the airport I went the further distance into Kona and bought an air ticket for Oahu, and also replenished my stock of Volcano perfume. They were still playing Hapa in the shop which I now listened to ceaselessly on CD while driving. I had learnt it quickly off by heart. It seemed that compulsions also overtook me on the Venus line. The pink, I understood – but the macadamia nuts, a particular perfume and Hapa! I seriously doubted whether I would ever be able to live a day without any of them. Maybe the loneliness of my existence caused me to look for friendship in other ways. Nuts, music, perfume – they are all sensuous things too, so maybe Venus was the cause. But I am always cautious not to push to the astrological connection too far.

While in Kona I bumped into Rex, yet again! So far we had met in Kona when I stayed at Patey's Place and we bumped into each other both times I had stayed at Arnott's in Hilo. Then he was with me at the Tahitian dance festival where I chilled my back and here he was again. We were really pleased to see each other, marvelling at how it should be that we were meeting once more. Refreshingly, romance seemed to steer clear of us, although when I found myself quite lonely at times and would quest around for solutions to this, he came to mind. But never when I saw him.

It was such a strange holiday – I found that I was planning for California and yet I was still to stay in Hawaii for another week – the length of a holiday for some people! I was without any physical ties, except for finances and my back. My life felt quite free of boundaries, which was good for me as Neptune is dominated by Saturn in my chart and so tends to be over-shadowed.

Back to the present. I had enjoyed the photographic session with Hannah enormously and knew that it would only be possible on Hawaii with Venus. Once I had gone away it would be different, and such a photographic session would feel frivolous and irrelevant. Venus on the Ascendant, my line in Hawaii. I had chosen to visit this place first on my travels because it seemed an easy option. In the Caribbean would come great challenges, so I felt sure there would be no room for fripperies like photos of clothes. I put in my 'fashion show' films to be developed; I hoped that they'd turn out well.

So, was this the lazy useless life? If so, did I like it? Well, not the loneliness, which seemed to be tied in with it. How was I to be sure that I had milked the Venus line totally – was I missing some depths of uselessness? I was unlikely to come to Hawaii for three months ever again, so I did not wish to miss a trick.

Reviewing how Venus felt, however, I found that I still con-sidered men as sex objects, a hangover from my adolescence, but my attitude to women was vastly different. I looked to women for friendship, getting me out of scrapes, and for their conversation and guidance. They were my refuge and strength.

Gradually, the remaining days disappeared as all holidays speed up towards their end, although for me, it was just the end of part one. I would think of painting my diary and then not do it, think of going to visit new places, just the few I had not seen, then not go and then drive once again down the coast to Beach 69. There the beach was ideal for me. I could park the car without travelling too far on dirt tracks, walk less than five minutes to the beach – the extent of my mobility – and then sit under the shade of fallen trees on the beach, just five steps from the water's edge. Just a couple of houses stood back from the beach and usually only one or two families gathered there.

Bobi invited me to dine with her in the evenings, initially because she said she had bought in too many vegetables and would waste them if she didn't share them with me. As the supply never diminished, I thought she must just like my company. So, I made salads and she cooked something hot each night; we ate and then she washed up. Was this the nearest I would get to useless laziness?

My life revolved around Bobi and her world, meeting her visitors and friends and once even going to a beach resort where her daughter was playing tennis. I could eat with her, so no need to go shopping; I could do emails on her computer so no need of Internet cafés. All I did was go to the beach (usually 69) and swim and drive back, listening all the time to the Hapa CD and feeling thrilled to see the black lava landscape each day. For cultural life, I went to Waikoloa Resort where I discovered there were free afternoon concerts and I went each time there was one. So, I heard local music, saw hula dancing by a troupe of wrinkly grey-haired American ladies, in their late sixties if a day – but in my state of immobility I found myself marvelling at their ease of movement. One time a ukulele festival filled my day. But these events at the upmarket resort never led to any friendships or even conversation. Rex came up to see me, bringing with him the photos of the fashion show Hannah and I had done. He had picked them up for me at the chemist in Kona. So there was no need for me to travel far.

Little moments of humour arose, such as going to the post with my letter of appeal to say (in my very best quaint English) what a good, law-abiding person I was; explaining how my parking would have been perfect in the UK, parking under a street lamp and in a marked bay; never mind that I parked against the flow of traffic. On this journey to the post box I passed through 25 and 35 mph limited areas. So, when I saw a blue flashing light in my mirror I looked to see my speed and the blood rushed through my skin and banged in my ears. I realised I was doing 45 mph and had no idea whether I was 10 or 20 mph over the limit. I stopped instantly, apologising profusely to the policewoman. And it worked… I got let off and continued with my 'law-abiding' letter, which also worked: I did not pay the parking fine.

The following day I went to all the little beaches and attractions of north Kohala that I had not seen. Chastened by my speeding, I drove sedately. My back still gave me much trouble, even with a further visit to Dr Willey. I recall going to the nearby Lapakahi historical park and fortunately found there were benches along the path that linked the ruins of the old village. From each seat I spied the next one and my main aim was to see as much of the old village ruins as possible while focusing on the next opportunity to sit. How different it felt from the time that Hannah and I went to the ancient Place of Refuge and just wandered around soaking up the atmosphere! I visited the Pololu Outlook which rewards you with a view down the coast where no road has ever been built. The scenery is wild and the cliffs green right down to the ocean. The sea licks the base of the cliffs, moving in and out to give glimpses of black sand. All was silvery and misty, but I couldn't stand long enough to take it in. I hopped around somewhere close to agony.

Diary 14 March 2002

The day started with a trip to Waikoloa to pick up Bobi's camera which I had taken in for repair earlier. Then to Beach 69 in the afternoon. I go as usual to my spot by the tree, five paces from the water's edge. I settle down and then notice three people arrive. They stop on the other side of the fallen tree from me. I have nothing better to do than watch, and they get into the water together. Two men, one is obviously with his wife. They hold hands as they walk into the sea. The other one is bronzed, slender and with a long ponytail. I enjoy the view and then when the single man comes out of the sea, before the others, I decide to have a better look. So from my side of the tree I stand up and stretch and look through the branches to be able to say hello, who are you. Except that when I look through the tree I see the keenest pair of blue eyes I ever saw and blurt out, 'Hello, oh! What beautiful eyes you have!' The reply comes back equally candid: 'Oh, what a beautiful body you have, I'd love to make love to you!'

Well, I leaned through the branches and kissed him. Oh! Venus, you minx! Next I walked to his side of the tree and found him all embarrassed because I had aroused him. What would his friends think! I had no idea that American men from New York would be so uptight about such things. So, I found out that he was showing two friends around the island because he knew Hawaii quite well. It was a whistle-stop tour taking in what I had done in three months in a matter of days. So, their visit was short and later in the day at sunset I spied them on Spencer Beach, a regular haunt of mine for sunset watching. In the meantime, John 'the Eyes' and I had agreed to meet that evening. He couldn't do dinner with me because he was already committed to his friends John and Sue. I said that that was fine. What could I do with him over dinner, anyway, when both of us had a lust to satisfy? Better just to wait out the evening separately.

★

So, at 9.30 p.m. John 'the Eyes' arrived at Kohala Adventure Centre games room, three days before the end of my holiday in Hawaii. What sort of timing for a romance is this, Venus? However, all we wanted to do was to assuage our passion and so we closed the door and window blinds and he shyly came towards me. I think this is just his way of getting women into bed and I was willing both to watch and play the game. I felt I had met a true Casanova: a man who loves women. This was his life. We had moments of humour as my back restricted me and he had a bad cut on his knee and that restricted him, so our gasps were not only of pleasure! So, we enjoyed each other and then he had to leave. I felt that we had really respected our bodies and our desires and been gentle with our shared vulnerability. We released each other gently.

I asked him if he would like to see me again and he said he couldn't because... and I finished his sentence for him: because there were so many other women? He nodded quietly. I felt a bit sorry for him. How could he ever develop intimacy in a relationship? Although he gave me his phone number I doubted I would ever use it. By 11.30 p.m. our relationship was over. Two and a half hours in total. But where did this leave me? In a spiral of faster and faster relationships. Almost like a revolving door they came in and went, but the tempo must by then have reached its peak. However, it had been most enjoyable and those few hours felt so tender and loving.

Musing on what little I knew of John I could make sense of what occurred. He was strongly built and monumental, rather like a Red Indian in his bearing. And his bright blue eyes were the colour of the sea when it stirs up white sand – almost powder blue. He told me at the beach that he was Libra sun sign, Cancer moon and Scorpio Ascendant. I am Cancer sun sign and Libra Ascendant and his Scorpio eyes gave us a magnetic attraction. I felt that I had consumed the love of Venus and the fire of Pele in a pure form. And maybe I had put to rest the strange anxiety of whether it is right to sleep with someone so soon. In our case there could be no later. Many different feelings.

In meditation I felt Venus and Pele as internal forces. No need to step outside of myself to find them. I felt that my journey to Hawaii was complete. The only love I could not understand was my deep love for the black lava landscape of the South Kohala coast. I just loved it as a bee must love the nectar of a flower.

Greg, a friend of Bobi's whom I had been chatting to on and off as he came around to do odd jobs for Bobi, had got a whiff of the evening's entertainment and I realised it had made him more remote. I felt that he thought he knew the score with me. I felt it was likely from his demeanour that he thought that I was one of those girls whom you wouldn't wish to get close to because they sleep around. And the perception was not all incorrect and so my feelings that it had all been OK the previous night received a knock. I felt I must change it; somehow Greg mirrored the other part of me, which said that what I was doing was unacceptable.

Diary 15 March 2002

Greg takes me on a trip to collect driftwood and to visit a *heiau*, or shrine, near to the small Upolo airport, a place inaccessible by ordinary rent car. Even his van has difficulty because the rain has made the going very soft. There is no driftwood, but the *heiau*, described as rather forbidding in the guidebook, seems extraordinarily peaceful. We enter at the beckoning of a local who has gone to sit there. There are offerings to the spirits: flowers and pebbles with leaves wrapped around them. The place is obviously used as a place of worship. Outside, Greg and I lie down together on the grass and chat to the sky as I ease my back against the turfs.

I enjoy Greg's company. He's gentle and amused by me. He teases me too and is considerate of my back. I kiss him at one point. Then I realise that this is what I really love doing. Just kissing men when it appeals to me. All the men I have had relationships with in Hawaii I have kissed first! Maybe not Mike, I don't recall. I just have a compelling desire to just kiss.

I leave Greg and go to the ukulele festival where I learn how to make a lei out of orchids and which, later on, I give to Greg. I select eight photos from the fashion show and get them on the Internet, knowing that I will not do this once I get to California and beyond to the Caribbean…

I kiss Greg again, very tenderly, when I give him the lei. Then we have dinner with Bobi and Dante. Maybe I have shifted what I consider to be Greg's perception of me because he no longer feels distant but quite happily gives me a back massage and I kiss him again and again.

I would have liked him to stay the night.

Diary 17 March 2002

The inspectors are coming today to check the facilities at the Centre. So, I get up early and clear the room so that the games room is available for its advertised purpose. Dante, who has come to stay for a while in his tent, must take his tent down. Ronald was supposed to take me out, but it's raining very hard and I feel distracted by all the preparations for the officials. I agree to meet Greg between 1 p.m. and 3 p.m. He will be working at the house.

Then I have a change of plan and hope Bobi tells Greg of it.

Dante, without whom I wouldn't have found Kapaau, wants to go way down the coast past the Kona airport, so I take him and then I return to Beach 69. The weather there is beautiful with bright sun and I stay longer, knowing that this is my last visit to this favourite beach. Ah! With memories of John too. I contact Sai Baba and ask him for help with my emotions and to have greater joy within myself. This causes me to fall fast asleep.

I awake at 5.30 p.m. and hope again that Bobi will have told Greg where I am. But when I get back to the house a note from Bobi says that the inspection was cancelled and that she has gone to the beach. No sign of Greg. So, I have missed him. I hope he has not been inconvenienced by me. But I am glad that I did not return earlier because I suspect that he has not been at Bobi's all that day, given how wet the weather has been there. Hawaii, a place where you can choose your weather.

Ah, but later in the day I find a note from him saying he is sorry to have missed me. So he had been here! I am sorry too.

I make a salad as usual for both Bobi and me and then go out and leave a message for Greg on his answerphone. But I know that the message is unlikely to reach him because Greg lives in a tent at the moment.

★

It was the second goodbye message of the day, because while I was near to Kona during the afternoon I phoned Jerry and parted nicely from him, agreeing that we would not meet again. It felt good. Rather as it must feel preparing to die and getting your papers in order.

I also spent time putting thoughts into words about the black lava. 'I love the black lava because...' And came up with the words: 'because it represents destruction, chaos and beautiful renewal all at the same time. New land is formed as well as old land covered over.' So simple in the end, but I had actually to say it. I really felt the energy from the lava; it surged through me expanding me as well as Hawaii. Everything seemed to be ending, not with drama or sorrow, just with conclusions, very quietly.

My last notes in the diary for that day, my last day in Big Island, sum up the time I had spent with Bobi at Kapaau.

Diary 17 March 2002 (continued)

A life of Kapaau, Beach 69, travel by car and music, with little to do in the way of food preparation, no shopping, no painting, men passing aimlessly through my life. My life has become totally useless, lazy and leisurely. The useless is still a little difficult because everything is in some way productive, but I am happy with it. Content. And with Dante, I met him when he was thumbing a lift, he caused me to go to Bobi's place and now I have moved him on to live down the coast. We both felt it was sweet. Things feel to be wrapping up nicely. And tomorrow I shall meet Hannah in Oahu. She will pick meet me at the airport so I can spend a little supportive time with her before leaving Hawaii for a timespan I cannot judge. Will I ever return?

★

For my departure, I made an early start – pre-dawn! I signed Bobi's visitors' book and went to the airport to catch a delayed flight to Honolulu, leaving a message on Hannah's phone to say I would be late. Standing in line for boarding made me realise that at Oakland (a bigger airport) I would need wheelchair assistance, because I could not walk and then stand to watch the luggage arrive on the carousel and then carry it. It seemed a bit dramatic, over the top, but I was in pain whether I walked or stood so I didn't really have much option.

At Honolulu I didn't know just where I would meet Hannah, but, as with my contact with her before, there she was for me. Off in her sister's boyfriend's car and away to see the sights of Oahu. First breakfast, and then to a lookout in the mountains and then to a waterfall and a river through a jungle area almost in central Honolulu, finally to the beach for a last swim. Three and a half hours in Oahu and off I went with lots of kisses goodbye. So, although I had resisted going to Oahu because I felt the built-up area of Honolulu would have repercussions on the whole island, there I was. Having not made a visit to Kawai, I left that for a hazy future visit.

Diary 18 March 2002

Hannah has been such a good friend; Oahu would have been anonymous without her. On this day my gold shoes fell apart and I gave them to Hannah to put in the trash. I cannot believe how accepting of me people are. They're all in their twenties and I am pushing fifty! I hope I act as a role model and note that I too have friends in the UK who are twenty and thirty years older than me. On the flight to Oakland (with wheelchair to meet me) I muse on whether it is my enthusiasm and energy that people like. And my self-doubt, even at fifty! Venus has taught me to love myself, no doubt. She and Pele are still in my heart.

I thank Archangel Michael for protecting me so that my life of laziness allowed me still to leave on time and not stay in Hawaii for ever. A thought that had actually occurred to me as I got more and more idle.

I sit on the flight to Oakland a bit nervous about the wheelchair and meeting my friend Fiona whom I have not seen for probably ten years. And, of course, the new husband of nine days!

A new friend (Hannah) leaves and an old one (Fiona) comes back.

Chapter Seven

CALIFORNIA SUN AND MARS

My journey to Oakland was transporting me to another astro-cartographic view of my self in the world. I sat on the plane from Hawaii without a book to read, just musing and sleeping and letting the time pass. Not quite taking stock, more a gentle drift allowing any expressions to be at a level below conscious thought, fleeting and unrestricted. The trip to California had not originally been planned. At one time I thought I might be seeing Jerry in Los Angeles and Mike in San Diego. I would not now see Jerry and while I might see Mike it would not be as a lover, but merely because he lives near Maggie, my Findhorn friend, and so, why not! Finding out that my old friend Fiona was now living in Pacifica near San Francisco would allow me to see a friend (the first on my travels) and one whom I had not seen for many years. And I would meet her new husband.

Then, via email, I had made arrangements to see Maggie in San Diego. I had met her – and shared a caravan with her – at a flower essence conference in Findhorn back in 1997. I could also meet Mary, a woman I had met at Sai Baba's ashram in 2000, or was it 2001? Never mind, I had not seen either woman since and this was my opportunity! And what an opportunity; their credentials were formidable. Mary was living in Malibu and was a Reiki Master, a direct Master from Mrs Takata who brought Reiki to the West. Maggie made flower essences and knew Deepak Chopra. I felt I would be in good hands!

My back still hurt me plenty. I had been able to board the plane without the need of a wheelchair at Honolulu because the airport was small and I could just check in my bags without having to walk far or stand up for long. At Oakland, a wheelchair took me from the plane to a special buggy with other infirm people and I was whisked away to the baggage reclaim, where further assistance was given, but was little needed, because very quickly my greeting party was upon me. I felt something of a fraud, wearing walking boots, and well-worn ones at that, while being in the cripples' parade.

I was glad Fiona recognised me because I was not sure whether I would have spotted her quite so quickly, particularly as I sped past her in the buggy. How nice to see her, after three months of new faces. She was quick to assure me that anything goes in California, so walking boots and wheelchair assistance would not cause an eyebrow to stir.

We drove to the Pacifica apartment, overlooking the ocean from a lofty vantage point. All you could see from the window was the ocean; it was as if we lived on the beach. Pushing midnight I bedded down in their office and looked forward to the next day.

Fiona had told me there was not room for me to stay and I had thought that this might cause me to return to the youth hostel in San Francisco. However, I had joined a group of women called 5W (Women Welcome Women World Wide) and had a list of members with me. Fiona and I perused my list in the morning and there was a member living just two blocks away! Now, the protocol is to write first and get a rapport and then visit. However I phoned and left a message on her answerphone to say I was here and, although I had not followed protocol, I was there for her inspection and if she did not like me, I didn't have to stay with her.

So, I had a quiet day, getting to know Todd and re-establishing my friendship with Fiona. In the evening Deborah rang and came round immediately. She seemed to find my novel approach unusual but not alarming and soon she asked me if I was ready to go with her. I was so pleased. This was my first 5W contact and it worked! I was able to spend my days with Fiona and the nights with Deborah, so everyone had breathing space from each other. Deborah even reminded me, in looks, of Fiona. Shana had said she could accommodate me (she being the woman I met at Papaya Plantation, Kurman's place) but that would have been twenty-five minutes away by car. However, I did get to see Shana and her boyfriend one evening and it was fun to resume our relationship and talk about our time in the steam vent near Pahoa.

I also managed to find a local yoga class, with easy postures, and so explored the extent of my back pain.

Diary 20 March 2002

All I do is sleep, eat, snooze, look at the ocean and go to the post office and do my emails. Dave says that my back pain is spiritual. Well, I realise that the triggering cause may not be spiritual, but the solution is! God heals us, so all is spiritual. I feel I need more joy in my life to heal my back. Since coming to California I have started to explore more deeply what is the cause and the solution to my back pain. What must I do or be. Stayed up late talking to Deborah about travel, men, spooks versus sensible caution.

As I walk from Deborah's to Fiona's I practise holding joy in my heart. It feels wonderful. Fiona is largely occupied in trying to meet a deadline for a translation job. It's nice because we are company for each other, but can just sit around without any need to entertain, or in my case stay awake. We are comfortable with each other, but I am concerned for her and Todd and their future together and their ability to remain in Pacifica.

Diary 23 March 2002

I spent the final night of my stay here with Fiona and Todd, ready to be escorted away and down to Malibu on the early morning train. There are two trains. One follows a coastal route, supposedly beautiful, and the other goes inland. I hope to go the coast route and pass through Santa Barbara where Hannah hailed from. However that train is many hours late, coming all the way from Vancouver, so I have little option but to go inland. I take photos of Fiona and Todd at the train station as I leave. They smile for the camera. I have no idea when or where I shall see them again. But it has been so nice refreshing our relationship with a meeting! A bonus: Fiona and Deborah are now friends.

★

To get my breath I will now tell you about the astrological implications of being in California. You will remember that I had been there before and in San Francisco I was influenced by the

114

Sun and Mars, both on the Ascendant; but these lines move further away as I go south so I would expect their influence to diminish. And I feel that is just what happened, but I was to receive from both Mary and Maggie a lot of help analysing my back, and the strength from the Sun and Mars to be active in working with it. I had felt to be an observer of my circumstances in Hawaii, allowing Venus and Pele to draw me away from my 'normal' life; in California I felt able to analyse the issues that had arisen. I felt I had only been able to touch on this in Hawaii before I was off on another merry dance. And what better people to analyse with! Both had fine healing credentials.

The rail journey south was a little tedious. I slept, dreamed, ate and looked at vineyards, fruit trees – apples, then oranges. I had to transfer to a bus part way and then I looked at sand hills. Oh! How nice to meet Mary!

My first analysis came the next morning when I got a red itchy lump which had occurred intermittently, for the previous three or four years. I had come to the conclusion eventually that this was herpes, caught from an affair I had in Greece (part of the death knell of the loving partnership I had had with Dave). Knowing I had the condition had in many respects been my salvation. No risky sex for me in Hawaii. Safe sex. It was about protecting men from me, and I enjoyed the caring and careful role that put me in. Realising I had herpes (from a description of symptoms on the Internet) had made me also aware of the difficulties of kinesiology self-testing when the emotional stakes are high. When I had delved into what the cause of the lump was, before the net surfing, I found that when I asked questions about the lump my eyes would dart all over the place and I had to get my eyes to stand still, otherwise the kinesiology result was likely to be flawed. When my eyes were still, I found I was holding my breath – another no-no in kinesiology testing!

Diary 24 March 2002

My back has become worse. Why had it occurred now? Maybe the effects of travel. Or maybe my back feels that it has permission to manifest pain now that help is at hand. Mary and I go into Malibu to take breakfast. Malibu can look so grey – sea, sky and dehydrated scrub on the cliffs. I can see it is attractive, but certainly it is not, for me, a beautiful place. Mary tells me about her landlady who lives in the other half of the house. She is a former Pet of the Year from the 1980s. She certainly is still very pretty with an obviously enhanced figure and with one of the biggest faces I have ever seen. Next to Mary, she looks monumental. Possibly these features all help you to star in the erotic world!

She invites us to watch the Oscars with her. It is the first time I have ever seen the programme, never having lived in a house with a television. Many people here are having Oscar parties and I have noticed that in the walled housing complex where Mary lives the chat around the pool is all about commercials, acting and films. I don't recognise anyone because I don't watch American films or TV. As an aside, Mary's landlady tells me to visit Tortola on my travels in the Caribbean.

I have started to treat the herpes with the aromatherapy oils and flower essences that I carry with me. At least that seems to be working, though my back is just worse! Things must come to a head. Mary has asked me to think what words I use about my legs, to see if I can identify what is causing the sciatic nerve problem that is so painful in my back and right leg. All I can think of is put my best foot forward. This doesn't seem to trigger any type of helpful response.

Diary 25 March 2002

A second trip into Malibu and I have the greatest energy experience of my life. A huge cream and rose quartz crystal in a bookshop (esoteric books) gives off so much energy I can even feel it from the photograph I took of it! It was priced at $9,800 and I found myself almost buying it. Oh, but how can I carry that on my travels? It stands tall and wide on a table-sized pedestal. Time has been passing and it is nearly Easter and soon to be Dave's birthday, so I get him a book on Tibet. How the time has suddenly moved from Christmas and New Year to nearly Easter! The same day I am given a feminist book by its author, a friend of Mary's with whom we have lunch. Then to another bookshop to get me a copy of *Frommer's Caribbean from $70 a Day*. With no youth hostels listed, I am concerned for my finances. I never considered how much places might cost when I worked out my tour, only their astrological significance. The book provides me with a map of the Caribbean and so I am able to see that Tortola sits right on the Pluto line – I intend to visit! Another of Mary's friends informs me that in Martinique fries and a coke cost her $120. I'll give that a wide berth.

★

Mary and I spent much of our time discussing astrology and Reiki. She is very keen on Chinese astrology and she had told me, when we first met in India, that my sign, the Snake, made her understand why I had difficulty being 'faithful'. So, we discussed men and our feelings. This was the way life was now – confide, discuss, feel good, support, help and love. I was so glad I had come to see her.

Mary uses Sanjeevinis too; in fact, she introduced me to the system. She has the whole set of cards so I started taking vibration medicine for my back and herpes. I also began to meditate on the Sun to see if that would throw any light on my back. I was given an esoteric sword as a gift to help my back. To give me strength and support, so that felt good.

I started to plan my trip to the Caribbean. The travel guide only covered East Caribbean, not the Bahamas, but I didn't think I would have time for the Bahamas too. Plus with the Pluto line kicking in around Tortola, why go further north and west? This is not a sightseeing tour! I mused on whether to start in Puerto Rico, flying to San Juan, and then go on from there. The A★C★G information which I had originally bought included descriptions of how three cities would be for me. One of these had been San Juan. It had sounded pretty horrendous. It advised that it was not a place to stay long in and was associated with death (by any means) and flies and dogs. Not my favourite animals! The animals were not necessarily for real, but indicated the nature of the place. Puerto Rico is a little distant from the Pluto line and so the effects would be more limited, and I intended to go all the way to the line. After Tortola, the line curves through the whole chain of the West Indian Islands, so I should be able both to travel and stay on the line. Right down to Trinidad. I decided to leave the details of my travels to the time when I was travelling. It was too good an opportunity to spend time with Mary. I really needed to get to the root of the back pain while I was with her. Reading could wait.

So, to hark back to San Juan, now that I have mentioned it. The A★C★G information I had received included information on three cities. San Juan influences were limited to Pluto on the Ascendant – nothing else was nearby. Pure undiluted Pluto, except it was diluted by distance. It said that Pluto's influence would be quite powerful – it would be quite obvious in my day to day life. However 'the more intense and threatening excesses are less likely to affect you as you are far enough from the exact centre to moderate its more extreme manifestations'.[1]

So, maybe a good place to start, rather than in the thick of it in Tortola. The details about San Juan start with: 'If you are just visiting, seek peak experience and symbols of change.' This, I considered, was good, given my desire (now) to make changes whether it be in sexual liaisons or climbing out of my back pain. Probably the two were related and so it came through both Mary's and Maggie's work with me that it was so.

Pluto was about change and so while I had had little idea about how to change and what to change when I planned the trip I had decided that the Caribbean was the place to do it. As the San Juan text went on to say: 'Living here is the first chapter of the rest of your life.' And: 'The fields must be burned before replanting.'

I was already picking up a desire to contact Pluto to announce my arrival and ask for assistance with the changes I sought. In deciding the overall pattern of my destinations astrologically, I had taken a route that I considered to be easy, difficult, easy, difficult. I didn't want all hard work. At least that was how I had seen it. But Hawaii had taught me that what I had thought would be easy was not quite so straightforward. It wasn't a bed of roses, but more a return to my life with a bed of men – teenage promiscuity.

---

[1] From 'Astro★Carto★Graphy Explained. Analysis of three locations for Juliet Green. Interpretation by Jim Lewis', produced by Equinox Astrology.

Mary suggested that the back pain that had come out of Hawaii was a masculine issue. She told me that the right side of my body was the male side and looking back I could see that it had been a perpetual problem: a growth on my right hip had had to be removed when I was sixteen years old and I had occasionally had sciatic pain in my right side, never the left. My father had always wanted a son, and although I was a much-loved child, I always knew of this preference. Living near the Mars and Sun influences with their male emphasis, as I was in California, was possibly not going to help me with this, but going to live on the Pluto line might give me the opportunity I needed. Change could be in the air!

I still didn't see the full connection between the right-sided back pain and masculinity until two things hit me. One was that in California I enjoyed talking of my exploits to Mary's friends and this included the 'sexploits' too and we all found them quite an entertainment. Then one night while at Maggie's house I found myself very much drawn to erotic and cruel fantasy. What does my A★C★G information reveal? Sun zones are where masculine consciousness prevails, with pride, arrogance, thirst for recognition (as a man!). The Mars influence gives a machismo complex, where even in women the masculine side dominates, perhaps for the first time. Cruelty and desire to dominate come in too – so that explains the fantasy. So, no wonder I was becoming aware of the masculine issues in my life. I remembered my childhood desire to do all things that my father did. For example, wanting to eat with a big knife like my father, a fascination with muscular development, smoking, etc. Sun and Mars lines were not the place to subdue my masculine side, just note its presence and shelve it till I got to Pluto.

To lard the emphasis on the masculine the book even refers to erotic stimulation and challenge and that you become a man, regardless of your sex. Powerful stuff! I was beginning to look forward to Pluto as my salvation, rather than a power that cast a caution over me. I began to feel that I couldn't get there fast enough. There certainly didn't seem to be any possibility of breaking away from the back pain here.

Astro★Carto★Graphy seems strange. So much of it I should be

able to work out in advance; it should allow me to predict, but it never does. I always seem to be on the surprised end of the spectrum. However, I feel that that indicates that nothing is forced; I am not trying to work at it. The effects occur, the events take place and then I study the text and the penny drops. What a comfort that can be.

My last outing with Mary took me to the Lake Shrine of Paramahansa Yogananda. It was a beautiful day and a wonderfully peaceful spot. Mary told me that I should get a copy of Paramahansa's *Autobiography of a Yogi*. It was on sale there. I eyed the size of the book (thick) and thought of my own small appetite for reading. Mary misread this and thought I was concerned about finances. After all, she knew of my desire to buy the book about travelling the Caribbean on $70 a day, and had heard my concern that the travel book assumed at least two people travelling together, in order to effect economies that would not be possible for me, alone. In fact, I could see the $70 a day escalating to at least $100 a day, if I stuck to the book.

Anyway, with reluctance, I took Mary's recommendation and bought the book. That proved to be a turning point in my life – but I was not aware of that at the time, only after I had read it. Hefty or not, I read it and passed it on to my partner in Crete, who was equally taken with it, and he has the advantage of a better memory than me, so he reminds me of what the Great Yogi says from time to time.

Mary and I then went to meet a friend of hers who had family contacts in the Caribbean. I perked up a bit at the possibility of staying with people, rather than the more lonely life I felt awaited me in hotels. (I had noticed in Hawaii that couples on holiday in hotels don't even notice you and so hostels were both my friendly and budget-conscious choice, but hostels were absent from the Caribbean.) Staying with friends in California had made me aware of how pleasant house life is, particularly with friends. As it transpired I never did enquire further of Bev's contacts. Strange.

That night Mary and I went home and stayed up late discussing Dr Agawal's system of medicine and Sanjeevinis, both of which we knew from India, where we met at Sai Baba's ashram. The Sanjeevini vibration medicine system has the ability to duplicate medicinal vibrations, but without the side effects caused by the chemicals in the medicines themselves. I had used this system in Hawaii to duplicate the pain killers and muscle relaxants prescribed for me by the doctor. But Mary had used the little cards that come with the pack and these describe body parts and symptoms. So, I made up a vibrational medicine for me and for my partner for herpes. There's a birthday present for you!

Thinking of birthday presents, it was getting near to Dave's birthday so I sent him this and other goodies from my travels and in so doing had the pleasure of speaking Greek at the post office. The counter clerk was Greek and so it was my first visit to the language for some time. Delightful! I had worried in case my Greek started to fail me. (I have these thoughts each winter when I am away from Greece; the difference this time was that I would be away not for five months but about seventeen months.)

Back to my painful back. I made another meditation to the Sun and asked for assistance with my back. I had already received a sword in a previous meditation but now I learnt to keep it in my suitcase and that picking it up and looking at it will help my back. It was highly decorated and gold. The Sun said I should wear more gold; well, I was trying to buy a pair of gold shoes, but so far had not found any. The nearest I got was in Honolulu with Hannah, but time was short and I felt it would be easy to get them anywhere, but it had not proved to be so. Gold shoes have always been a favourite because they don't show the dust – the exact opposite of black patent!

Diary 26 March 2002

I must sort out today my travel for tomorrow to San Diego and whether I shall see Mike while I'm with Maggie. I muse about the further travel and think I might stay with Bev's relatives in Grenada. It's warm and sunny and I'm sitting on Mary's back step looking into her little garden, overgrown and secluded. I sit a bit hunched up and notice that my skin has a warm, slightly stale smell (a little like drying hay) and remember that when I was in Hawaii I just loved the smell of the locally made products – the scent Volcano I considered to be essential to my well-being. Now these products have little appeal. Maybe in the Caribbean, when it is warm, their appeal will return.

Then I remember it could be pretty cold in Honokaa and that hadn't at all depressed my enthusiasm for the scent. Pele and Venus now feel rather external, but not too remote.

Mary has given me a three-hour Reiki session and she tells me I need to deal with death, loss and rejection (by my partner, when he said he would be ill if he continued our love relationship). She suggested to me that when I feel myself agitated by feelings associated with loss, etc., to note the change in my voice tone and to let the feelings run through my body, close my mind off, just let the emotion run through me and it will run through. At the end new thoughts would come and that would be the end to the matter. She suggests that I can't induce it, only deal with it when the time is right. She suggests that I ask the help of Sai Baba.

Bev has given me a pair of shoes (not gold!), something else to do with feet/walking or whatever it is I need to resolve. One thing that remains from Hawaii: I still feel I look beautiful, and I enjoy that!

★

The following day, Mary left to see her new lover. That was making her really excited and it took the edge off my sadness at leaving her. I was excited for her – and for myself at the prospect of seeing Maggie. Maggie of Crete Street, San Diego; we had shared a caravan while studying flower essences. I had always felt the management at Findhorn put us together because our addresses both included Crete.

On the train journey to San Diego I slept and intermittently read *Frommer's* book. I traced out the Pluto line down the Caribbean Islands. The line so closely followed the line of the islands I would never need to be far away. I marked on other influences too. There were no other planets involved, just that where two lines cross, the effect of that crossing is felt at that latitude right around the globe. I made a note to myself to read up about these impacts when I was due to meet them. It seemed more important just then to sleep to the rattle of the train.

In deciding where exactly to go I determined I would talk to Pluto and get guidance, but not on the train. As the line has much to do with death and renewal, it occurred to me that my mother, then eighty-three years old, might die during this part of my travels. As she had not enjoyed good health for a few years this was not a dramatic thought, just matter of fact.

At the railway station Maggie was there to meet me. She recognised me straight away. It is always fortunate when you have short-sightedness to find the other person makes up for your disability. We immediately went to an Indian restaurant. My favourite food and in short supply in Hawaii, so I was delighted with her choice. It was good to see her and I could tell that she would do me good straight away. She looks at you in an in-depth way, maybe a little disconcerting if you aren't happy with that, but in my case, I relaxed instantly, knowing I was in good hands – and I could stop moving for a while. The changes from Hawaii to Fiona's to Deborah's and to Mary's house felt quite like a whirlwind, even though my time with Maggie was due to be short too. At least I had only just arrived.

We talked about her flower essences and my journey. She told me she had an address for me to stay in Rio, although I never did pick that one up. Also, she had a friend in Miami whom I could visit. She was not well, so the desire to help her came out in me and I did, in fact visit her.

We got home: Maggie's house. As an aside, a feature of my being a Cancerian is that I carry my home with me, so I always feel at home, even in a hotel room and before even spending a night there. To recommence: once home, Maggie probed me about how things were. She told me I was kicking myself about something. Ah! I remembered Mary's advice about finding words that would fit my legs (although it is back pain, the right leg sciatic nerve pain is what tortures me). I opened to her all the things that had happened in the split-up between Dave and me. How ashamed I felt of the herpes, how I felt I had ruined a wonderful relationship, and how the 'fling' I had had was so much more damaging than I had thought it would be.

The story was as follows: we had already moved to Crete, but Dave had been away in the UK for three weeks – we had never been apart for so long before – and I had found myself in such pain that my body ached all over, and with such overwhelming sexual desires that I could not understand. No wonder I did what I did, but I had not expected that when I met Dave at the airport, for a lovely rendezvous, that I would feel as if I were greeting a stranger – after twenty-three years together! Even our neighbour in England, who had come to meet me too, looked more familiar than Dave. I remember feeling absolutely horrified at my reaction, realising too, that my 'fling' would be more likely to be resumed, which it was. That was when I got herpes. Back in spring 1997. After that, no matter how hard Dave and I both tried at the relationship, it just wouldn't rekindle. By 2001, it was all over; we were no more than brother and sister.

I told Maggie how I felt that I had ruined my life. And yet, this was four years later and I was on a holiday that I could never have done with someone else. It had to be my own experience. If we had still been together, as lovers, there was no way that this holiday would have been possible. In any case, the finances allowed only me to do it and the business in Crete had to continue. We couldn't both take a sabbatical at the same time.

Maggie broke it down for me. The root of my shame was not my herpes, but the relationship that caused it. I had been kicking myself about it and so had a bad back and leg. It was right side, as everything had been in my life starting with a tumour on my right hip which started to grow around puberty. Some girls got breasts, I just got a lump on one hip! The kicking was even indicated by a very tight muscle down the back of my right leg. As the right side is masculine this started to fit in with Mary's saying it was a father issue and, as Maggie continued, so I realised that my father had wanted a son, and although I had always been a loved child I had mimicked masculine attributes – way beyond my father's own show of masculinity. He had been a headmaster of a junior school and showed no inclination (as I did) to having muscles! All he did I would try – like eating at the same speed as him, using a big knife like he did. When we went to the seaside I wouldn't wear a bikini top, because father didn't, until it became necessary as my own femininity was starting to creep in. I was on the quest for men! So at ten years old I was already interested in men and saw them as sexual objects (again mimicking how some young men feel about women) and sexual acts as conquests. This also explained to me why the proximity to the Mars line in California felt good. I felt at home. I realised during my stay with Maggie the changes I sought were: to let go of the need to be a boy for my father and to acknowledge the feminine in me and to stop seeing men as sex objects and sexual relations as power sources. The promiscuity had to stop! That would certainly keep me busy with Pluto.

However, I didn't want to wait to get my back sorted, so I started that night by visualising a heart-shaped box (I placed my hands over my own heart) and asked for all things that I was kicking myself about, remembered or forgotten, to be placed in the heart and taken away. The unknown was particularly to capture all the items that had made me embarrassed as a child, now forgotten. I can remember lying in bed many a time, squirming, with flushed cheeks, years after an embarrassing event – and kicking myself! My heart-shaped box had to be expanded several times as more things were added. As a result (I felt) of my affair, I had become very irritable and this had led (I felt) to Dave meeting and falling in love with Christa. So, all that went in the box too. I gave the box to Sai Baba and received the box back, full of love and to be placed in my heart. This was so I could love myself, not despite these things, but because of them.

My pain was still there and I figured I still had to work on my grief at the loss of the relationship with Dave. Maggie had picked up that I needed to recognise loss and death. She held my attention completely, given my expedition to Pluto where death would be paramount feature. All my relationships on Hawaii I could now see as being about loss. The tighter the screw turned, the faster the relationships went. It almost started to feel as if my relationships with men in Hawaii had just gone faster and faster, almost like a revolving door turning faster and faster. One in, one out, with the cycle turning and tightening all the time. And every one ended in a loss. I looked back and saw how the length of time I had sustained a relationship for had gone from a few hit-and-miss weeks with Jerry, to five days with Mike, right down to a few hours with John. And what more could I have done with John? I remembered being quite satisfied that it was all over so fast. A three-hour relationship. A sense of conquest and loss. Was this the sort of thing I felt men were into? Is this the sort of man or person I wished to be? Well, change!

Maggie gave me flower essences to help me to change. Grid-buster I particularly remember – for breaking old patterns. What a wonderful woman she is! She lightens everything too by saying it's all a play we are acting in. Don't take it seriously. This should be written on my wall.

We went to see a film, always a time for rumination, I have found. Sitting in the dark, skimming the plot and thinking. I recall the few occasions I went to the pictures as a child and finding I could almost have panic attacks. Things that I needed to do, particularly if exams were in the offing, I would panic about, and then feel utterly helpless because sitting in the picture house there was nothing I could do. Just sitting, fidgeting, feeling hot and miserable and waiting for the movie to end so I could take some action. Then the lights would come on and I'd see my friends and realise it was almost like waking from a nightmare and all my anxiety would evaporate. Teachers described me as highly strung. I didn't know what it meant.

What, however, I did come to realise during this movie was that my lower chakras didn't agree with my higher chakras. They were refusing to give ground and to love me and take part in the healing processes Maggie and I were working on. From my solar plexus down they all said no, I was still at fault, still to blame, a distinctly unsavoury character. No wonder my lower back still hurt! I held each chakra in turn, going down my body from my solar plexus and told each one that I was loved, and that I was loved for the very reasons that the lower chakras took exception to. Then I heard myself say, I have ruined my life. Good grief! I thought we had got over that.

Next day I had developed a really nasty cold, so I stayed home, but that just gave Maggie and me a further opportunity to talk. We had now pieced together: kicking myself, shame, guilt, loss and the father issue. As well as the grid buster she gave me breathe-easy tea, eucalyptus oil and a releasing flower essence spray. For my part I gave her the information on Sanjeevinis. She found the idea of the replication of vibration by a piece of paper a bit hard to swallow. Strange, because she was open to so many things. We sat up late and she told me of her clairvoyance and clairaudience gifts. As a child she said she could always tell truth from falsehood. As an adult she attended a course that helped her skills and so she hears voices telling her things such as my father being part of my back and leg pain.

During my stay with Maggie she told me that she had arranged to meet friends in Carlsbad, just where Mike lives. This seemed highly fortuitous, so I rang Mike and he agreed to meet me at the fish restaurant where Maggie was meeting her friends. Mike and I would then eat elsewhere, because I am vegetarian, and I would meet Maggie for the run home. This could be interesting – how would I be with a man I had met in Hawaii?

Not to be! At the restaurant Maggie and her husband and friends met and went in. I waited ages for Mike to arrive and I eventually made contact with him on the restaurant phone. He told me he had been waiting at another restaurant. It appeared there was a chain of fish restaurants. Then when I didn't show, he went home. So, I asked him to come out and meet me where I was, but no, he didn't have time for that. I realised he had allotted me just half his evening and so it was now too late. Feeling exceptionally sore, I left to find an indifferent Italian restaurant where I sat with some anxiety hoping that Maggie would not be forced to wait for me at the fish restaurant. In fact, the service had been quite slow so I was back in time with angry tears just below the surface. What was the matter with me? My annoyance with Mike I knew to be out of all proportion, but it had me in an arm lock.

We drove back to San Diego and Maggie picked up my spirits a bit by asking her husband to drive us around in the dark to show me different parts of town. I remember particularly La Jolla, where Deepak Chopra lives. So, the day finished well, although my experience with Mike had left me very upset. He seemed to blame me for the misunderstanding about the venue, but how was I to know there was more than one restaurant? My eyes pricked with tears of victimisation. I had had a most miserable meal, barely able to taste anything through my misery. This had got to stop.

Mike had asked me to meet him the next day, instead, and

that, I said, was possible. I had to phone him at noon. However, when I did so, he told me that something had turned up and that he was now going to Palm Springs and couldn't see me after all. I felt cut up once again and felt myself both burst with anger and disappointment. How could he do this? To me! Then I realised, twice in twenty-four hours I had experienced rejection – part of the cycle of loss that we had already identified as a problem for me. One more thing to add to Pluto's busy agenda!

As Mary had introduced me to Mike I wrote to her about how it had turned out with him and we both agreed it seemed to be the end of the line. I thanked her for introducing us because he had been so instrumental in showing me how and who I am. And what has got to change. I realised that one thing I had wanted to do in meeting Mike again was to prod at his decision to be monogamous and I was thwarted in that by not seeing him. So, sexual power was at the root of that, too. Oh! The addiction to power and to the masculine stereotypical behaviour brought on by my wish to express male characteristics to show to my father! And he's been dead for more than twenty years!

In the night, I spent time asking for my own, unknown, sexual truth to blossom, rather than remaining with this pattern of maleness. Maggie's grid-buster, pattern-breaking essence to the rescue – ding ding!

Diary 31 March 2002

So much to work upon. Even issues I thought that I had worked upon. I feel rather like a librarian, collecting and classifying books, but in this case my library contains the issues that are making me ill. I have loss, grief (father, Dave and possibly soon to follow, my mother) and rejection. I also have a fear of illnesses that my mother has: osteoporosis, which is bending her back so she no longer stands upright, deafness and such poor eyesight as to be registered as blind. Also, I recap, shame over herpes and the affair I had, kicking myself about losing Dave, ruining my life, repetition of sexual objectivity. (Strangely, Dave never appeared as a sexual object to me, but then he has lots of female energy so maybe the male identification comes out in a competitive way only with people with more male energy than me. I had also met him in the neutral environment of work.) I also lacked love for myself and forgiveness – and this after Venus! And I lack a sense of detachment that causes me to be absorbed into the drama of things, instead of seeing life as a theatre stage setting, as Maggie counsels.

This final night with Maggie sees me still with a cold, causing me to sweat profusely and ready for my trip to Miami tomorrow, with wheelchair support at the airports.

★

So, had the Sun and Mars had any effect on me? Probably not much, because I was a little distance from them, but I certainly felt able to catalogue problems, even if not to deal with them. The guidebook says of the Sun that I should feel positive (yes, except for managing to feel a victim regarding Mike), an urge to become master of my own fate (yes), humour, leadership and hope. These I felt were pretty neutral, though you, dear reader, may see more than I can. The book continued, 'circumstances constantly demand loyalty and affection'.[2] I certainly received these from Mary and Maggie and not finding them in Mike was particularly acute for me. The book adds that I would have a thirst for recognition, even to the point of ruthlessness, but I did not feel I was touched by that. And yet, afterwards I realised that while eating my Italian meal alone I could have killed Mike for failing to meet me. Ruthless? It's not a strong enough word for my torment. Health is good – not really! I make things happen, having an inner urge; for me it felt that I was only able to note the areas of activity and store them for later. Logic, will and energy are strong, well... I certainly went through problem identification, with help. But my desire to face all of these issues could well have been a reflection of my strongest drive towards self-realisation – enlightenment, with the help of Paramahansa Yogananda. The Sun on the Ascendant would also bring out the artist in me. And I had painted a big silk scarf for Maggie, and developed an idea for one with Mary (realised later).

And of Mars? This was further away, so the effect might not

---

[2] From Jim Lewis, *Astro★Carto★Graphy Explanatory Handbook*, produced by Equinox Astrology.

be noted by me (I have never considered myself to be very energetically aware or to know who I am, so things have to punch me on the nose for me to see them). The book says that 'Mars's power is intense, should be respected and used with caution.' I would be boisterous, opportunistic, domineering and overcome by passions like jealousy and anger. No, that did not ring any bells with me, except for my interactions with Mike. Of relationships with men, the book added, 'Woe to those who affront you under a rising Mars.'[3] And perhaps my getting advice regarding my health. That was an opportunity seized. Neither was I accident prone. I would be given to more dominating sexual fantasy than normal, so Mars could be responsible for that! And I had got a certain pleasure from entertaining Mary's friends with my time in Hawaii, with Venus. That certainly had got milked for its social points. Cruelty and adventure didn't feel to be a part of me, except that perhaps my continuing to feel negative reactions – guilt, etc. – could be considered as being cruel to myself. And, as I said, I could have killed Mike for mucking me about! 'Life is rarely dull', that was certainly true.

With the Sun and Mars I never had the same surprises to my reactions as I did on the Venus line when I felt I should look over my shoulder to see who was speaking. Maybe the Venus sign represented a greater change from 'normal' for me than the more comfortable masculine Mars and Sun. So I will have to leave you, the reader, who may be more astute than me, to notice things that I can't see!

I felt, when nearest to the Mars and Sun lines (with Fiona, in the Bay Area) at first happier, in fact, more joyful than you would expect me to feel with such back pain. Venus still made me feel beautiful, but where had the self love gone? Let's see what Pluto has in store for me, or rather how I can work through the agenda I now have – the fields are ripe for burning!

---

[3] From Jim Lewis, *Astro★Carto★Graphy Explanatory Handbook*, produced by Equinox Astrology.

Chapter Eight

A MOMENT AS ME

First of April. I arrived in Miami, with wheelchair assistance at the airports. This journey taught me how helpful people are. As long as you make your needs known, things happen. I flew from San Diego to Miami, arriving pleasantly in the afternoon, and took a taxi to the youth hostel. And what a nice place it was. Quite palatial and definitely downtown, so I didn't have to walk far for anything. I met Ginny, Maggie's friend, and went to a travel agent and bought an air ticket to Puerto Rico. I had wanted to leave myself completely free from the constraints of a round-the-world ticket, so at Miami I would head out into the unknown ending up in Trinidad where I would resume my ticketed journey. I judged that from Puerto Rico I could island hop down to Trinidad, by flights and ferries.

Not much to report on the astrological front because in Miami there were no lines near to me. However, as I was in Miami and it's a place people visit I decided to enjoy a few days, basking in the sun, visiting Miami's wide and lengthy beach. It is lined by high rise hotels and condos (one where Ginny lives) but the beach is so expansive that the condos don't dominate the beach. They are back there and the sea is just here.

Ginny took me to a really good vegetarian café out near Sunny Isles, with wholefoods, spiritual music and Internet. I felt I could have eaten the shop! I did some healing work with Ginny, as Maggie had suggested, and saw her again the next day to continue the treatment. I even managed to sort out the buses for the second visit.

Sitting on the beach, I also decided that I was not responsible for all the results of all of my actions. If I inadvertently did something that had a big effect on my life (like having an affair and then finding it devastating to my long-term relationship) then

I should not see myself as to blame, but rather to see it as change coming in and change being necessary and good, so I should welcome that change. Also, I gave myself another statement: men are for having fun with, sex is for later and, most importantly, men are people! This would have been impossible in California.

I went to the beach at Sunny Isles and the sky was overcast, but the water was still turquoise and the white undersides of the seagulls' bodies and wings caught the reflection of turquoise from the sea as they skimmed the surface. Kindly, Ginny agreed to drive me to the airport, which is incredibly helpful for me. It's always nice to be seen off, by friends old or new. I gave Ginny a Sanjeevini card so she can avoid taking tablets with side effects. Otherwise Miami consisted of sitting at the pavement café outside the youth hostel, imbibing Miami's atmosphere.

The last night in Miami, I started to prepare myself for Pluto. I meditated upon my back and its pain, found my guide, this time Sai Baba, in my heart and we went together to the painful area, using my vertebrae as if they were rungs of a ladder. I have told my back that I love it and it is OK and that I am supported in life. Down the rungs of the ladder to my lower back with Sai Baba, where I released the muscle tension, but I know there are more issues so it will not be better in the morning, but you have to start somewhere.

Then I took a meditation direct to Pluto. Last time I did this Pluto was just a black nothingness. This time the scene was night-time – and the fields were on fire! My guide, a solid black ball bearing (as before), was less heavy than before. So, yes, the fields are burning and the experiences I shall have are my gift. I feel I now understand the phrases: be true to yourself and know your own truth; don't act out a role that you have been taught or that conditioning has caused you to adopt. I can become who I really am.

This is new to me, as I really never felt that I knew who I was. When self-development books talked of discovering myself all I could do was to invent a person. I looked back to my teen years of promiscuity and sexual rivalry and felt they could be put behind me. Truth and the dawn broke.

And with that dawn, one last item. I was sharing a dorm. One of my room mates, also with the surname Green (that's how I came to know her – the hostel management got us confused) was in the next bunk bed to me. She was really black-skinned. In the early morning light I sleepily looked across from my top bunk to hers and her arm was outside the white sheet as she slept peacefully. Now, her very dark blackness I would have usually found aesthetically challenging, but seeing her contrasted against white bedding made me realise just how stunningly beautiful she was, not just her, but that very dark pigmentation that I had not before been able to enjoy. That change held me in good stead for my time in the Caribbean and my experiences there.

Chapter Nine

PUERTO RICO AND PLUTO

Puerto Rico, the start of a new time and new line. I couldn't wait! I arrived in the evening of 3 April. On the flight I checked my finances. The *Frommer's* guide said that there were no youth hostels in the Caribbean. The nearest approximation was in Guadeloupe, so I thought that I might go there. My finances, kept so meticulously every day of my holiday so far, showed I spent on average £57 a day. That seemed all right, but the odd extra such as medical bills, car rental and buying presents – flower essences from Maggie – for people whose services and friendship I had appreciated in Hawaii had made a bigger hole than was comfortable and didn't leave me with a great deal of slack as I entered what must be more expensive territory. So there I was in Puerto Rico paying $79 for a room, including an extra for parking, and $50 for a rent car per day. So much for *Frommer's $70 a day*! I remembered that one of the features of the Pluto line was that miracles could happen. I had better watch out for them in the financial area of my life.

On the flight to Puerto Rico I did a meditation to Pluto and still found the fields ablaze. The changes are that the fiery fields now remind me of the glowing lava flows of Hawaii and my guide is no longer a ball bearing, but a dashing young and dark man, maybe of Spanish or Arab origin. I wanted to focus on my back pain, but found that I couldn't draw it into focus – no walking down the vertebrae like rungs of the ladder. I just couldn't focus either on the causes of my back pain regarding guilt, shame or any such things. Have they already gone? I did not think so, the pain was still very much in evidence. The cold that started in California had settled in my left lung. That at least was not on my right side! The last concern on the flight was that as we touched down I felt that a tremendous weight had come down on me, particularly around the temples. Perhaps the weight of personal responsibility for change. I hoped so.

In San Juan the hotel I had chosen from the guidebook was comfortable, with a lovely open area and a green oasis of a garden, where little birds twittered as I waited for breakfast, served outdoors. It was there that I met Sue, who had two children and was finding it a bit expensive to do the organised island tours. We agreed that we would travel together. That would help me to pay for the car and give her a tour for less money. This sounded like a good start – women's cooperation following the fine examples of Hawaii and California. My mother had never valued women friends and so my ability to show appreciation of women had been new to me and so welcome.

My coughing continued through the first morning in Puerto Rico – and then it just cleared. At the end of my tether, I had just said, for God's sake clear up – and it went. A miracle! I began to feel that I could have fun here, particularly if Sue helped the finances. With four people together we were much more likely to make *Frommer's* assumed economies of scale.

Sue went to ask her children about the arrangement to travel with me, which immediately fell through because they wanted to go shopping in San Juan, rather than go south to Ponce as their mother suggested. Maybe tomorrow. That was a shame, but never mind, it would give me a day to get myself acclimatised without going as far as Ponce, which had been her plan. However the arrangements were never to stick. Her children always put a spanner in the works and I got the feeling that Sue regarded it with a certain amount of embarrassment. So, in the end, I didn't even get her company after all, let alone any savings.

There was no public transport in Puerto Rico, hence the car. I couldn't possibly see myself able to thumb a lift while my back refused to allow me even to stand still. So, I made use of the car by starting a small sightseeing programme, visiting first El Yunge to see a rainforest and waterfalls. I found it quite fascinating that a rainforest could be an attraction in itself when in England rain is considered to be such a dampener of spirits, events and holidays. However, it didn't rain on me so the only thing I really felt was a bit lonely because it seemed (probably truthfully) that everyone else had companions. Local family groups, speaking in ringing Spanish, made up some of the parties going along the little way-marked paths from waterfall to waterfall and to other sights deemed to be attractions. They were all able to linger longer than me – I would stop at a waterfall, enjoy it for half a minute then my back and leg would ache so much I would hop around and so leave to go to the next point of interest.

With the assistance of *Frommer's* I added into my day a visit to Luquillo, marked down as a good beach and near El Yunge. I stopped at an area of food shacks, by the roadside. I could see beaches beyond the shacks, but all looked rather litter-strewn. I stopped to get some lunch and tried to explain what I wanted (no meat, no fish). I ended up with a veggie plate: a somewhat tediously bland set of side dishes with an undressed salad, which, as I was to become aware, was the standard non-meat food in the Caribbean. While making my order, a woman sitting at a nearby table turned round and asked me (in English) if I needed help. I said I didn't – I tend to think it's up to the stall holders to sort you out, not strangers on hand to help. However, I struck up a conversation with her and sat down with her and her friends, who like most people there had no English.

So, Janet became my interpreter and I was able to chat to her and her group of friends. She had lived in Chicago, hence her English. She also volunteered that she'd had a Canadian room-mate. I picked up on this: did this mean she was interested in a new room mate? Well, maybe. We agreed to speak later, so I took her phone number so she could consider it and we could arrange to meet if she wanted. That might promise a let-up on the finances and also give me some much-needed company. I was aware that now I was outside the land of hostels it would not be so simple to make a dorm-mate and then travel together as I had done before. The travel arrangement with Sue was still a pos-sibility, however, so I felt some obligation to honour our joint travel rather than move on immediately.

After eating, I ventured to the beach. It had dark gold sands, blue sea with fresh white waves, palm trees and hotels to the rear. And plenty of parking. Not really my scene. The sea, sand and waves were lovely (and the parking – given my back) but I prefer all to be nature; and a hotel and the car parking had made their handprint. My book said it was one of the best beaches in the Caribbean – I did hope that this would prove untrue. And fortunately it did. The sea was a bit rough for me to swim comfortably because it was so easy to jar my back, or just overarch it while doing breast stroke and keeping an eye on the waves at the same time.

As agreed, I phoned Janet. It's always a new learning process handling public phone boxes in a different place. So, I was a bit edgy by the time I got through and not thrilled to hear Janet ask me to call her again at 7.30 p.m. Again, a feature of public phones, now so often lost with mobile phones, was finding one (in working order) at the appointed time. I wandered around in the car and made my way to Fajardo. This I knew would be where I would board the Saturday ferry to St John, via St Thomas. Just as well to reconnoitre the place first.

Fajardo seemed to be falling down, with some municipal efforts to shore it up with fancy paving and uncomfortable metal seats in the square and precinct. The *Frommer's* guide had mentioned a fairly good restaurant which was on the road to Fajardo, but I had failed to spot it, and wondered if on my return, in the dark, I would spot it. I did in fact spot it, but by then I was on my other mission. Janet had been a mixture of reserve and agreeableness and had asked me to visit her. She had given me her address which, being mainly composed of a series of numbers with slashes and hyphens, didn't mean much to me. I could not picture how it would be at all. After a few attempts and repeated phone calls, I found it.

The house was on a fairly modern cheap housing complex with some shabbiness in evidence among the detached bungalows which had gardens but no gardeners. It would do. She had another lodger, but had three bedrooms (mine would be shared with some boxes) and a kitchen and lounge. Oh, to be able to cook and avoid Caribbean veggie plates! She had told me that the Canadian had paid her $10 a night, but then she had been long-term. I was really only looking for something for a couple of nights. In fact, at that time I had arrived on a Wednesday I was due to leave on Saturday's ferry (a weekly service). She wanted me to pay $20 and I felt I couldn't argue without just being shown the door. So, I accepted. I could move in the next day. I chose to make that evening time so I could go out with Sue during the day, if that plan was to work.

Janet's house was about halfway along the north coast (not actually on the coast) between San Juan and the east coast. So, I would be closer to Fajardo, though I would still have to return my car to the office near San Juan airport. Finding a house felt quite important financially. Night fell as I drove back to San Juan to the hotel and then another miracle occurred.

This is the story: I had originally driven into San Juan from the airport along the national highway and was really heading the same way again. However, this time I found that I had suddenly peeled of the main road and was heading for central San Juan, and no signs mentioned Condado where my hotel was. It was dark and I had no idea where I was and my map was impossible to read except by stopping and craning my neck to read it with the help of street lighting. Trying to do this with a bad back was not easy, nor did I know most of the time the name of the road I was on. So, I began to stop frequently and ask.

Each time I said Condado, people said yes, straight on, and on and on. They were absolutely right and I found myself on known territory right by the hotel, with immeasurable relief. Later, I was to look at the map and realise that of the many turnings I might have taken off the national highway this was the only one which sped through the city on a dual carriageway direct to Condado. All the others led to the sort of complexities of roads and traffic systems that lost motorists dread. Hence the miracle. At least I would not have to replicate the journey again, now that I was going to live in Canovanas.

During that day, while on the beach, I had also worked on my back, trying to pull the pain out of the hypertonic muscle that runs from my groin (towards the back) down to my knee. I decided to try some flower essences to help release it. No release. I must meditate, was my conclusion.

Next day, goodbye to hotel Casa de Caribe, hello to Janet's house. Again, Sue's daughters had decided against Ponce. So, I went alone. One reason for wanting company was to get road guidance. Navigation and driving in a place unknown to you, and busy, is always difficult. But despite numerous problems throughout my days in Puerto Rico I didn't feel the despair or the frustration I might expect. Plus I learnt coping mechanisms, such as signalling to the passenger of an adjacent car to wind down their window and then asking, by pointing along the road, is this the way to...? The effect was great. People either said or gesticulated yes or no, or pointed in the direction that I needed to take: turn right, left or U-turn. Better still I learnt to route-plan and write down key points where I would change road or where I might expect to find new signposts. I began to feel that Puerto Rico was giving me some good life tips!

I went alone to Ponce and arrived around midday, in brilliant sunshine. Just right for the beach that I had been promised would be good. Maybe my life in Crete had made these unforgettable Caribbean beaches exactly that – not for how good they are, but for how poor they are. I had some trouble finding the beach because I just kept feeling that I must have got it wrong. It was stony and shallow with reefs too close to the shore to allow swimming. I spoke to a passer-by and he put me right as much as possible, and he also showed me where to eat. It was in a complex of stalls on a boardwalk near the beach. He also told me what food to ask for: corn sticks. So for a dollar I had corn on the cob and a packaged dip while looking over the marina and at the sea birds, swirling and swooping for fish. Then I swam around the corner away from the reef, though my greatest memory of the beach there was getting sunburnt.

I then headed into Ponce town which my guidebook said was an interesting colonial town with many preserved buildings. Yes, they were right, once I had navigated myself from the beach to the town centre. I've noticed this before – that people assume that once you are in town you know where you are and there's no need for signs. Well, of course I got lost and kept seeming to go round the same circuit till I tried a route that, to my surprise, got me out of the loop and to my destination.

So, I arrived in the centre, still feeling a little jaded by the drive down to Ponce and then by the paucity of the beach. It didn't feel a very relaxing time. The town grew on me as I walked about and found fine classical buildings around a grand square and a fabulous red-and-black former fire station, now a museum and tourist information centre. This, I came to realise, was shown on most postcards of the town. Red and black stripes certainly are an unusual arrangement for a building. Everything spoke of a prosperous past. Some of the wonderful buildings, not fortunate enough to have an owner rich enough to afford upkeep, were almost beyond repair, but certainly not beyond recognition as being former fine buildings of character. Many of the buildings had a fine use of colour, blending kindly with the golden-yellow mimosas in blossom in the street.

I was not able to give my all to the pleasure of the town because I knew I would be driving back in the dark. Would I be able to find Janet's house? I made the route back to San Juan feeling that once I hit the north coast road from San Juan I would be fine. But, seemingly as ever on my drives around San Juan, good was to come. By 'chance', I found myself on a route along the coast, rather than the slightly more inland national road. So, suddenly, I was passing delightful beaches, barely visible in the evening light, but the gleam of pale sand and the light coming off the sea promised turquoise, seen through a thick fringe of palm trees.

Then the route turned slightly and I found, or rather heard, shacks playing upbeat, live local music, I saw people dancing, and caught the smells of food. OK, meat smells, with grills aflame, but at last I realised I had met the Puerto Rico that I had been searching for. Not that I had known I was searching for anything, but I knew now I had found it! Beaches by day, music at night. I felt that I breathed a new force. And, I was living nearby!

A glance, later, at *Frommer's* mentioned the area as having a cycle route through the mangroves, that was all. That would have not drawn me at all. The bad back sounded a cautious note even at the word 'cycle'. No mention was made of these delightful beaches frequented by local people (and therefore rather littered) but otherwise offering a touch of paradise with the fringe of palm trees providing a green backdrop to the sea and sand. Sorry, this might sound like a commercial opportunity, but they really did give me a great deal of pleasure. My veins felt a different pulse.

When I had booked in with Janet, I had wondered whether it was a folly to move since I had arrived in Puerto Rico on Wednesday and intended getting the ferry out on Saturday – the day of the weekly crossing to the US Virgin Islands. However, by the Friday morning I had decided to stay another week, just to find out why people liked Puerto Rico – there must be something I was missing, I hadn't really taken to Puerto Rico. That had made me decide to stay ten days, instead of three – to find out why anyone should come here. On that Friday night I had found it. The excitement and energy of Puerto Rico was there! It had seemed a little strange to decide to stay longer in a place I felt lukewarm about when most folk would have just been pleased not to be scheduled to stay longer. But I needed to stick it out.

And, in that one moment my endless playing of Hawaiian music came to an end. It now sounded soft and insipid. This was the Caribbean and a new beat! To my untutored ear it was a mix of calypso and reggae and salsa. I drove through this exciting area grinning my head off, breathing with difficulty as my heart beat against my ribs. I took another wrong turn, overshot Janet's house so I arrived later than promised, but it was OK. I moved in, then went to the top of her road, where a small shopping mall enjoys custom from both the highway and the population of Canovanas. To a bakery, open late, and where vegetarian options did not exist. In fact, I wondered if I existed as the stunned serving girl looked straight through me. The phrase 'dumbed out' seem to fit the bill.

I began to accept this as a new way of life in the Caribbean. If you want any convenience food to be vegetarian, expect again. The response is either a nonplussed silence or a rather hostile response that suggests that you are not only afflicted with a mental illness, but that you are deaf as well. And oh my, can West Indians sound harsh when they decide you are a shouting case! At least the sandwich cake and sweet drink I had were cheap. I was out of tourist land.

I thought about cash and decided to go to the ATM, which was a drive-in affair in the mall car park. I walked there though because I couldn't see how I would deal with an ATM, which would be bound to be different from all others I had ever used (a new country always means a lack of familiarity with banking systems and public telephones – it's just life) and driving through would just create stress. I am the sort of person who can never get near enough the automatic pay point on a toll road to be able to pay without getting out of the car.

Even without the car and having a short stretch of the legs (good for left/right brain integration) I was still unable to get the machine to accept my card. So, I just had to bear being surrounded by car drivers totally incredulous that I was using legs rather than wheels to get the cash – or not. Then a little miracle happened. I got back in the car to drive away, reversed out of the car park bay and had quite forgotten that the queue of cars for the ATM went right behind my parking spot when bump! I had hit a car. A black four-wheel drive had been side on to me and right behind me so that when I turned round to back out I couldn't see either its front or rear lights. Oh dear, the crunch of cars always sounds formidable. I got out of my car and the big guy in the big car looked like he hoped for drama. So, we both looked for damage – to his, not mine – and there was none! Not a single dent or scratch, much to my relief and his chagrin. He looked at me as if I had got him out of his car under false pretences. His horns retreated, he got back in his own vehicle without a word and I then checked my car, likewise, not a blemish.

Back down the road to Janet's.

Diary 5 (I think) April 2002

What has happened to the immaculate record keeping – I don't even know the date!

Things at Janet's seem warm, homely and cooperative. I agree to give Janet a lift in the morning so she doesn't have to walk up the hill to the main road where she catches a ride to work. It feels good to have the chance to help out. Family life. The door to my room doesn't close and Janet showed me a way of crushing a towel through the gap in order to hold it from falling wide open or knocking in the wind while I am asleep. I slept knowing that I was now paying $20 a night, instead of $79 after parking and tax at the hotel – and I was now living with two friendly women and visiting relations, rather than Sue and her family in my life, who just continued to let me down.

The news here, however, made me prick up my ears. There's been a murder today on the estate where I am living. Oh, Pluto, is this the start for me of death events, ranging as my book says from murder to suicide? Fortunately my interested response is taken as a natural reaction to local news and if anything the response I get is one of reassurance that murder is not usual here. Even more interesting to me, of course that it's happened while I've been here.

Diary 6 April 2002

Janet got a lift from her uncle in the morning so I didn't do my good deed for the day. But I was up early, so headed out to the beaches I had seen in the evening light. My most local one I checked out and found the area under the palms to be too heavily littered to sit there and find shade. So, I sat out in the sun, with only two fishermen for company, and rather remote at that. I wasn't sure whether I should find their presence threatening or reassuring, given that I was alone. Sometimes people arrived, scavenging the beach and then disappearing. I decided they wanted firewood and not my wallet. I felt a little company would assist me in knowing the local ways and whether leaving my bag unattended on the beach while swimming was sensible or foolish, I didn't know which.

I was a touch restless, so, after half an hour or so I decided to head off to Isla Verde/Miramar, between Canovanas and San Juan. I really had no idea where I was heading, but as 'luck' would have it, I parked the car to ask and found I was right outside an Internet café. So I could write to friends and tell them I was OK and now in Pluto land. Then I went off to Dollar Rental to renegotiate the car for an extra week. Maybe they'd give me a better rate for the second week.

That had me heading into trouble. I stopped a couple of times at petrol stations to ask directions to Dollar Rental's office. I knew how to get to the car rental office from the airport, but not from here. I kept seeing the office; it was on a road running parallel to the major road, and I was either on the wrong side of the dual carriageway to access it or I couldn't find the right slip road to get to it when I was on the correct side of the road. I waved at it several times. Eventually, and I hardly knew why, I suddenly got it right and there I was at the rent car office – thank God! Then I realised I had no wallet. So, back to the petrol station where I had last asked directions – don't ask me how I found it again or even how I recognised it having gone in and out with a head full of 'how do I get to' and then coming out full of directions: 'Turn left at… turn right', or was it the other way round? They didn't have my money.

For love nor money, I couldn't find my way back to Isla Verde to the first garage. After an hour of driving I had retraced my entire route and there at the Texaco garage was my wallet! The woman on the till gave signs of recognition the moment I appeared, but only when I said the word 'wallet' in Spanish did she pass it to me. What a relief!

During the drive around a tropical storm blew up and so it was a difficult journey for that reason too. I've never been good at busy roads with spray from lorries. I went through much the same rigmarole getting back to Dollar Rental. Except that at one point I stopped to ask someone and it was just as though a new route had opened up, just for me. I drove straight there. Another little miracle!

At Dollar Rental I couldn't renegotiate a better price or get rid of the insurance accident waiver. Maybe there's a good reason to keep the waiver: today I had to do an emergency stop, testing the ABS system big time. I didn't think I was in the wrong that time but I had noticed on my way around to Dollar Rental that I had gone through a red light.

Back at Janet's I did some silk painting, always a sign of feeling settled, and so put the finishing touches to the scarf I had made for Maggie. It looked lovely and went off in the post.

★

On the Saturday night, following this run-around day, I went with Janet and Denise (her housemate) to Pinones, the delightful place of shacks, music and beaches. More of her family were at the shacks and we spent time there. I told them about my day and how I had lost my wallet. They rolled their eyes at me. I made light of it, just relieved that I had recovered it.

Janet and Denise danced and we generally spent time getting to know each other a bit better. The food was all meat and not possible for me, of course, but I got the most wonderful non-alcoholic pina colada, all made from fresh coconut and pineapple and decorated up in front of me with a concoction of fruits and ornaments. I came to think that this would be the norm, but I was in for a shock: elsewhere in the Caribbean all the ingredients came out of tins and so the taste was far from exceptional. No wonder they normally put alcohol in, it's probably the only way to cover up the 'tin' flavour. Janet told me that Puerto Rico is the home of pina colada. I certainly came to believe that more and more.

After Pinones, Janet wanted to meet friends and go to a night club. I had no idea that this would mean a drive right over the other side of San Juan. We drove for more than an hour and had to wait at certain points to see if her friends would rendezvous. It all began to feel rather tedious after my already-busy driving day. The night club arrived and had salsa music and people dancing. They all looked really good. I have never mastered partner dancing and, with my back... so I sat and watched. I felt tired and a little withdrawn. Loud music and smoke rattled my nerves, and it was 4 a.m. before we reached home. So, I slept till late, did a little silk painting and read *Que Pasa*, the local magazine with a tourist slant.

Music was to resume again at 5 p.m. at Pinones. Janet had told me that it's only a weekend thing, so I must make the most of it. By next Saturday night I would be gone! To fill in the day, I decided to do a forest trip, but then Denise, still in dressing gown, told me it was already 1 p.m. She also said that the roads were particularly busy with daytrippers on a Sunday, so I just went to a local beach and found it busy with local people and huge pelicans. A busy beach made me feel happier to leave my things and go swimming. People seemed very friendly towards me, but my lack of Spanish was a great drawback.

To save the problem of meat food at the shacks, I had been to the bakery having reduced my expectations of the food there. I ate my 'normal' bocadillo with cheese and salad for $1.50 with some fondness for its familiarity. Good food and cheap! But the air conditioning in the bakery was so powerful my glasses steamed up when I entered. That was a first. I had only experienced this before in England the other way around – where you can walk from a cold street into a hot public house atmosphere and get the same steaming problem.

However, that day a rain flurry drove everyone off the beach and I discovered that I could get rice and beans and salad at the shacks, which was bland but passable. After that, I went home to Janet's to get ready for an evening out doing music at Pinones again. I felt overdressed in Hawaiian finery, they were very informal there. Well, I stood out anyway in the company of Spanish people so it hardly mattered what I wore. Denise was quite volatile and Janet said she was a stickler about the 'correct way to do things'. Denise made a comment to me, which I nodded at because the music was too loud to ask for an explanation, and thus I seemed to be a catalyst for her getting rid of an old boyfriend who was in the band that night. It all seemed inexplicable to me. I really wondered what I had done. It all seemed a trifle to me and that my casual nod was to lead to this outcome seemed so strange. I remember that her boyfriend had put his arm along the back of my chair, but that didn't seem much of a crime. In her eyes it was getting fresh with me. After this altercation and in my case because the evening was a touch chilly, we left.

I went to eat at a dreadful Chinese at the shopping mall and then went home. Denise and Janet had gone straight home from Pinones but then had decided to return to the music. So they were out when I returned. I didn't ask how things were with the boyfriend when I met them at breakfast.

The next day I took Janet up the hill to get her lift to work and then went to the post office. There was a long line, totally unacceptable these days in England. It surprised me that people seemed quite content to wait very long times for service. But then I had recently read an article about waiting and expectations. If you expect to wait, the time passes faster with less frustration than if you expect immediate service when an unpredicted waiting period can feel like a life sentence. It did not help having a bad back, which caused me virtually to dance around the little poles and ropes that cordoned the queuing process.

Eventually, I hit the road for Guanica, the start of a tour, my guidebook said, of the different forest types in Puerto Rico. I chose a slightly fancy route so that I would take in a piece of road that looked fun. However, as this was not the conventional route there were no helpful traffic signs and so I ended up further away than when I had started, but it didn't feel awful, just part of the adventure.

So I did then follow the more usual route and got to the first forest. There were trails and I coped with a short one which took me by a 700-year-old tree with blue flowers where I sat and contemplated the nature of life. I felt a great tenderness to the tree. I set up a deva and called in nature spirits to assist the woodland. Then a honeymooning couple came by and told me about a mountain yoga retreat centre on Puerto Rico, near Utuado. While I had no interest in staying there, it might be worth a visit. One of the things I was prepared to look at on this holiday was possible winter vacation places so that we could operate a winter season, as well as in summer. I made a note of the place, then headed off to the coast to see another woodland type.

There, I followed another trail and saw red-headed vultures, many pelicans and a fabulous insect that I thought was a type of damsel fly. So struck was I by the black bands across its clear wings that I drew it so I captured its likeness on paper. I also found two blue flowers whose likeness would go on to a silk scarf for Mary. One from the tree, the other a small blue convolvulus I found in the woodland. I pressed both flowers. I swam a couple of times, alone, at the most beautiful off-the-beaten-track beaches. Delightful calming water. Then I fell asleep in the shade of a tree; it all felt very peaceful.

Back to the house. On the way I got lost only once (congratulations), found a petrol station (phew) and ate at a sandwich shop. Then I returned delighted to have company for the evening. It had felt a bit of a lonely day. It rained heavily overnight. Janet's uncle was doing the lift that day and so I was free to go and visit caves, west of San Juan. However they were closed owing to the rain. So I decided now was the time to visit San Juan and actually visit the old city, instead of just negotiating the hotel area by car, which was all I had done to date.

I hung around at the house till the rush hour was over and then headed in. I found there was a tourist bus around San Juan and parking on the edge of town was easy, so I got to San Cristobal castle – and really enjoyed it. There were sobering accounts of how Puerto Rico had been exploited over and over again by imperialist powers. Massacres and petty wars made me feel really ashamed of being English. Most of the city I then just saw from the bus. Narrow streets with tourist shops and other fortresses, but I had seen one castle and that was enough for my back.

I then drove out to the Botanic Gardens and got permission to drive around it, which meant that I kept having to reassure garden and security staff that it was by agreement. It was a pity not to walk: the park had a lovely dreamy quality to it with a wonderful bamboo and Monet garden. Another blue-flowered plant – a water hyacinth – caused me to change my mind about the flower choice for Mary's scarf. My only instruction from her was that it had to be blue.

It was still early, so I went to Isla Verde to the Internet café and had a fresh juice. Their computers were all down. So, as I wanted to speak to Dave I bought a phone card and tried my best to use it. Trying to stand still (with my back) in a public phone booth where the order in which one should do things was not clear and the international codes a total puzzle to me, I became pretty frustrated and quite upset about how difficult it is to do the most simple things in an unfamiliar place. I had spent a small fortune and had not managed to make a single call! I went to the ATM, having spent such a lot on the phone, and so that I could make it through the next two days of trips and pay for the ferry to St Thomas, now only three days away. So, I got $200 out, again walking to the ATM – I still couldn't handle drive-thru. Then home to a small feast of fresh vegetables and cheese. I felt as if my communications with the world were breaking down. No Internet, no telephone.

I went to bed early and was surprised to wake to the sound of my door banging, caused by not having the towel wedged in place. It was lying on the floor. I was puzzled by this; I was sure I had fixed the towel as usual, as Janet had shown me. I got up and put it to rights. I lay there thinking about it and fell back to sleep.

Diary 10 April 2002

Got up early and took Janet to the top of the road. Decided against the caves visit, in case they were still closed from flooding, and went instead to the Carite forest. For this I would need more petrol so I called at the gas station, only to find my wallet depleted of the $200 I had got out the night before. Then I remembered how the door had suddenly started to bang during the night. I had left my wallet on the side table, in the bedroom, near the door.

I felt dizzy at the discovery of theft. All of me felt weak and pale. It must have happened in the house, so it was probably Janet or Denise as they lived there, or it could have been Janet's family who sometimes stayed late. That seemed unlikely: a visitor wouldn't know where my wallet might be. But would either Janet or Denise really be able to enter my room, take my wallet, empty it of its notes and then put it back, all while I slept? The corridor outside my room would have had to be dark; a crack of light would have woken me. And if the corridor outside was in darkness, would they have been able to even find my wallet on the table, among other things – and empty it?

I decided I must check everything before deciding what action to take. At least $180 was gone. I had probably broken into one of the $20 bills while shopping after the ATM visit. I distinctly remembered putting the money away in my wallet; I could not have left it in the ATM. I felt terribly unsettled. What to do? Nothing for now: go on to Carite forest, don't be hasty.

*

Carite is a dense jungle type of forest. Wonderful tall palms and other exotics unknown to me. I found a track and walked some way along it. Deep in the forest was a landmark of an upturned car, a wreck, at the side of the track. It had been there a while, and I noted it for navigating my way back. Strangely, on the way back, I looked for it – but it had gone! Well, there was a very slight mark which might have been made by dragging an object (the car had no wheels) out of the ditch, but it was amazing to find it gone. Had it been a figment of my imagination? I would never know. It just gave me a bit of a strange feeling: what is real and what isn't?

Is this another miracle or not? I needed to steady myself and so I called into being a deva for the forest and called nature spirits to help the forest, adding a bit of tangible magic.

Next, I went to a dwarf forest, high in the clouds but with not enough rain for high growth. Then to a highly acclaimed blue lagoon, Charco Azul, where I swam in the cool water. A charming place. Again, I was all alone.

I began to observe how differently my life flowed in Puerto Rico and with Pluto. In Hawaii I was keen to stop doing things and chose not to sight see. Here I didn't seem to be able to stop.

On the way back I called in at a small hotel, at Coama, which had a bath fed by a hot spring. Back to thermal water, so nice – and so good for my back. I stayed a while enjoying its warmth, just able to swim up and down on my own. The pool had been laid out in a classic style: rectangular, with a smaller semicircular extension at one end. Beyond were views of the hills. That is something I shall always remember about Puerto Rico: steep, sharply pointed hills, and so many of them. Little sharp peaks in clusters across the vista, and all very verdant. On the subject of views, I caught sight of myself as I entered the pool and thought how lovely I looked. So, a bit of Venus is alive and well! Maybe a revisit by Pele and Venus, given that I have returned to thermal waters. The hotel, Parador, needed just $5 entrance fee. I struggled to find it. The theft had left me with just small change.

After this wonderful pampering, I headed back, losing my way in San Juan, but that led me across a delightful, almost ceremonial bridge (unfortunately requiring a toll fee) so my entry to the city was quiet, sedate and somewhat stately, with flags flying. I felt a little like royalty! And they say the Queen of England never has any money in her pocket.

After that, a fill-up of petrol so I could hand the car back to the rental office with the right amount of fuel and with just five minutes to spare. Another miracle – and one to follow. I had arranged for Denise to pick me up from Dollar Rental, but a telephone call quickly showed this was not going to happen. In a land of no buses and a pocket empty of money this felt an impossible situation. So, as I was still in the rent car office, I turned and asked the couple behind me in the queue if they were going my way. I knew the answer would be yes. All that was necessary for me to do was to pose the question.

The lift stopped at the top of the road and I started to walk down to Janet's house. Then a woman kindly stopped and gave me a further lift. Now that I was near to Janet's house, I was mulling over what to do about the theft so, after I got to the house I found that I had left a small bag of groceries in the car – and my wallet! Or at least that was what I thought I had done. I obviously put them down absentmindedly in the house without thinking and then couldn't find them. Denise was in the house and heard my commotion and then relief that all was well. So, in the last two days Denise had known twice over how careless I could be with my wallet. It wouldn't help my credibility if I was to announce that money had been stolen. I felt a bit of an idiot. I looked around my room for the lost $180 or $200, but they were nowhere.

I had decided during the day that I would have to mention it to Janet. She was my landlady after all. See what would come from that. Intuitively I felt Denise had probably taken it, but I really had no idea. Janet's uncle and a grandchild had also visited the house that evening. The only suspicious circumstance had been the way my bedroom door suddenly started to bang in the night, as if it had been opened, disturbing the towel, and then closed again without the towel. And the towel was on the floor by the door, so I had not gone to bed without putting it in place.

I decided that I was unlikely to call in the police. My stay at Janet's had cost me less money, even when the theft was included, than if I had stayed in the hotel. I had had company, even if someone had turned out to be untrustworthy. I was leaving soon and so I didn't want to hold up my trip to St John via St Thomas by a police enquiry and lastly I didn't want to leave a sour taste in Janet's mouth which might stop her from taking a lodger again.

So, that night at 10 p.m. I had Janet's company on my own and I told her of my loss. She immediately got up and went to Denise about it. They returned to the living room together and both of them treated it very seriously and were most concerned. So, although one of them might have taken it their manner gave me no inclination of it. The enquiry stopped there. The money was still missing but I wanted my stay to be peaceful, not full of police, even if it did mean I could not claim the loss on my holiday insurance because I would have no police report. I had thought when I told Janet that I would threaten to report it, but what did it matter? And, as I had already shown a poor sense of responsibility towards my wallet, I felt it was unlikely that the police would work hard at it. Worse things happen at sea. Denise reminded me that as I was to leave early on Saturday we must celebrate by going to Pinones again on Friday evening.

Thursday morning and up early. This time, Janet and I both walked up the road to take a lift with her friend because I wanted to pick up a rent car at Fajardo so that I could drop it off there before getting on the ferry. I even managed to make an arrangement (with no small amount of persuasion) to return the car and then be picked up by the ferry people, at the car hire office, and taken to the quayside. The rent car guy was actually extremely helpful and sorted out all the ferry information for me. All I had to do was phone and remind Lydia from the ferry company to pick me up and get me there on time. Well, for most people that would be easy but with my luck with phones it was not! Interestingly, the ferry company would pick up four passengers, even from the airport, to take them to Fajardo, but not just one person. The difficulties of being alone.

Diary 11 April 2002

I now know I am kicking myself not only for losing Dave, but more particularly because the affair I had caused me to lose my 'in-love' feeling towards him. It is now six years since I was in love – that wonderful cloud nine feeling. That's a long time to go without feeling in love. What I felt for my Greek lover was an overwhelming heat. When people say they have the hots for someone I can seriously say I felt the furnace. I listen to myself, carefully, to hear what my inner voice, the chatter, is actually saying to me. I feel I need to know the full measure of my thoughts before I can start to work on the issues. When I want to go on a meditation to Pluto I am still only able to see fields ablaze. I have not been able to make contact. I think I have some distance to travel along this road; getting closer to the line might help. Oh

Tortola! I can hardly wait! Listening to myself – and a good time to do this is when I am driving – I hear, 'I blame myself'; 'It was my fault the relationship split up'. I notice my true colours, or true guilt, six years on! Me, who had never before knowingly experienced guilt, knowing that all life ever merits is a feeling of regretfulness, not guilt. Yet this has racked me.

★

As I was at the east of the island and had a car again, I decided to stay in the east and go to Las Cabezas, a nature reserve. It was part of my agenda of finding out about Puerto Rico. At Las Cabezas, a notice informed me that the public were only allowed in on Friday, Saturday and Sunday. Today was Thursday, groups only. However, I persuaded the staff to let me join an English-speaking tour in the afternoon. Good, and no mean feat.

So, I still had a morning to occupy: I asked about kayaks. There were two problems: the sea was choppy – and I was on my own (the kayaks are for two people). I agreed to call by later and went to Seven Seas Beach instead. This turned out to be as good as the text. The water was protected by a breakwater and the sea was even better than the book said. It was the colour of John's eyes. Remember? The man who I met at the Beach 69 with the wonderful eyes! I smiled gently at the memory. Never again would I act like that, but I had still to learn a new way to be.

So, I swam in the turquoise-and-blue eyes of my former lover, basking in the delightful calmness of the water that let me swim freely without concern for my back. I was in for about an hour, coming out and lying down. Then I sat up to sing the Gayatri Mantra, taught to me at Sai Baba's ashram in 2000. I closed my eyes and saw the orange of Baba's robe and felt total happiness. Just great! Good inside and out, with palm trees fringing my vision and different, big, birds, flying aloft. Quite rightly I expected I'd find out more on the nature tour in the afternoon.

I still had lots of time so I considered a boat trip for the evening (not a kayak) and then went to the reserve and waited for the 1.30 p.m. commencement of the tour.

It proved a very informative tour of mangrove swamps, saying how important they were as spawning grounds for young fish, away from the big sea predators. Mangrove swamps are being lost throughout the world, adversely affecting fish stocks. There are also different mangrove species and these were explained. So, I came away knowing about buttonwood mangrove, red mangrove (which produce a red resin which colours the swamp water), black mangrove (where the seeds develop into new plants before being released from the parent plant) and white mangroves. A boardwalk through the mangroves and buggy rides took us around and none of the stops were too long for me to stand and yet long enough to be informative. Hurrah!

At the end of the trip I went back to look again at kayaks. Fortunately the name is the same in Spanish; some things are easy in life. Well, it appeared that the boats (shared) were considered a better option for me as I was alone. OK, I would join a party. I had just enjoyed one group trip, so why not have another?

There was an element of doubt about the boat trip. As yet there were not enough people for the boat to go. By the time they could tell me if the boat would go all the kayaks would be gone. As the boat was $10 and the kayaks $40, I decided to put my trust in the boat. It would work. And it did. I waited till 7 p.m., then the boat set off for its hour-long trip. We were propelled by oar power through narrow channels, sometimes having to duck down to avoid the low branches of the mangroves and then we were at the lake, acclaimed for its bioluminescence.

As we entered the lake I was immensely disappointed. It was nearly dark and no light at all appeared to come from the lake. But that was because it was not how I had imagined it would be. The light shone through the water only when it was disturbed, so the luminescence appeared with the turbulence from the oars. In our wake the dark water became bright turquoise water and my jaw dropped open. Our fingers dragged through the water had the same light effect. Then you could see fish and as they moved so they left a flow of light in their wake, just for a moment. I already had my swimsuit on, so I asked if I could swim – sure – so I dived off the boat into black water which immediately lit up and I watched the light flow away from my breaststroke arms and legs. Some others followed me in. By then I was able to see their plumes of light too. This really is magic! The more the night darkness came, the more spectacular the show.

On our return, we passed through the trees and then the crew caught iguanas from the trees and people had their photos taken with them, before they were released into the water to swim back to their perches. I am not happy about this 'abuse' of wildlife so I wouldn't partake. They were certainly big and impressive creatures. Little did I know then how important iguanas would later become in my life, at least for a while.

On my travels in this corner of Puerto Rico I had managed to find an acclaimed restaurant for the evening: Pasion por el Fogon. They had vegetarian specialities and so I had booked straight away! The restaurant lived up to its reputation and I had an excellent meal, conversing with three people at the next table who were working in Puerto Rico. I drove home feeling less lonely than I normally did and with as much of a skip in my step as I could manage.

Diary 11 April 2002 (continued)

It's been a real squealing day of pleasure; maybe I am going with the flow, including how I treated the theft yesterday. The drive home ended a perfect day, even if I was a bit sunburnt. I returned and phoned the yoga retreat centre, Casa Grande, in order to pay a visit tomorrow, my last day in Puerto Rico. Another little miracle with the car – having gone through a red light, and hit a car waiting for the ATM without scrape, now I have backed into Janet's car port, an extension to the house supported by pillars, and felt I didn't go in quite straight. I never do; reversing is not my forte and of course it was dark. So, feeling that my reversing was not too good I got out of the car to inspect whether I needed to try again. Yes, I did – but, the distance between the pillar and a back corner of the car was less than I could insert my finger into. I had stopped absolutely at the last moment. How easy it would have been to have damaged both car and Janet's property, and just before leaving! Someone is looking after me for sure.

★

My last full day started later than usual. I had no need to drive Janet to the top of the road. I was on my way to visit the caves washed out earlier in the week. They were on the far side of San Juan so I took in the morning traffic and somehow got through the San Juan road network without a single mishap. That's a first. I stopped for petrol and wanted just enough to leave the tank half full when I returned the car the next day. I suddenly said 'stop!' and had just the right amount to leave the car on half. All of these small matters are not life-shattering, but then my life is quite simple, so I have to be aware of small miracles.

The caves involved a lot of cordoned waiting. School parties obviously knew the ropes – they'd been before – but for a newcomer to the caves it was quite perplexing. Don't queue here… queue there, etc.

The caves were worth seeing, although parts were still closed by the bad weather. I suspected a lot of that was due to their safety procedures and insurance, rather than a real problem. This was the litigious United States, after all. The sections with archaeological remains were closed. That was a pity. I bought some expensive sweeties to give me a boost on my journey and set off for Taino Indian Center. See how the original Puerto Ricans had lived.

Well, I came to a road block. The road was blocked by maintenance vehicles and would be for four to five hours. I stopped and looked at the map and found another route, noting down my route as carefully as possible so that I could refer to my list of directions, rather than opening up the rather voluminous Puerto Rican map. This way of working, with a list of instructions, often makes me feel as if doors are opening, instead of being in a maze.

When I arrived at the Taino Center car park, there was a sign to say it was closed owing to slippery conditions. However, I was not to be put off, but donned my heavy walking boots. They went well with the chosen outfit for the day: the Hawaiian strapless, boned dress in shocking pink with a flowing skirt. However there is nothing like being distinctive if you are alone. So, I went down to the pay point armed with the knowledge that I was well shod and wouldn't slip in the mud. No need to gird my loins, the ticket office was open. So, they would take my money, even if they were closed. They admitted they had left the closed sign there as a deterrent.

In the end I could see why. The site was mainly a large ceremonial playing field, which I tried to walk on as little as possible because I did have the feeling it was a little soft underfoot and therefore easy to damage – and it did feel like hallowed ground. The main ceremonial field (there were other smaller ones) had stones around its perimeter with images of people carved into them. It is not clear what the images represent, but I would think they'd either represent the person who had 'bought' the seat or represented his/her station in life or, possibly, that the seat owner had carved an image of a favourite player. It was the sort of place where the imagination could run riot.

I was busy taking photos of the arrangement of mountains around the site – somehow they looked very special – when I was approached by two men. They were the only other visitors; you can see why loneliness can be a problem! I was in the presence of Jose, an archaeologist, and his photographer friend, Angel, both from the Puerto Rican University. I was in good hands. Yes, I had just photographed a significant view: the hill was like a cemi, a god overlooking the site. Angel, the photographer, took my photo with the archaeologist, who, as we lined up, quipped, 'Here's one for the *National Geographic* – Puerto Rican Native with English tourist.' I certainly looked extremely like an English Rose, but no other UK tourist would look like that! Everyone seems to wear beige shorts, blue T-shirts and trainers and maybe a baseball hat advertising a restaurant or other such. If I went missing, how would anyone ever find me from that type of description? Much better to wear a flamboyant and inappropriate frock and big boots!

I learnt quite a lot about the site and the people who lived there, now being in the informed hands of English speakers instead of the smudgy photocopy in Spanish I had received on arrival. We got on well and the place echoed with our laughter. Jose said that I wouldn't leave Puerto Rico the next day. I assured him I would, but there was certainly a dynamic attraction between us, even though he was rather rotund for my taste. It pointed up that since leaving Hawaii, where suitors had flowed in and out of my life, this was my first attraction to the opposite sex on the Pluto line.

I told Jose about my astrocartographic journey and he was sensitive in his understanding of it and his interest was marked by questions, which, although the journey is inwards, were not too personal, just nicely searching. We all exchanged email addresses and I felt very warm towards both of them. Jose finished by saying that Cabo Rojo (which I had not visited) was a lovely place to meditate. So, it was a lure to make me stay, but I wouldn't be drawn. A more profound taste of Pluto was what I sought.

I left, driving quickly to Utuado, the Casa Grande retreat centre, arriving only a little later than I had suggested. The journey there took me through grander mountains than I had seen before and near to a lake, just before arriving. So, the area would furnish walks and probably boat trips on the lake. Now I was wearing my work hat. Would this be a potential centre to bring people to for yoga as a winter retreat?

I found Steve quite quickly. He is the owner. He had originally been engaged in his own yoga practice, but found others wanted to join him, so he had accidentally become something of a teacher. However he was quite happy for me to bring teachers too. In his six years there the place had changed into a meditation and yoga retreat. The yoga studio was well equipped, the pool and garden attractive, although I felt the place would benefit from a new coat of paint. It had a gentle, slightly dilapidated feel that I wasn't sure would go down well with people who had paid a high air fare and might expect a more upmarket resort for their money. But it seems nowhere is perfect, unless you run it yourself when the imperfections are often blocked from your view. He gives love to the centre and certainly the early evening meal I had with him was good.

I left and headed to the north coast for Pinones, a long way on a narrow road; it must be really beautiful in the daytime. However, perhaps it was a good job that it was dark because I found my camera, bought especially for this holiday, would not accept a new film.

I haven't mentioned before, but at the top of the Janet's road, the main shop was a chain supermarket where I seemed to have had endless trouble. They really were my bête noire. Whatever I bought there I seemed to take back and whatever service I asked of them the result did not meet up to the specification. I had had one film printed by them five times before they got the specification and colour right. By then they were miles off their agreed time schedule. The film I was now trying to load unsuccessfully was their own make – ha!

In order to pick up the final version of the photographs they were doing for me I had to leave the wonderful music of Pinones at 11.30 p.m. on my last evening – at least they closed late! It was as well to leave Pinones early, given my early start to the ferry, but terribly hard to leave the Puerto Rico I had discovered and loved so much. I tried to load a Kodak film in the camera, but that was no better, so it was not the brand of film that was the problem. But I was so coloured by annoyance that I felt that loading their film had probably caused the problem. So the chain got more of my custom as I grudgingly purchased a disposable camera for my sea trip to the Virgin Islands.

I packed my bags and went to bed at 1.45 a.m. Janet asked me to send her postcards from future destinations. I said I would – and I did. I was just so pleased, and still am, that I didn't call in the police about the theft. The leaving would have had a very different flavour – not worth the insurance claim for the $200.

I got up at 5.15 a.m. and Janet's uncle gave me the bad news! He had noticed I had a flat tyre. (Maybe Jose and Angel were right after all, I wouldn't be leaving!) But the uncle fixed the spare while I had breakfast and off I was able to go. I left Janet in a very disappointed state: she wanted a man she knew, Edgar, to come and stay, but he hadn't shown. His car broke down, he said, so no licking chocolate and cream off each other as Janet had hoped. She had cleaned the house too. She looked a bit crushed.

Diary 13 April 2002

So, off to Fajardo and then the ferry to St John. Nearer the Pluto line. I looked back over my time in Puerto Rico. Lots of little miracles. In fact, as I sat in the car I remembered another, where I nearly hit a stationary car in Pinones, at night, while I was parking. Oh-ho yes! And my car has received a little scratch (but that's all) from going through some automatic gates in Isla Verde that opened towards me and hit me before I'd had time to reverse.

Puerto Rico has been strange. I have had to stay longer and so change my plans in order to understand what the Caribbean was about. Most people would have been glad to stay only three days in a place they didn't like, but I had extended it to ten days. That could have felt like a very long time! I have had no real contact with Pluto in my meditations. Just the fields burning. Perhaps the changes are unconscious. I have decided what I want to change and perhaps it is just happening for me, or to me. I am sure time will tell.

★

On the way to Fajardo, I looked out for tyre change places, so I could get a new tyre, rather than be charged for one by the rental company. But it was Saturday and only just after 6 a.m. I couldn't find a petrol station open, let alone a tyre shop. I was quickly on half a tank, the amount I had to have in the tank when I gave it back. I asked Sai Baba to hold it on the half. It worked!

Lydia, my contact for the ferry, was waiting for me at the rent car office. I poked my keys through the office door and headed out with her to the dock. There I bought my ticket, found a phone booth and tried to phone the campsite on St John. No luck with that. I felt unsettled: whether to stay in St Thomas or St John. Maybe I would be able to get my camera repaired in St Thomas. But it was not a difficult uncertainty, just a little tickle in the side.

I met a man on the boat, travelling with his three very well-behaved sons, at least two of them under ten, yet quite prepared to sit and watch as their father chatted to me. Jesus was from the Dominican Republic and was travelling to St Thomas. He told me of a small hotel, the Island Beachcomber, where the prices were low, although he couldn't tell me the price. It was near Charlotte Amalie, the town on St Thomas, but by the beach. In fact, he told me we would pass it on the ferry and he would point it out.

The journey was smooth and passed peacefully. One of the children was cold so I wrapped a sweater around him and another fell asleep with his head in my lap. A small coal-black head. All the way we chatted and saw small islands passing. I had no idea there would be so many. Little pointed triangles pushing out of the sea. I am now invited to the Dominican Republic too! My new friend did indeed point out the hotel, a low-lying building partly hidden in greenery with a stunning white beach. I decided to stay in St Thomas.

Chapter Ten

PLUTO GETTING CLOSER

We disembarked at Charlotte Amalie and Jesus and his sons got into the minibus taxi with me. They lived quite close to the hotel so we did a little detour to drop them first and then me at the hotel. Ten dollars for the short ride – I paid. In the hotel, my eyebrows nearly shot off the top of my head when the receptionist told me it was $100 a night, plus tax, plus, I expected, 20% service. No food, just the room. I was a little surprised to find that a man from Santo Domingo should think this cheap! But I was there, so I agreed to stay for one night.

I was taken to my room, a spacious room with two double beds and easy chairs. Outside I had a balcony overlooking the garden with glimpses of the sea beyond. A deep sense of calm came over me and I breathed in the view, excitement suddenly growing. Perfection: a hotel overlooking the beach with a garden bar and restaurant between me and the sea. Then I suddenly felt very tired. Staying in the house in Puerto Rico had been fun, but perhaps rather more contact time than I cared for – strange considering I often felt lonely. Being on my own now, I just took off my clothes and climbed into bed. It felt a real relief to be on my own and yet never had I felt bombarded with attention at Janet's. Falling asleep saved me from my enquiring mind: why was I suddenly so tired?

When I woke, I thought: I have surrendered myself to spending more money than I can sensibly afford. I have left Puerto Rico having had money stolen, a car tyre left unfixed, needing to buy a new camera and now this hotel is too expensive. So, I will live beyond my means. I decided that there would be no more daily calculations and recording of how much I had spent, something I had done every day till now. It hadn't mattered how tired I had been, I had sat each day and done my accounts. No more. I would live beyond my means. It seemed to roll of my tongue very easily and gave me a sly sense of fun. All my life I had been careful. When I was a child, my father had kept a saving account for me, and odd shillings that came from visits to family friends and relatives were squirreled away there. This, my father had said, was for travel. Each year I saw an amount of interest had been added and thought that it was called interest because it was interesting. With some pride my father showed me the little bank book, with its interest and I came to believe it was virtuous to have money in a little book. So, here I was about to empty the coffers.

I put on my bikini, skipped down the dark-wood staircase with no shoes on and headed to the beach. Just like that! No roadways to cross, I could walk barefoot from my room to the sea – and it was turquoise. Soft white sand and turquoise sea, made creamy by the sand in the slight turbulence of lapping waves – a pot of white paint mixed with the turquoise to brighten it and it just looked like a playground to me.

At the bar – I wanted a bottle of water – I found the barmaid, Leanne. She was from Barnsley, South Yorkshire, very close to Sheffield where I had lived my life from being eighteen to forty-two years. For me, Barnsley is the least attractive place in the world to live. I am sure this is an exaggeration, but it came as no surprise that someone should want to leave and come here!

Barnsley people are down to earth. They are known to call a spade a spade and be blunt in so doing. So, I felt comfortable to ask Leanne if she knew somewhere cheaper to live. May as well be pragmatic, even if I was happy to live beyond my means. Leanne mentioned some condos, but while they were only $500 a month, a month was too long for me! But if I stayed just five days it would be cheaper than the hotel. I certainly wouldn't need to stay a month; I was still not on the Pluto line.

The lure of the sea was great. I swam, I sunbathed – and met Mary. Mary worked for the *National Geographic* – maybe they'd be interested in my form of travel, but I didn't ask her. I just smiled sweetly at my memory of Jose and Angel. My trip was not about filling column space or having experiences for recording, it was a personal, inner journey, where nothing noteworthy might happen – what then? That was not the sort of pressure I wanted.

Mary endorsed both Cinnamon Bay and Mahoe Campgrounds, both on St John. She was in St Thomas for one night only, but we got on well enough to exchange addresses. I stayed on the beach, sitting while she slept and then went to dress for dinner. Slacks, and gold nail varnish. Now, there's a change from the girly look of Venus.

I ate at the hotel, though the food was very limited for a vegetarian. But the setting was lovely, the garden was full of little white fairy lights and I had to cross a little ornamental bridge to get from my room to the restaurant. It sounds rather kitsch but it looked terribly romantic. I leaned back in my chair and decided that this was the Caribbean. I had had no idea beforehand what the Caribbean would be like, but now I knew. I have never lived in a house with a television and I don't read newspaper fillers about travel so I had no impression in my mind about how it would be. But something must have filtered in because I knew that the sea and sand colour, the ability to walk barefoot from my room to the sea was it! I had arrived.

In the night I dreamed: I gathered an assembly hall full of people together with the assistance of one other person (unknown). They came because I said I had a big announcement to make. When I stood before them, the announcement turned out to be that my parents had been given two bottles of wine! My assistant then turned into Maggie from San Diego. She was highly embarrassed – and so was I! Very kindly she told me that before she would assist me in anything like this again she would need to know more about it, in advance. I felt embarrassed because I knew it was no big deal to receive two bottles of wine. The audience were restive, but in the end they just filed out. Maggie was diplomatic, but I knew I had goofed. What did it all mean?

Day two of my new paradise. I swam before breakfast and then walked with Mary to the airport, which was nearby. I then walked on in search of the cheap condos that Leanne had suggested. Nothing. I couldn't really work out where she meant, but there was a large hotel, largely closed. Later I deduced that she had meant some 'backrooms', in other words rooms that didn't come up to the tourist specification. But they were beyond the beach where the rocks meet the sea, so I would have lost my

Caribbean. So, I paid for another night at the Beachcomber and went into town to see the crowning ceremony for the carnival, carrying with me my defunct camera in quest of repair. On the way, I met Jesus and his sons. I agreed to meet him later at my beach, Lindbergh Bay.

I also had my *Frommer's* guide with me so I went to Bunker Hill, a cheap hotel mentioned in the book. Oh, but it was tired. The bed I was shown, by a matter-of-fact owner, was limp and almost filled the room. I couldn't imagine staying there, it was so dingy. There was no view of the sea. A woman who had given me a lift into town suggested I try the homeless shelter – in fact she was very encouraging – if I couldn't afford a hotel I was homeless, wasn't I? I went to look, but there was no way I could go and talk to the Sister there and tell her I was homeless with £30,000 in the bank and jewellery including thirty-eight diamonds (mainly small) in my luggage. And Bunker Hill was still going to be $80 a night so I would still be 'living beyond my means'. So why not do it in style?

I looked at one further hotel, the Mid Town, but its name was not in its favour and the ambience was poor – and it still cost $60, so it would still be beyond my means. I would live beyond my means; my new favourite saying – and so liberating! I turned my quest to an Internet café, but at $3 for fifteen minutes I only read and didn't reply to my emails. Living beyond my means had its comfort limits. Then I went further to look for camera shops, all the way to the cruise ship dock at Havensight, only to be told that no, they only sold new ones and no they didn't know of anywhere for repairs.

On the way back, I called in at a bar where a young man, who was drunk, bought me a drink. Maybe I should extend my new carefree ways to 'spending' money too: he obviously survived even though he was a drunk and he still bought drinks for strangers!

On the street, I seemed to be quickly becoming known as I walked about. I was dressed in my fifties-style Hawaiian clothes and looked very much the English lady tourist. That was good, I like to be remembered, it makes me safe. If I was remembered and then went missing people would know if they had seen me. This actually was taken further to its limits later.

The ceremony for the Carnival Queen and King crowning was late starting, fancy! Very amateurish and sweet. The winners from previous years, right back to the 1950s, made a guard of honour for the new arrivals. Everyone was dressed up for the event, so I felt quite right in my smart clothes – but I was nearly the only white face there. Do none of the white people care about these traditions?

I left the town in the late afternoon in order to rendezvous with Jesus and his sons at the beach. But I saw them on their way from the beach so I hailed them and went to their house and had home-made tamarind juice. It was just delicious, and so nice to get local specialities. There was a tension between Jesus and me, both of us feeling attracted to each other. But his wife was due to arrive in two weeks' time, so this was no place for a dalliance – and I didn't want to dive into a fast-flowing river of relationships with men when that was what I had come to sort out! But we agreed to meet that night for dinner.

At last, time for a swim in the sea, then an idle look through the accommodation pages of the local paper, putting a circle around any ads which looked interesting, but all in a desultory way – nothing else to do at that moment. Jesus arrived and had actually eaten already, but he brought me sweets and some garlic bread and more tamarind juice. After sitting together while I ate dinner in the restaurant we sat outside my room. He wanted to kiss and cuddle and then make love. I didn't want to be a possible cause of him losing a love relationship for a sudden passion, as my Greek neighbour had been for me. I refused him. But there I was again, blaming myself for the collapse of my relationship with Dave. However, if that was what it took to keep myself from Jesus's advances, then that was all right with me!

I felt responsible for protecting people against herpes and against having a disastrous relationship, ending with them feeling no love for their partner. I said I would only see him again if he was prepared not to approach me for sex. I said I would release him. This was a new statement for me. To release him. It felt nice. And, I had held to my resolve not to have sex. It was 4 a.m. when he left me and for me the next place to go was to bed, feeling triumphant!

The next day I realised I had lost my pinhole spectacles. I wear them to help to improve my eyesight and never like to be without them, particularly as they are also my sunglasses – sunglasses which don't change the colours of the world. They just sharpen my vision and cut down the amount of light coming at me. Why have they disappeared now?

Every day in the morning I paid the hotel for another night. I wanted to leave the door of opportunity open so that if something cheaper came my way, I could take it, and as there was no discount rate for the week I troubled the management to handle my credit card each day. I had said to myself that if I finished my travels with £5,000 I would donate it to Sai Baba, so I trusted all would be well, even with the cost of living there in St Thomas. The fields of distrust and anxiety over money were slowly burning.

I still found no joy in getting the camera repaired despite more trips to town, but I did find a jeweller's shop (among the hundreds there) that did free Internet. So, that was for me! I felt tired that day, not too surprising going to bed at 4 a.m! So I returned to the hotel and after a small sleep I finished off the final outlining work on my silk, Hawaiian diary scarf. I felt a desire to get the Hawaii scarf completed before my enthusiasm for it faded.

The broken camera went off in the post for John, Dave's cousin, to sort out for me. I had bought it from him and he was now expecting it, following a correspondence by email. The queue for the post was long and I ended up hopping around, dancing around, trying to stay out of pain. My back still was not right, but then I had not done anything there to get it right, except to say no to sex, just once.

I found a wonderful place to eat veggie burgers. Willie, who ran it, was a personal trainer with a desire to feed people good food. And he did! He also told me that his landlady might be able to help me with accommodation. It turned out that I had already seen her – she was a Carnival Queen back in the fifties. But I did not think anything would come of it. Her house was away from the sea – and I lived beyond my means as a way of living with Pluto. The fields must burn!

Buying a new pen is a bit like having sex with someone for the first time. Will it be rough, smooth, a good write or leak ink right through to the other side of the paper? My diary has enjoyed or felt abused by many different pens on my trip. Here I am buying another.

Every day I swim early and then seem to be drawn to visit town once again. There is a series of little open buses called the dollar ride. You go wherever you want (within the parameters of the route) for a dollar. Accidentally, today, I found myself leaving town and going not towards the airport and thus to the Island Beachcomber, but right across the island to Red Hook, and then back into town. On the journey I decided I would buy a tent and go to St John. The only camping shop on St Thomas has closed down, but a passer-by near the now empty store told me to try the supermarket Big Kmart. Cinnamon Bay camp ground on St John, here I come!

Went again to Willie's for a burger and found his landlady was there. Indeed, she told me she was Carnival Queen in 1954, when I was but one year old. I took her card, but no, I didn't now need accommodation, although she could offer me a room. I was off to Cinnamon Bay. But first to Tutu Park's Big Kmart for the tent. I came away with tent (smallest possible), sleeping bag with mattress and a pump. The whole lot cost me less than $60, so I was very pleased. Just one night and it would pay for itself! Armed with such goods I went home to the Beachcomber and threw myself into the sea. But before my plunge I sat and chatted to Guy, who runs the bar. He had a tall man sitting in the bar and it was he who called me over, otherwise I would have gone straight into the sea. On being summonsed, I crossed the low fence from the beach path to the bar and wondered why I was bothering to be sociable. But I was in an exuberant mood and was quite happy to talk of my successes that day.

★

Little did I know at the time what a momentous meeting that would prove to be. Victor, the tall man became richly influential in my games with Pluto and other planets to come.

After our chat, not even noted beyond a mention in my diary entry for 16 April, above, I just walked away from them and swam in the sea, finished my diary painting – a little confused and hurried, probably Pluto wanting me to get away from all this Venus stuff and concentrate on the present. Or perhaps it was just me. I have always been a person who enjoys the end product, to the point of rushing it. My mother said that as a child I used to say with obvious emphatic satisfaction: 'There!' when I had completed something. My diary suggested that I perhaps felt a time drawing to a close and if I didn't complete things now they would never happen. Either Pluto would strangle them or I would be holding Pluto at arm's length in order to finish them.

So, my diary informs us that, 'All I feel I would like to do here is get my clothes washing up to date, paint Mary's scarf, see Magens Bay (said to be one of the top beaches in the Caribbean) and do my emails.' The man at the bar, Victor, still didn't feature, except to say I met him again at the hotel and we agreed to meet at Magens Bay the following afternoon. Victor warned me that a work commitment might prevent his joining me, but I went anyway, accomplishing something of a difficult task in so doing.

The taxis in St Thomas were mainly minibus size – and drivers did not want to transport just one person – and no one else wanted to go at that time. People from the cruise ships had already gone. Eventually a driver took me, but by then I was a little later than Victor had suggested as a time for us to meet. So, I arrived at a fairly crowded beach and searched the long strand for an absent Victor.

I was not impressed with the beach. It had a shack of a bar so you could order a drink from your towel, and toilets, but there was no shade, unless you went under the trees and then the sand was full of leaves and had no immediacy of sea. The beach, where it was wetted by the gentle waves, cast a grey sheen of pollution on the pale sand. Not a friendly sight, and when you entered the sea the water was a little murky grey, until the light turquoise took over further out. I began to realise just how wonderful our local beaches in Crete are. I ached for them. Clean water, shady cafés – just behind the beach and the brightest turquoise water you could imagine at my favourite Balos Bay.

At about 4 p.m. I realised that all the people were going, in fact nearly all gone, from the beach – back to the ship. I stayed on, trusting that I would get a taxi. I stayed, quietly dreaming till 5.45 p.m. and then found a taxi to take me at 6.30 p.m. He was there to take the stragglers, the last to leave. This was fine because I saw the sunset and felt that great calm that a sunset gives me. A sense of completion to the day – there!

I went home a little disappointed at the lack of company, but decided to take a meal at the hotel next door to the Beachcomber. This was a good plan. A table with four people at it; immediately they invited me to join them. I felt like a new toy. Everyone fussed over me and I was the centre of attention. Kelly, Anna, Lol and James! Lol is ill, James is in pain. I agreed to look at them both the next day.

Diary 18 April 2002

I stayed home during the day. Nearly finished Mary's scarf and worked on Lol, clearing the weight from his chest, energy balance and reconnections. I went for a swim with Victor, who turned out to have the body of a fit twenty-five-year-old, even though he was fifty-eight years old. He looked stunning, having been a medal-winning wrestler and still in training and coaching kids in wrestling.

Then, just as I had finished showering, and a little before the agreed time, James came round for his treatment. Now I am always most professional in what I do, particularly if there is a bed in the room. But I had to answer the door with just a towel wrapped round me. I invited him in, wishing to excuse myself and withdraw to the bathroom for my clothes. But not to be! The pesky towel dropped off me while I was opening the door and I revealed all to a rather surprised – but pleased – James.

I was so embarrassed. Oh – how could this have happened? I picked up the towel and rushed to the bathroom, located at the far end of the bedroom and James let himself in. I regained my clothes and composure and went out and did the work on James. The work required him to be lying down, so we used the bed and to my intense professional discomfort I found myself attracted to him, even though he was grossly overweight and that's not normally attractive to me. Both of us seemed to find the towel event and the therapy sexually stimulating. I was just not prepared for that! I managed to draw the line at making love, but it felt a close-run thing.

Just after the height of our passion there was a knock at the door and Victor announced through the closed door that he had come to see me! I could see his outline through the door. I had no idea whether he could see through the thin blind that covered the glass part of the door and see us, and I was so embarrassed I could never bring myself to peer through it myself from the outside to see what he could have seen of us.

I didn't open the door to Victor, being naked and not wishing to let him be a party to my sudden lack of professionalism. My head reeled with the juxtaposition of things, the confusion of roles and both men arriving at inopportune moments. It had the makings of a farce. But the good thing was, I had not let James make love to me. Another chance to explore saying no. So in a way it had been very opportune. The bedside phone had been ringing all day too, with another James wanting treatment to stop smoking, but, in the end, he decided he wished to stay a smoker – at least for the time being. I was quite relieved because I needed time to re-establish my professional role. So, I pulled a Medicine Card and got 'Otter': laugh at your antics, balance work and play, reclaim vulnerability. Perfect.

★

Dinnertime, so downstairs, first to the bar to chat to Leanne, a soulmate for keeping me sane or, just then, for regaining sanity. Then I went in for dinner – and Victor turned up! We had dinner together, I paid. Then we went for a stroll on the beach in the dark. Always a romantic thing to do. He had a habit of turning our conversation to biblical matters and I was getting a little tired of one preaching episode, but I was otherwise enjoying his company, strolling along hand in hand. So I decided to shut him up by turning to him and kissing him. Even as I did so I wondered just how many bad matches must have been made in moments like that! I could certainly not be the first person to

171

hush a person up who was beginning to be boring by kissing them. Well, he kissed very nicely and I found myself held gently in a most loving embrace. I later discovered that he had the largest hands I had ever seen (perfect for wrestling, of course, but also for giving hugs that feel totally supporting).

Victor found out about my painting and asked to see it. So, being aware of the corny 'come up and see my etchings', I took him up to my room. He was greatly taken with my work and he told me he had just written a story and the publisher needed illustrations in order to use his work. Would I do it? Yes! That is, if it felt right. We agreed that I would read his manuscript. Then we forgot all about that and sitting on my veranda found we had a mutual attraction for each, beyond the artwork. I told him I would not make love to him, but we went indoors and lay, where James and I had lain, and I went through a replay of no sex, too soon. Victor appeared to have good control over his body and emotions and so I didn't feel any pressure to go further than I wanted.

Then, and I shall never know how he did it, he lifted me up and my dress was suddenly lying on the floor. I have never been disrobed so fast. One second I was wearing a dress, the next I was naked! In this hot weather I was short on underwear and now I was bare. I lay back on the bed, while Victor went to the bathroom. The day's events seemed to have had an attritional effect on my good conduct.

But, in the end, the herpes saved me. I told Victor of the affliction and passed him a condom and that stemmed his ardour. He blustered slightly, seeming to be lost for sensible words and took his leave of me, saying he'd have to think about it. Another time and another way of not having sex. I found myself almost elated. It also made me feel even more fond of him because he had given me an experience of how not to make love. I loosely agreed to meet him the next day at the post office, where he worked. But he didn't show up. I went nearby to see Willie and have a veggie burger and he told me how pleased he was with the Chinese fluorite I had given him as a gift for his new shop. I had carried the fluorite since my trip to Maui with Elle and it seemed the right time to divest myself of it.

I was now ready to go to St John – one step nearer to Tortola and the line. In fact, the map made it difficult for me to see exactly where the line was drawn, but I would certainly be proximate to it if not on it when I was in Tortola. I would not see St Thomas again until Carnival Weekend when I intended to take the twenty-minute ferry ride back from St John. I had already arranged to stay in the hotel manager's flat for the carnival because the Island Beachcomber hotel would be full.

Chapter Eleven

ST JOHN

I left from the small Red Hook ferry dock and found myself lulled to sleep even though the journey was both short and new to me. Maybe the events of the past days were telling on me. Whenever I opened an eye we were still looking at land and in fact there was scarcely any open horizon – always there were islands sliding by the ferry. I missed the broad, free horizon, and searched out any small opening where the sky and sea would meet.

I looked back over my stay in St Thomas. I realised that the Island Beachcomber, apart from being the cheapest good-quality, beachside hotel on the island, had a conference room. It would make a splendid yoga holiday space. The walls are made of slatted timber, perfectly vented to let the air in and keep the feel of an outdoor space while restricting the views to the sea which, while charming, would be available all day and would be better limited for the intense inward-looking yoga. I had looked at two other places, Mahadeva's retreat on Maui and Casa Grande on Puerto Rico. But this was it. With the possibility of nightlife and shopping too – being near to Charlotte Amalie, where diamonds are as common as sticks of candy rock on my childhood trips to Blackpool. The only problem was that the hotel seemed to be popular and might not be able to hold vacancies for me. Nice to be thinking of something other than personal development!

Cinnamon Bay campsite was a good taxi ride along the island from the dock at Cruz Bay and I got lovely glimpses of creamy crescents of sand, like little smiles, backed by green hills and fronted by a margin of bright turquoise sea before the deep blue hit in. Being a National Park, it has its advantages over St Thomas, which seems to have a hotel in every bay. I set up camp near to the sea, where the uniformed park staff directed, under the trees for shade and in a clearing big enough for about six other tents. So, I would have company.

Straight away I went to the beach, just a short distance away, and sat there and tried to make contact with Pluto. I approached Pluto only to find a hard shell, no entry, but then my view opened up and I was let in. I asked, as per the meditation formula, if Pluto wanted anything from me. The answer was: more spirituality, more trust and more fun. So, I went for a swim, always a pleasure.

The campsite had a restaurant, so I stopped and had a mediocre dinner, in a sea of mainly deserted tables. There was information about walks (not when I wanted them) and snorkelling – but I do that already. So, I just went to bed and had to pump my mattress in the night. It went flat – and it was brand new! I still had the receipt so I would return it, maybe the next day. I couldn't stay on St John with a faulty air bed.

The next day I woke to a feeling of being at a loss, what to do, with whom, how to make my time good here. The campsite breakfast was no help. It was less than mediocre. Decidedly bad. Not only was the porridge lumpy and like concrete but I noticed that the cook and the serving staff were at daggers drawn. No wonder the food tasted so hateful – it was exactly that! I decided that I would not eat there again. I had not bothered to buy any cooking equipment and so I would have to go into Cruz Bay to eat, but at least that might give me a little company. I had cut my accommodation bill to $27 (for a bare site with a cold shower) and so I decided I could splash out a bit on food. And, I reminded myself, there was to be no account keeping!

The day was overcast, decidedly grey and my mood matched it. I went off to make some phone calls. I had sorted the phones out by now and so was successful at phoning both the supermarket regarding the mattress and calling Victor at work. We agreed to meet. Dave, in Crete, I couldn't get. It was his birthday – 20 April – the first time we had been apart on his birthday since we had met in 1974.

I spent the whole day around the tent, seeing if I could get the air mattress to stay inflated, putting final touches to Mary's silk scarf, doing a design for a scarf for Victor. Lol had said that he and his friends might come over, but they didn't show. By mid-afternoon it was raining. I chose that moment to swim. Have fun, Pluto had said!

With some difficulty I got a taxi in the evening (I had to wait a while – the camp site is beyond the range of average town-based taxis). I went to Mongoose Junction on the edge of town (Cruz Bay) and found an excellent Thai restaurant. What a change from American-style, West Indian bland veggie plates! I met a lovely woman in the restaurant and she was camping at Cinnamon Bay too – but it was her last day. And I thought I might have found someone to have fun with! It seemed I must remain in some isolation. My new friend, Joy (yes) had come to Cinnamon Bay every year for fifteen years, the same week of each year. She would have been very informative as well as fun. Never mind. Pluto, a life apart from others, the book had said.

The next day I woke to rain, had a swim, dressed in pink and went off for breakfast in Cruz Bay, got a printout off the Internet on herpes (to show Victor) followed by a trip over to Red Hook. I was really keen to see him and more than a little disappointed to find him not waiting at the dock for me. Maybe he had got caught up in traffic, it can happen. In the end I had come over without my airbed because my efforts to get it to stay up had been successful and it had lasted the night. So I had come over only to see Victor. And where was he? I looked lovely too, with the pink fifties-style dress and matching nails, with a pretty white lace shawl over my shoulders.

Anyway, Victor did show. I saw him making enquiries about me and so ran over to him. I was so pleased to see him. I considered him to be highly disciplined (keeping up a difficult training and coaching regime) spiritual (even if it was the Bible – maybe, I thought, I would learn religious tolerance) and good fun – with a laugh like smooth, dark chocolate with little nutty bits in it. He moved about as if he were fifteen, looked as if he were twenty-five (from the neck down) and from the neck up he looked fifty, not handsome, but somehow striking with a huge smile. I realised I had dressed up for the occasion because I could feel dowdy and droopy next to him.

We went to a couple of bars and discussed chasteness and herpes. We then both got the ferry to St John, to be together for another hour. I complained about my back and Victor said he knew a good chiropractor whom he worked with in his wrestling life. I agreed I would go again to St Thomas to see Kevin.

On St John, Victor is very well known. Everyone seemed to hail him. He explained that for some time he had been a policeman on St John, before moving to the post office and St Thomas. I found myself continually kissing and holding him and he just lapped it up! He asked me how I felt about our relationship and I didn't really know what to say. The Ascendant lines are very much about self and one's own needs, not necessarily about communicating these in order to meet someone else's needs, or plain curiosity. That is why in Hawaii I didn't care that Jerry was an alcoholic and I was certainly in no position to help him because all I could think of were my needs. So, there I was again, not knowing what to say because it would sound selfish. It felt easier to talk on a subject that we both had an affinity with and in my case I had no desire whatsoever to ask him the same question: how did he feel? So I really felt that I liked his company because he assuaged my loneliness and that just kissing and cuddling was fine with me, if he could handle that. We parted in Cruz Bay, at the ferry dock and I went back to the campsite and then headed back out for dinner – only to find the Thai place closed. However, a nearby bar with food did its duty and I went to bed on a good full stomach.

I had got to know the family in the tent near me. So, we went snorkelling together, on another cloudy, dull day. The shoals of fish were legion. Patches of little fish were so thick that you couldn't see to swim through them. We snorkelled between two small, rocky outcrops out in the bay, which was a bit scary for me, the water surging through and foaming up in front of you, but with company I was OK. Later, I painted the nails of the two daughters of the family – pink – and taught them a little Greek. One daughter also had a Greek project for school so I gave some attention to that too and then taught both parents yoga for an hour and suggested a book on partnership yoga as they wished to work together. I had been enthused by the prospect of seeing a chiropractor to look at my back and already it did feel a bit better. I deemed it required energy moving between chakras.

I ate lunch with the family at their tent and then a camp

warden came to tell me to expect a phone call at four o'clock. That was kind, them coming to find me. The phone call had been from Victor who wanted to give me the phone number of Kevin, the chiropractor. I waited by the phone at 4 p.m. and, like a stood-up teenager, I was still there at 5 p.m. Just after that Victor phoned. Hmm... Obviously the discipline I liked didn't run to time scheduling. Victor gave me the phone number for the chiropractor and also said he had prayed for me in the night. Maybe that was the time I was wakeful and wondering what I was doing with my life. Going to bed early didn't always suit me.

I made an appointment to see the chiropractor the next day and hoped I might see Victor too. I was still musing over his question of how I felt about the relationship, but I had also become acquainted with a single man staying in the same tent enclave and I liked him, Jon, and was relieved to feel no desire for him. I also had the feeling that no one seemed able to give me enough to satisfy me. I demanded constant physical attention – kiss me quick!

I spent the nights working on my health, asking for assistance from Sai Baba, Pluto, anyone who came to mind to clear old energy out and allow new energy to come in. My focus was largely my back. Trying to get a change in my back – and a change in my life. Almost anything would do in order to indicate to me how Pluto was working with me. I did feel that a better under-standing of how Pluto worked (shown by example) would assist me in making any change I wanted. I wished to feel omnipotent. To be able to effect any change I wanted. Certainly the need to set the agenda for change was apparent. And this proved to be useful.

As my time with Pluto on the Ascendant went by I wanted miracles, self-transformation – and that's what I got. I had expected the time to be difficult – 'great personal changes may occur, but these could be more than the organism could bear,' said the A★C★G book.[4] Speaking to my astrologer friend I had to say it felt to be going smoothly. What she told me was that because I chose an agenda of change I was working *with* Pluto, whereas if I had wanted my life to stay constant and static I might have been tossed around

---

[4] From Jim Lewis, *Astro★Carto★Graphy Explanatory Handbook*, produced by Equinox Astrology.

in a state of flux, with Pluto in control. So, what a great place I had chosen for my second major astrological place!

The old energy I was clearing at that time was related to my father wanting a son and the weight of this childhood energy was colossal. Offloading it took some amount of almost physical strain. But in retrospect there was little resistance. The fields were to be burned. Death was inevitable. I filled myself with Pluto's energy and sought to look at how I was behaving. I realised to the full extent that my time on the line was about my needs and not those of others, hence why I couldn't even answer the question of how I felt about Victor, when he asked, because his very need to know caused me to not be able to tell him. It was his need and not mine, so I just couldn't engage with it. I couldn't even tell him I just wanted him because he was lovely and I was lonely.

At the end of the week I said goodbye to the camping family. Their week had consisted of grey skies on all of their full days, only their arrival and departure days had there been sunshine. They left in bright sunshine, turning the sea from grey green to bright turquoise blue. I felt sorry for them, but at least they had not got sunburnt.

Plans meant returning to St Thomas and staying at the manager's house at the Island Beachcomber so I could go to the St Thomas carnival – and this meant I could pursue my search for lost pinhole glasses, still missing but maybe at the hotel. I had tried to fit the chiropractor and festival into the same visit, but it was not to be; festival fever was in the air and the chiropractor would be closed. So, two visits to St Thomas.

My first visit to St Thomas would include seeing the chiropractor and, hopefully, Victor. So, the Friday morning ferry took me over to St Thomas, to Red Hook. Straight to Kevin Lenahan who cracked my back this way and that and took a look at the X-rays I had brought from Hawaii. He thought my hips were out of alignment, whereas Dr Willie on Hawaii had muscle tested that they were in alignment. But that might have changed. He said that the misalignments could be put right, but it would take time. I made a further appointment to sort out my more immediate and acute back problem. I wasn't sure whether he saw a bankroll when he saw me, so I refrained from giving my back his wholesale attention. Let Pluto have a share of this too! He had a nice open face but somewhere I detected a cloud that I couldn't define. Maybe money, maybe something else. Certainly, I felt I didn't get a discount for being Victor's friend. Maybe he felt ill at ease with me because he felt I could perceive something in him. In any case the book said that Pluto can leave people feeling uneasy in your company, so maybe that was enough.

I noted in my diary that I had gone to the chiropractor's in a little slip of a silk frock (the legacy of Hawaii – and a way of feeling glamorous) with just a lace shawl for extra cover. I was glad of the shawl because in the waiting room there was an Indian couple so I was able to cover my shoulders and chest, and feel comfortable in their presence – something I hoped would be mutual. All day I felt loving and caring thoughts about people, even for the taxi driver in St John (whom I described as a real sweetie – a real accolade for me as far as taxi drivers are concerned).

After my appointment, I waited an hour at the chiropractors' surgery for Victor to show. It was lovely to see him. We went to a nearby bar and I sat near to him, drinking him in, more than the soft drink in my hand.

We talked of the future and that he might come over to Tortola to see me. He was also due to go to train as a wrestling coach at the next level, so he would be off-island. Time seemed slim for us. My travels, his training. I started to consider whether I wanted to curtail my travels to stay with him. But, no, whenever I asked – and it became a regular subject for me to ask myself – the answer was always no, I had to move on. I could tell it even as I asked the question, even though I hoped the answer would be to stay; I was always relieved to be told that I was to go forward.

As I returned to the ferry to St John, Victor gave me a magazine to read. I looked at it on the boat and found it to be a religious text all about heaven, hell, sin and Satan. This was really going to tax my drive for religious tolerance. So, I gave up reading it, I just didn't want it to interfere with my liking of Victor. I could feel myself thinking – just pick out the good bits! I was very fond of him but it was only as he addressed my needs. I was aware that as my needs changed then I might feel differently towards him. Oh, how manipulative all this seems to be!

I wrote in my diary that I loved his humility and service to the public. He had chosen to do public works (police and post office) and he had once joked that maybe he would make a good maid, because of his need to be in service. His wrestling coaching was an extension of this, in a more refined fashion. He had no desire to take money for his coaching services. He had worked also as a model, including as Mister Power for Guinness ads in the Caribbean and as an actor. I wrote emails to friends to say I had met an ex-Olympic wrestler – and before anyone got anxious about this, I added, 'who now works at the post office'. It sounded so meek and mild; no one was going to worry about my safety.

Diary 23 April 2002

I've found out quite a lot about Victor. He is fifty-seven years old, has seven children, the youngest is nine. Two grown-up sons are models in England. He looks much younger than his years with an incredibly slender waist, largely hidden by his liking for loose trousers and T-shirts that cover him well, no tightness around his muscular form. He expects to live to 120 and I think it is possible. Although I can't agree with his religious bent he is totally sincere in it. We have spoken again about sexual activities, but I am managing to keep a healthy sexual distance from him and we both expect to refrain from sex so early in our relationship. This is helpful to me in my desire to change my attitude. I feel as if my hand is being guided by him in remaining celibate, rather than being encouraged to explore what the bedroom might hold. This is very relaxing and, of course, it is also meeting my needs.

Victor David Levitt; this name had a particular significance for me. When I was young my cousin married a man called Victor on 1 January at noon. I thought Victor was a very romantic and racy name. When I met Dave, in a moment of childish fun, I noted that his middle initial was 'V' and I had hoped it would stand for Victor and was very disappointed that it stood for Vernon, a name neither he nor I found favour with. I liked the name David well enough so that would do. Finding a Victor David Levitt was really special, in the same way as watching the numbers on the car's milometer go over all the nines to 100,000! Not really significant, just a bit of fun.

★

I took the ferry boat back to St John and as no one asked me for my ticket I kept it to use a second time. Maybe my fear of poverty had still not left me. I decided to watch that too. I had been deciding to act always in the best way possible. Holding onto my ticket was a reversal of this. Hmm...

So many areas of my life I was watching how I was, asking for change, then seeing it manifested. Sometimes my life felt like a film screen, with me acting several roles and watching at the same time. I observed closely all my thoughts, words and deeds, looking closely for possibilities for change. Nothing else mattered. Except Victor David Levitt.

I arrived back in Cruz Bay and would have eaten at Panini's, an Italian I favoured. But the staff there were arguing when I arrived, so I just left. I need food to be the best. A US naval boat was in harbour at St Thomas, and the little town here on St John was crowded with white-clad sailors, attracting a lot of attention, and lapping it up. This exacerbated the problem of getting a taxi to take 'just one' to Cinnamon Bay. I felt I was touting for trade – anyone willing to take me to the camp?

I have said that I had made a friend of a single man, Jon who was camping nearby. Well, we had a wonderful day together, with a rent car, sampling each bay for snorkelling beyond the limits of the taxi run. Driving on the left with a left-hand-drive car. That was new for me. I had noticed how vehicles pull over to the right as they go around steep corners and go blindly around the steep, winding roads. I was trusting in God that nothing was coming the other way and meeting me nose to nose. An amusing sign painted in the road said MON LEF STAY. A reminder in local terms to drive on the left.

Jon and I hit it off well and snorkelled comfortable together, and there was, at least for me, none of the sexual tensions that had vexed my time in Hawaii. No debate about whether I wanted him as a lover. It felt perfectly natural just to be neutral. That had been unthinkable in Hawaii.

We had the car for two days, the irony being that I had felt a car would be useful to get into and out of Cruz Bay in the evening in order to eat, yet there I was eating just cheese and crackers at Jon's tent that night when, with the car, freedom was mine! Then, I suddenly noticed that a message had been left by the tent asking me to call Victor. A spurt of activity, but I only had his work phone number and I had missed him. I would have to wait for the next day. When I did call, he was fine and I made a mental note to be as kindly as he was when people don't pick up messages or forget to phone me.

My life became based on the sea and meditation. I recommenced looking at father issues, getting my back better and living my own truth. Be the woman I am, however unsure I was about what that meant. I found looking at the sea and mourning my young (male) womanhood to be helpful. I had no wish to change what had happened, no bitterness, just a sense of loss. But what exactly had I lost? I didn't know. I had still to experience the change to being a woman to know. Venus was certainly helpful – and my time on Hawaii coming to appreciate women friends – and pretty clothes could help point the way.

Meditation became standard practice for me. I allowed an issue to develop in my mind and then would sit quietly. After allowing the issue to surface I entered a process where I imagined a calm pool with dead (grey) sticks breaking the flat surface. The sticks represented my thoughts, nipped off before they had time to develop and so I was able to hold off thinking about the issue, but just let my unconscious deal with it. However, one time I watched the bare sticks produce leaves and then flowers as I watched them. I wondered whether this was a new phase or my mind just trying to reassert itself. I let it rest

The second day of the rent car had us exploring Leinster Bay where the snorkelling was lovely with lots of large, plump starfish. We just stopped and snorkelled every bay possible – a bit like chocoholics in a sweet factory. Around lunch, I excused myself to phone Victor, but he was not available; then again I tried an hour later and he had left work – I had missed him! Ha! How it was to live without easy access to a phone.

After a full day trip we got back to the tents. Mine was laden with messages to call Victor. I called from the campsite office, but he was not at work. I stood around uncertainly considering my plans to go to Tortola and whether Victor would feature in that, when the phone rang. He had had a tooth out – it had been knocked loose while he was wrestling, and had not settled down – and so his voice was difficult through the anaesthetic. I agreed to catch the morning ferry, drop my bags off at his car in the post office car park and then go to my next appointment with the chiropractor.

With pleasure at having sorted out some plans I skipped with excitement down the drive, back to the tent, conscious that I might just be undoing all the chiropractic work, but what the hell! Such is happiness – and excitement about Victor who was the subject of my happiness and seemed so warm to me. I felt to be in good hands, Victor and his chiropractor friend!

I spent my last evening in Cruz Bay and discovered from my emails that I had both lost and found my X-rays – you remember, taken in Hawaii. I went to retrieve them from a courier's office and eventually heard the story. I had written my email address on the huge X-ray envelope (just in case I lost them) and I had accidentally left the envelope in the taxi after I returned from my first visit to the chiropractor. I had never missed them – too much thought on Victor – but the driver had taken them to the courier's office and they had emailed me. I could have gone months before realising that they had gone. By then long gone! I didn't hear this story right away because that evening the courier's office was closed. I had to wait for the next day to know how the couriers had come by my X-ray packet.

Next morning I broke camp, said goodbye to Cinnamon Bay and climbed aboard the ferry to St Thomas, laden with all the paraphernalia I had deemed I needed for the whole holiday, and also all the camping stuff.

I met Victor at the post office. There he stood with his regulation pinafore and toothy grin – the gap is central. I was so pleased to see him. I have always been given to moments of joy and excitement, when I am wont to squeal – this was one such. Starry-eyed, I went off to the chiropractor who made lots of adjustments again. This time he didn't charge me highly.

Perhaps it was just the initial consultation that made the price high before.

I decided I had just time to go back over the water and see the courier to collect the X-rays, but I missed the ferry by a whisker. It started with me missing the stop on the little dollar ride bus because I had not realised it had reached Red Hook ferry terminal. So I went most of the way back across the island before realising my mistake. I took a taxi back, but I saw the boat go… So often the ferries run late, but not when I needed it. I found myself all agitated. I still had time for the next ferry, to pick up the X-rays and get back on the ferry after that, but somehow the agitation I felt in the taxi hoping to catch the boat had stayed with me – even though it was not appropriate. It had only been my plan, it didn't have to be the only plan. I watched myself and wondered why I couldn't just change mode and be calm about it.

Back to St Thomas, armed with X-rays (just don't put them down – anywhere!) and I still had time to watch part of the carnival before returning to the post office to meet Victor out of work. The carnival featured the children's parade that day and was somewhat small-townish with some of the children just improvising a dance, rather than having choreographed steps. It rained hard too, umbrellas up restricting the view. A Hawaiian-inspired float went past which amused me. It showed just how little understanding of the Hawaiian culture had been integrated into the exhibit. The child hula dancers danced hula in grass skirts – to reggae music!

I met Victor outside the post office, still in his uniform, navy blue with a pinafore to protect him from his work loading trailers and unloading trailers of their postal contents. The photograph I took of him, grinning his head off, shows his arms flung high and wide so that they dwarf the view of the post office building behind him. Something in the gesture made me feel as though he were the post office. I knew he was conscientious: a safety captain, trade union rep and also worked diligently to clear the post so that no one needed to wait for their mail. He told me all this, very much in earnest, as if the service's quality very much depended on him. A real public spirit!

Diary 26 April 2002

Victor and I are pushing our chasteness a bit. We get rather more physically involved than we can cope with and then cool off by conversation, only to engage once more in the physical. It makes for an uncomfortable relationship or rather the stress of not having sex makes me quite glad when we part. It is a relief. Funny time, when we are hot for each other I feel myself change to the person I used to be: wanting to have power and control. So, it's still too soon to try out sex in my new persona. It just isn't established enough. I must be all of that new person first. It's a lovely experience changing who I am and observing the process. The great thing is I am getting to know Victor so that I can decide to have sex once I know who he is. When I feel we have some *intimacy*. There's lots I still need to know about Victor, in case I am easy prey to lies and deception. This suspicion is getting smaller and then I have to ask myself. Why should I judge? Why not take it all at face value, go with the flow and enjoy! Does it all have to be so difficult? Well, yes, if I want to make the changes, I think it does. But maybe the next pattern to break will be that of judging.

★

We both went back to the Island Beachcomber where I would be staying, courtesy of the manager. Gosh, he, Blare, was a tense man. He said that he was all laid-back, but continually swilled back a caffeine drink and he chain smoked. The devil may care! I gave him, the manager, a massage, then did a tie cut with my father via Reiki and Victor did some work on my sciatic nerve, stretching my back. That felt good: a combination of non-sexual physical attention and the remedial effect on my back. Victor said he might return that evening, but no, he kept away. Tomorrow we would go to Tortola.

Tortola meant changing from the United States Virgin Islands (USVI) and going to the British Virgin Islands (BVI). Changing country meant the end of easy and cheap ferry rides that had been the case between St Thomas and St John.

Victor wanted to go to Tortola on the early boat, but was late meeting me at the hotel. So, thinking he wasn't coming and feeling rather nettled, I had arranged a taxi, but then, when we got to the ferry terminal, the boat had been rescheduled by forty minutes. So, we were early. Victor, in his optimistic way felt that this was good. I just felt that I could have stayed in bed longer! I was not helped by being hungry, having a period headache and not having drunk enough water. At least that was my excuse.

Chapter Twelve

TORTOLA AND THE PLUTO EFFECT

The boat to Tortola was noisy and precluded conversation as it roared and shook itself through the sea. Victor asked me not to snuggle him because there was a woman on the boat from his church sitting near us. So I said I would sit on my hands. A phrase we came to use from time to time.

Why were we both going to Tortola? Well, for me it was to be close to or actually on the line – I never was fully able to satisfy myself as to just where the line was, unlike in Hawaii where it was obvious. Here, the A★C★G map of the world just showed the Virgin Islands like a series of scattered crumbs, no knowing what was supposed to be what. The black Pluto line itself was broad enough to cover several islands.

In Victor's case, he was going to Tortola because he was supposed to be meeting someone about a land deal. He was also coming to say goodbye to me on my new territory and then would leave.

I have been really remiss in giving you a précis of what Pluto on the Ascendant is about. Well, the A★C★G book says that the Plutonic force:

> ...is perhaps the heaviest of all and residence or even travel through this zone can cause total upheaval and change in life ... miracles can happen ... Pluto burns the fields for new planting and life takes on a miraculous form.

It goes on to say that after experiencing Plutonic forces 'people will never again be able to live in the illusions in which most people exist, so they make most of us feel uncomfortable.' On the Ascendant there is:

> a tendency to be secretive and a tendency to relate to everyone on a sexual or competitive level. You feel passionately about what

moves you but keep this to yourself. People remember you because you make them feel uncomfortable and remind them of things they'd prefer to forget. So, you spend time alone, which exacerbates sexual needs. You identify with personal transformation and are constantly trying to better yourself … Under this line great personal changes may occur, but these may be more than the organism could bear. West is less intense than east.

And I have just sailed closer!

The boat docked at West End, a taxi ride away from the town where Victor would have his meeting. We travelled together and I left Victor in Road Town, Tortola's main town and went off over the mountain to Brewer's Bay campsite. Now, the guidebook describes it as a bit of an odd place, but seemingly liked by the camping buffs who stayed there. That is as may be. I arrived by taxi at the reception bar area and no one was there to meet me. I felt a bit miffed. I walked around and found lots of broken-down tents along the seashore and found no one camping at all, nor did it look as if this was a new phenomenon. It was deserted. However, the bay itself looked pretty and from the number of big brown birds there – pelicans – there would be plenty of fish to look at, if no people. Snorkelling could continue.

Now, the British Virgin Islands are a bit strange. Typically, I had a new set of public telephones to contend with, but the currency is the same as the US Virgin Islands – US dollars. Anyhow I managed to work the public phone by the beach and call the people who should have been there to meet me. I felt a bit temperamental at their lack of welcoming presence, but they said they would be down later and that I should just pitch my tent.

Diary 27 April 2002

I am the only one staying – oh, the isolation! I pitched the tent on the opposite side of the track from the beach – only those renting a tent can have the sea view. It feels a very vulnerable spot. Just a little tent beneath the tall, dark, towering coconut palms, a very childlike tent in bright yellow, green and blue. It's plain that only one person could dwell in it. I headed for the bar at the far end of the beach – I realised I'd not eaten since lunch yesterday. I picked a Medicine Card before leaving the tent – and took the one for blending in and not being the centre of attention. A bit difficult when mine is the only tent and the odd stroller on the road points to it and says is that yours. So, I sat in the bar and watched the St Thomas carnival (main day today) on the telly, like everyone else. Then a man walked into the bar and made my hair stand on end. He asked me my name, I said 'Juliet' and he then said, 'Juliet Green?' Who on earth here knows my name! He turned out to be Victor's taxi driver – he had come over the island from Road Town to see me.

So, Victor was waiting for me at the camp office. We ate together, kissed, cuddled and talked endlessly. We talked of his work – he was writing a paper that spoke against privatisation of the US postal service – and we discussed spiritual matters. He showed me some rocks which reminded him of the ones at the start of the novel he had written. Then we walked to my tiny tent and, like teenagers cramped in the back seat of a car, played with each other till we felt the release of orgasms. I didn't know what to make of this, was it OK? Had it been all too soon? But we hadn't actually made love. How far can you bend the rules? What is too soon? I decided it was a bit soon, but not so soon. And anyway, we hadn't actually made love.

I did feel warm and close to him. We both went off in his taxi so I could see him back to the ferry, still with my head feeling as if it was continually expanding with the pleasure and contentment of sexual release. But Victor told me this time that it had been months since he made love, not a year as he had told me before. I just noticed the discrepancy. In the taxi I could put my hand on his leg without feeling as if I was engaging in dangerous territory. Those days are over, we are lovers. It felt good to have waited, thank you herpes! His skin is so dark, but I learnt the beauty of that back in Miami, with the woman in the next bunk bed – her skin so dark against the white sheet was fabulous. In a way the velvet blackness, with an underlying tint of redness, reminds me of the lava flows flowing out of the rock in Hawaii Volcano National Park.

I went all the way to the West End of Tortola to see Victor away and then went to the, by now, nearby Jolly Roger eating place. It's said (in the guidebook) to have the best key lime pie ever. Well, it was my first key lime pie so I didn't know, but it was highly delightful. The restaurant faced the sea and most people came via tenders from yachts, not by land like me. So, when it was time to go, nearly 8 p.m. could I find a taxi? They don't exist at that time. There was no possible way I could walk back; it was perhaps twenty miles and going dark already. Eventually, I walked around the harbour to Pusser's, a drinking hole and full of nightlife. No taxi there either, but then Ort and Davidia appeared.

Diary 27 April 2002 (continued)

Ort was a taxi driver, out for the night with his wife, Davidia (another form of David in my life!), but they decided to take me home. Got back about 10 p.m., spending another $40 on taxi fares. This will have to stop! I could have rented a car for days on the amount I have spent on taxis today. Davidia was comfortable about the taxi man's cap coming back out on her night out, she's a sweetie. At the tent, went to bed and slept well, no rustlings or frightening noises. Suddenly it was daybreak.

Diary 28 April 2002

Looked at my watch, and it still said 11 p.m. – now I have no camera nor a reliable watch. Can't find my alarm clock and I seem to have lost my pinhole glasses for good! Never mind, go for a swim. I then walked to the rocks and was moved to sit where the fictitious man met the iguana. Victor yesterday pointed to this rock as being the type of area where the man and iguana would meet in his novel. I sat on the rock and cried, not much, but I suddenly felt deadly sad. Alone and driven to be alone by my journey. I know I can't give it up, what can I do? I have no circumstances here. If I stayed it would feel as if my life had ended, but to go on... I know I have to move on and so cannot gain the pleasures of longevity and familiarity.

The idea of settling down with Victor is as remote as it was to think about buying a house, car or boat with the money from the injury – it's not my life. I mourned the passing of the sweet time of chasteness. Now Victor and I are lovers and that time is over. It has felt as momentous as losing my virginity. I feel as if I will never feel like this again. It is the first experience of a relationship where I have held off sex; I've not had that overwhelming urge to consummate too soon. Next time I hold off it won't feel so special, because it won't be so new. It will start to be the regular way for me.

Last night a woman told me her two-week holiday here had felt like heaven. It feels in marked contrast to my struggle with things and changes taking place. Struggle, a funny word to use, because I want these changes and yet I mourn the old me.

Concerns with money keep nudging me. I look at how much I spent yesterday: taxis and ferry were 20+10+18+25+40 comes to $113, then a fancy meal! At least it's only $10 dollars a night to camp. What's the worry, Sai Baba will provide!

It feels good to get up, wrap a sarong around me and come to the beach. I tried phoning Dave today, just to tell him I had moved. I had to use cash. I just filled the telephone box with money and it still cut out after a few moments and swallowed every coin I had! I just couldn't physically put money in the box fast enough to stop it cutting me off. Tried a collect (reverse charges) call and to use my credit card but to no avail. I can't even enjoy a little nostalgic reunion. I gave up and found I was then propositioned by the man in the next telephone booth who asked me if I was staying alone in the little tent. I felt most uncomfortable admitting to that one, yes, yes alone, but I refused a cuddle from him. There's no security at the campsite whatsoever. I shall buy a padlock for my tent. A passing rainstorm, my watch says it's 7.45 a.m. Maybe.

★

Brewer's Bay is not quite the Caribbean white beaches and turquoise sea I was looking for, but it's pretty and quiet, with the campsite office at one end and a bar at the other linked by just a narrow road dividing the permanent (sea view) campsite from the tall coconut plantation (and my tent) on the landward side. It can rain in the grove and not on the beach the weather is so local. I was covered in mosquito bites and I had a blister from the snorkelling fins got while snorkelling, right foot, of course! I must still have father issues to resolve because my mental framework had not fully changed since the tie-cutting in St Thomas. Fortunately it felt that something would happen without me consciously having to work on it – good!

Diary 28 April 2002 (continued)

It's Sunday, so a no-Victor day. It's Sunday and he's not working and I don't have his home phone number. He should be seeing his artist friend (who has taken too long on the illustrations for Victor's book – it must be bottom of his in tray) to reclaim his manuscript so he can send it to me. I look at the rocks where the story starts. We'll see.

Pluto: I make a journey and find the fields are definitely still burning. My guide is still a great-looking guy. Today, however, he is old with a white pointy beard. Pluto wants change, not getting quite enough. I need to keep moving on, to work on illusions – how I look at life. I get a gift of silence. I will no longer be making old contacts, maybe the odd email, but only necessary stuff, not just for chat. So, I shall become more of an observer than a participant. I can go sightseeing – it is part of observing and change.

My sightseeing seems limited to fish – I'm snorkelling, sometimes alone and sometimes with people on the beach. You're supposed to have a buddy to snorkel with and not go alone so it's nice if someone goes with me. The Bay is hardly crowded, though, so it's not possible to expect company. So, I sit on the wall between the beach and the permanent tents and idle time looking at the sea, in the shade of the late afternoon.

★

Then a guy, Dale, came by. He slurred his speech a bit. I thought possibly he was a long-term dope user, but I was later to learn that he had an incurable progressive disease. Then Alexander came by and sat on the other side of me. Light blue eyes, fair, wild hair. Turned out he was fifty-nine but at a glance he didn't carry that many years. He was just slight and wiry.

Now, he was lots of fun and not doped up at all. His eyes twinkled with amusement and every slight wrinkle on his face spoke of laughter. Totally irreverent: 'You've never been married – *ever*?' I shake my head. He laughed and pressed on, 'So, you've never known alimony and divorce and lawyers?' Then he had Dale really rolling his eyes by chuckling and saying, 'Well, if you've come here to get laid, I can manage that one.' He was so light-hearted and fun, I just realised I had stepped back from such seriousness with Victor, all earnestness and biblical – and here I was with a real hoot of a guy. His eyes crinkled up with laughter all the time.

But what was going on? Victor had just left and the next day in walked mischief! His tent was made for two and at one time I would have been happy to go to bed with him, just because he was such good fun. Now, despite such hilarity and light-heartedness I kept my knickers on. It was working! I had a new saying: a relationship needs a period of innocence. That sounded nice. It's a bit like the doctor giving a name to a set of symptoms – you can feel relief already. A period of innocence. It has always been difficult for me to say no, to give something up that is enjoyable, but 'a period of innocence' is positive. Very positive!

Start of a new week. Into town at 8 a.m., the best time to leave the Brewer's Bay because other people are leaving then to go into Road Town to work, take children to school, etc. I wanted to get another disposable camera, get a film developed, do emails and get a telephone card. I also found out about a LIAT air travel ticket to take me down the islands making five stops before reaching Trinidad where I would recommence my round-the-world ticketed journey. All the dates would be open except for the starting date. So, I couldn't buy a ticket yet – I didn't know when I would go.

I had the usual problem of phones: with the new card, costing $20, the phone told me my card was upside down whichever way I tried it. Some phones were out of order, and standing in bright sunshine dancing around with my bad back just made the process totally unmanageable. At least Tortola's library had cheap Internet – very formal with handwritten receipts for using the services.

At a marina, I looked at adverts for people wanting to hitch a lift on boats, or help out on yachts, but there was nothing advertised that took my eye. Just noted it for future reference. A wander round town, and I bought a padlock for the tent and then got a taxi with Alexander back to Brewer's. He said that he was sticking to me like glue – he said that he knew a good thing when he saw one!

Eight dollars later, I managed to get the telephone to work and heard Victor's voice. Yes, I could use his post office box number for my mail. I wanted an address to get my repaired camera delivered to, whenever that might happen! Victor told me he loved me but my own feelings were very much dimmed by the excitement and laughter of Alexander. I felt greatly ill at ease. How could I be so fond of Victor one day and two days later he felt like yesterday's man?

Alexander once told me a story about a woman he had met. He told her that he had 'a little boat' at Brewer's Bay, and she was most put out to find it was just that! He had a red inflatable dinghy, meant for one person, but we did not weigh much, so when the weather was calm we could go out in it together, Alexander said. So, we spent a lot of time in Alexander's 'little boat', going right out into the Bay, tying up at mooring points and snorkelling. He free-dives and stays down for ages; no one seemed to know how he does it. I really loved our boat trips, particularly now I could lock the tent. That might seem a strange thing and most people had a good laugh about it. Yes, anyone could slit the tent and gain entry – but I would know they had been in. If anyone could just unzip and take my purse, passport, jewellery whatever – I just wouldn't know. So, before the days of padlock I found I was checking everything whenever I got back to my tent. I didn't want to find my passport was missing on the day I was leaving. Now, one glance and I knew the tent was OK.

Thinking of tents, I must just tell you a story. On my first night at Brewer's Bay, after I had come back from the Jolly Roger restaurant, in the dark I approached my tent – but what had happened to it? In the gloom of the moonlight in the plantation I quickened my step. My tent was all askew. As I anxiously surged forward I kicked something hard and it rolled – I gasped. For a moment I thought I had kicked a skull. I stopped dead. Then truth dawned: a coconut had fallen on my tent, knocked it sideways, torn the mosquito net and I had just kicked the offending coconut!

Every evening thereafter I spent at Alexander's tent, cooking and eating. In the tent Alexander always stripped off completely so I got to know how he was covered with lovely golden down. Every evening he would ask me to stay, but I didn't. He was an interesting character. He went dumpster diving, i.e. scavenging skips for food and anything that could be useful. It appeared that he used to have a rich wife and the divorce settlement meant that he did not have to work – as long as he was careful. A friend of his later told me two stories: one was that he didn't really need to scavenge at all; it was just the hunter-gatherer in him. Secondly, that security staff had warned him off while he was dumpster diving a supermarket skip. He told them – 'I have $100,000 worth of shares in your company, so I can dive your dumpsters if I like!' I could imagine his light cackling voice saying it too.

Alexander had been coming to Brewer's Bay for twenty-five years and generally keeps the place tidy by recycling stuff. So, I was able to give up renting a snorkel and mask because Alexander found enough bits and put them together and gave them to me. He slept on two air mattresses, one under the tent because he found it and it was not good enough to go inside the tent, but it provided extra padding. Everything has its place and use!

Our time together was short. I met him on Sunday and by Thursday he was gone, exchanging air mattresses with me because mine was really too big for my tent. When mine was pumped up it was about 100 mm deep and with the sides of the tent sloping inwards I couldn't actually lie flat out. His airbed was shorter and thin – just like inflated eggs, and so much flatter and more suitable. I also got his old tent to use for a while once he had left the island, leaving it, as he asked, at the campsite reception.

I did a meditation and included Sai Baba in the characters I opened to, along with Pluto. Sai Baba's words were to be careful. This didn't mean being cautious, but just to be full of care – for myself and others, whatever came into my life.

I went out again, for the last time, in the little red boat, I would so miss this, but already another person had come camping: a woman, Caroline, with a car. Now, that could be useful! I would now see how female friends would be with Pluto here. I had female friends in Puerto Rico, but that wasn't so close to the line – how would I fare here?

Brewer's Bay started to grow on me. There are old ruins from the old rum-making days. The coconut grove is really the edge of the rainforest but the two peninsulas that hug the bay are arid. The sea view is open and I felt that my thoughts could really get out there, not be hemmed in by islands as they were on St John. There were no limits imposed on me in Brewer's Bay.

Snorkelling meant seeing lobsters and all manner of corals, waving fan shapes and huge rigid ones like antlers. There were lots of shoals of fish, so deep that you just couldn't see through the shoal, only water gushing with fish. One day I walked out on to the peninsula to visit a cave. It looked like the huge maw of a cadaver. I sheltered within it, bent double, but out of the rain. Like being in a dragon's mouth, full of dripping fangs – and very dark.

Alexander and I talked politics and I found he had a very practical take on war: don't bother about the rights and wrongs, look at who is making money out of it. It's the corruption you're looking for. So nice to talk with someone practical rather than with a tendency to Bible-bash.

Caroline joined us for dinner, her first night, and then went to bed. I wasn't sure whether she absented herself because she was tired or whether she thought she might intrude on an amorous evening. We seemed to be able to just kiss and cuddle and then break the bond and separate, though it did seem a shame to miss out lovemaking with such a comic of a man. Chalk and cheese, Victor and Alexander.

I seemed to have learnt, perhaps from the book on watsu, the water massage on Hawaii, which suggested that if you felt roused by the close contact between practitioner and client you could send the sexual energy to your heart. I now seemed able to send the heat of sexual energy around my body and recover any composure I might have lost. Every little helps!

By now I had Victor's home phone number but he still hadn't been able to recover the manuscript of the book for me to illustrate. But I picked up a postcard to send to my mother and for some reason it had an iguana on the side where you write. I kept it. Victor was going to be away in Colorado Springs to update his wrestling coaching skills and there wasn't much time to go. But afterwards he was going to be off work for a few days – maybe a chance to get together again. Seriousness was beginning to take the lead hand over the outrageous comic.

A new month was upon us: May. I meditated on Sai Baba again and got the same 'careful' response. Out in the Bay to snorkel, savouring this last time. Alexander was going home to Virginia the next day. I cut his hair and beard and eyebrows to make him look presentable and he did look a lot less wild, but no less attractive to me. He was leaving loads of stuff behind – just moving on. I had only to leave his tent for his return and I could leave it either there or on Anegada. Now, that's a place I haven't spoken of. Let me introduce it to you.

My *Frommer's* guide, you remember – *Caribbean from $70 a Day* – well, I had read about each island and ticked or crossed off according to expense rating. Necker Island would cost me $32,000 for just one night, for example – I don't think so, I would be evicted part way through the second night! Then there were islands too far away from the line or that somehow just didn't ring a bell with me. Anegada was one such. My guide said be prepared for inconveniences such as mosquitoes. You could only go there by small planes. I had also heard of difficult reefs, currents and rip tides. I got the feeling of a gritty, grey place where I wouldn't be safe swimming alone – it just sounded dismal. I had no intention of doing that one! So when Alexander said to me, 'Go to Anegada, you'll love it there!' I opened my mouth to remonstrate, but it was waved aside. 'Go to the Big Bamboo and tell Diane that Alexander has sent you.' That was it. Now I have always felt inclined to take up recommendations, so I decided I would go.

Now, I had told Alexander I had herpes and, bless it, I now found it quite useful – people have got to be keen to take a risk of catching an incurable sexually transmitted disease. So that night, Alexander whipped out a condom and on our last night we made love. There could not be any navel gazing about it afterwards: I doubted whether I would ever see him again. Oh! But the condom burst and that left him scurrying off for a wash and me wondering about pregnancy. He read my thoughts and said that if I were pregnant he would certainly provide for me and the baby –

and I had no doubt that he would, though quite reasonably I thought that he'd be relieved if it wasn't necessary.

Next day both he and Caroline were due to leave. With Caroline I would do a bit of an island tour first but for Alexander, that was it – he would leave in the morning. I would be alone again on the campsite – after this time of companionship and change. But a change had already happened that evening – a new person had walked into my life. I was doing yoga on the beach and along came Kim with her dog. Alexander introduced us. Now she told me she walked the beach every day – so why had I never seen her before? And she was a yoga teacher! We agreed that I would come to her class at a resort near Road Town.

Diary 2 May 2002

The greatest thing that has happened is that I can now choose to have sex. The time before sex doesn't feel full of tension any more. It is just sweet innocence. Victor likes his title of 'the boyfriend on St Thomas' – does this objectify him? Well, possibly, but I still feel a need to put a distance between myself and men.

★

Email sent 3 May 2002

Dear Everyone,

Well, you can tell I have a cheap source of email, twice in one week, but some people missed out last time round, don't know why.

Well, I am still in Tortola BVI, a run-down place which looks like the Brits left forty years ago and just left the yachting set to run it. Wonderfully quiet at the campsite, a bit hectic in town. Road Town: a scatter of sheds and cheap buildings set at different angles across weed-strewn lots with parking between them running down to the nearby roads. Planned? I don't think so. There is an older street with pretty fronts, but for the most part it looks decidedly unfinished.

People come and go on the campsite so I lost my beach bum colleague Alexander yesterday. So that's the end of having a little dinghy to potter around in. Never mind, I have found a yoga teacher and classes.

Today I received a manuscript for a short story from the boyfriend in St Thomas, USVI. It arrived by boat and had to clear customs before I could make off with it. It is all so formal and yet so informal. Customs is really just a joke and you walk out to the boat if you want. There's really no separation. But I had my passport with me.

I have moved into Alexander's old tent as it is bigger than mine. I can scarcely lie flat out in mine. It is all pretty easy-going here, but I am already making plans to move on. Got to get down to Trinidad and then back to Miami and away out of the USA by 23 June, if I am to keep on schedule.

The most beautiful thing about this journey is being able to stay a few more days wherever I wish. That unties it from the usual week-long holiday schedule.

I have changed my way of responding to men and I am really happy about that, but otherwise the time here feels pretty easy-going, no difficulties in the way that happened in Hawaii and its wake. Nothing scary as I thought might happen. I am now about on the Pluto line, though the book says east of the line is more difficult and that is still to happen.

Still got to get a yellow fever injection for entry to Brazil (24 June).

I really appreciate all the help and support I

get from you and I just enjoy seeing all your names and I smile.

Love you, Juliet

Caroline and I filled her last day on Tortola by going from beach to beach around the island – finding some we didn't know of and missing others we had earmarked for visiting because of the tortuous road system. We ended up at the West End – at Jolly Roger's again – eating key lime pie. Caroline endorsed it.

Now Caroline was just coming to terms with sexual matters too and had just had an affair with a married man older than her father. She was really quite shaken up by it. Well, it happens and we agreed that there must be a purpose in it even if we can't see it now.

We went to the Prospect Reef, a hotel where Caroline was to spend her last night and also where Kim was teaching yoga that night. So, I end up shuttling myself back and forth trying to watch my laundry getting done in Road Town, visiting Road Town harbour waiting to see which ferry brought the long-awaited manuscript and trying to get to yoga at the Reef at the right time for the start of class. What a lot of hustle and bustle. The boat Victor told me the manuscript would be on came in, but the driver was not called Charlemaine as Victor said. No one had ever heard of a Charlemaine! Eventually I rang Victor and he would send the manuscript in the morning. Phantom manuscript was now what I called it.

So, a lovely evening with yoga which helped to reduce the scatter of my brain. Then back to Brewer's Bay with Kim. She was looking for a housesitter for July/August, but I did not think that it was a job for me. New people had arrived to camp! Then next morning, off to Road Town again, but first I needed to I take down my tent quickly so I would not end up paying for two tents – but it took ages and so I missed my lift with Kim across the island to Road Town. The two new people and I hitched a lift. I had decided to look more presentable without Alexander as a hippy role model so when I stepped out of the tent my two new friends thought I looked like a model – just stepped off the front cover of *Vogue* magazine. That's Hawaiian clothes for you!

At the dock, no manuscript, but I persisted and went to customs and saw the parcel was there waiting for me. Thank goodness for that. I had begun to think I had been listening to a pack of lies. This parcel represented the truth.

It proved a good day – almost like a turning point – I got a photocopy of a picture of an iguana from the library, got phones to work, photographs developed and the prints returned to me in the same day. I felt as if my luck had just turned.

Every time I had been to Road Town, I seemed to notice a hospital building. Eureka, it said. So, knowing I needed a yellow fever injection for entry to Brazil, and having tried unsuccessfully to get one in both Britain and Hawaii, I went in to ask. Ah! It was the wrong hospital. I needed Peebles hospital or a Dr Downing. I chose the hospital but, no, they told me to go to Dr Downing. As I walked in the direction of the doctor's house, a woman approached me and said in a very plummy English voice, 'Are you lost – I keep seeing you walking around?' No, I replied, I am not lost, just trying to find Dr Downing's house. 'Well, I am going there myself!' she retorted.

To make conversation, I asked if she knew whether the doctor would do a yellow fever injection. The reply came, 'I've just had one there myself and am going back to pay for it.' So, it would cost me $50, about the same price as if I had got it in the UK. But fancy finding someone who had just had the treatment I needed – and I didn't even approach her, she had accosted me. Heady stuff. Was this a miracle such as the book said could happen on Pluto?

After the injection and with my head still reeling from the uncanny encounter I got a lift from the doctor herself to part way back to Brewer's and then hitched a lift from the edge of town, only to find it was the same woman who had given us a lift in the morning. Then, to finish the trip, Kim came along and deposited me in the Bay. My diary noted: Ate well on pasta and salad, then to bed after so many 'coincidences'.

Saturday. I had been at Brewer's Bay for nearly a week. I suddenly remembered I was to meet Caroline at Prospect reef and go with her to the airport. Immediately I got a lift, all the way there – now that's a fine start at Brewer's!

I helped her to pack, something perhaps more useful than it

might usually have been – she was somewhat distracted by having had a new black boyfriend share her bed that night. An antidote, maybe, to a married man older than her father! She was busy getting his contact details.

We breakfasted together on the way to the airport and I suddenly felt low in energy. These 'coincidences' seemed to leave me needing a lot of protein. I saw her away and then asked at Clair Aero's desk about flights to Anegada. All I had to do was to telephone and they would put my name on the list of passengers. No money needed till I flew. I put my name on the list straight away. I would go on Monday.

I looked at the beach by the airport. It didn't entice me, so I got a taxi back to Road Town and it went via the mountain road to add to my exploration of the day. I must tell you, Tortola had begun to feel like a really inconvenient island. Road Town is on one coast, Brewer's Bay is on the opposite side of the island from Road Town, and over the mountain ridge, the main ferry terminal is at West End and the airport is actually on an adjoining island at the east end. It's a taxi driver's delight! Except the roads are abysmal.

By afternoon I was back at Brewer's Bay and my two new camping companions and I swam, snorkelled and ate together and got rained off several times. I sorted my photos: lots of photos of Alexander but the photos of the rock where the iguana story began were still to be developed. Victor's story was nice about a diver and an iguana. I have never illustrated a book before but I could see the story so clearly. I felt really captivated.

I had been making plans to go to Anegada. It had to be by plane and the plane went in the morning. Not easy for me at Brewer's. But perhaps…

Diary Sunday 5 May 2002

Today would be my father's birthday; he would have been ninety-three. Kim came by and I now have a lift with her to the airport. The timing is absolutely perfect. Listen to this. Sebastian, a man working on her house, is going back to Dominica and his flight is half an hour after mine. He needs to be at the airport an hour before his international flight; me, only half an hour beforehand, because mine's internal. His flight is 8.30 and mine is 8.00. We need to be there at exactly the same time.

★

Now, I am not good at asking for things and this was how the lift came about. I thought Kim had said that her mother was due to leave the island on Monday, but when I asked her on the Sunday, she said no, she was leaving on Wednesday. So, I was able to say to her: well that's a shame cos it would have been nice to travel together, get to know each other better (and incidentally, save me an expensive taxi ride; I would have to pay for the taxi to come first from Road Town and then take me to the airport). Then she said she was actually going to the airport on the Monday because she was taking Sebastian there and so I could share the journey. And the timings being so perfect. And, I didn't in the end even have to ask, just to say it was a shame. The 'coincidence' caused the hair on the back of my head to raise and prickle with sweat. When I waved goodbye to Kim, I had to go to bed to recover. These miracles were coming thick and fast!

Chapter Thirteen

ANEGADA, EAST OF LINE IS MORE INTENSE!

Email to friends later

On Alexander's advice I went to Anegada from
Tortola.. Still in the British Virgin Islands. Well,
Anegada is small, with just three shops (selling
food and plumbing gadgetry) and a post office.
All roads outside the main village (The Settlement) are sand and bedrock. It is an atoll just
twenty-eight feet at its highest point. No bank
or ATM to pay for the return flight. So I
actually had to use a traveller's cheque to pay
for the flight back off the island to Tortola. I
went on Monday and left Friday. It is completely quiet there. I camped by the beach,
Loblolly Bay, walked into the sea every day,
did yoga, meditated then painted the illustrations for the book, on silk. Had lunch at
Loblolly Bay at the Big Bamboo restaurant,
then I painted again, cooked for myself in the
eve and swam or snorkelled other times. Saw
nothing of the wild orchids or the flamingos.
Just didn't move around much. Total contentment. Didn't comb my hair or even clean my
teeth between Monday and Thursday night. I
wore the same clothes all day, a bikini, sarong
and a T-shirt. So, it was a real bohemian life.

Anegada is so beautiful. All turquoise water
and white sand flecked with pink coral. It even
surpassed Balos Bay in Crete for the intensity
of the turquoise. The moment I arrived and

saw the turquoise I knew I had come home.

Friday was the rude awakening. Would the taxi be there for 7 a.m? I got up at 5.30 a.m., broke camp and then bang on 7 a.m. I heard a strange pipping noise and realised I had just heard the BBC pips for the hour and the taxi had its radio on! The news! The world outside still existed.

Off to the airport, and a quick flight to Tortola via Virgin Gorda, so I visited VG after all. Just to drop one person off. Then, to St Thomas with me as the only passenger. Then, on to St Croix (pronounced Saint Croy). I arrived at St Thomas at 10.20 a.m. for the 10.30 flight to St Croix. It was delayed by fifteen minutes for me and another latecomer. There were four of us on the flight. It's low season and the biggest plane I flew on that day was a ten-seater and the longest flight eighteen minutes. I didn't have to worry about vegetarian food or in-flight entertainment.

So St Croix is back in the USVI. Still driving on the left and still using US dollars. It has a great Danish colonial feel. Not that I have been to Denmark, but the place has lovely two-storey buildings with colonnades and shutters. The view down the street is the waterfront, up the street to green hills. So it is pretty, light and airy. But I miss the quiet of Anegada. Will there be miracles as on Tortola – getting the yellow fever injection and the airport lift? Or finding pictures of iguanas and on Anegada finding that the illustrations for the book just flowed from me?

Just to backtrack for a moment: when Kim came to collect me to take me to the airport with Sebastian she was a little late. I got a bit anxious about whether I would make my flight.

Then I cooled it and said if God wants me on that flight I will be. All anxiety disappeared and I have decided that that is the end of anxiety. I make a plan and if God wants to change it, that's fine by me, I am sure s/he knows best! It sounds so obvious but it's taken a while... So, even with just ten minutes to go before the flight over to St Croix, I refused to worry. It saves using all that energy that is easy for me to fritter away on low-level anxiety and sometimes high-level grief.

Lastly, iguanas for the story. I didn't know what they looked like. I had seen them on Puerto Rico, but paid no real attention. No illustrator's eye. The library in Tortola had a picture of one, then I bought a postcard and for some strange reason where I would put my message was a drawing of an iguana. Finally, when I got to Anegada, next to the post office was a breeding programme for iguanas. There they were in cages ready for releasing into the wild! They were posed in all sorts of positions for me to draw, without causing them any fear or discomfort. They simply sat and posed for me. Even a tin of iguana food (empty) nearby furnished me with a picture of an iguana! Beautiful!

So, why have I now moved to St Croix? Well, Victor is here to attend an Olympic wrestling meeting after a week of coaching training in Colorado Springs. So it is prime time together. A whole weekend of his company and a chance to collaborate re the illustrations.

Just wonderful, particularly after the isolation of Anegada.

That's all for now, dear friends.

Love Juliet

Backtracking for a moment, the trip to Anegada went well and when I arrived I did a meditation on Pluto. The fields had been burnt – there were new shoots emerging! I decided to take stock. The changes I had noted so far had been: that my sexual energy was no longer rampant; I had started living my own truth – not that of my father's desire for a son; I was happy with my physical appearance; my need to keep moving overrode the need for human relationships; I had no concern about money – it would arrive; I had no concerns about whether I could do something – it would work, always, if it were my own truth; so, no anxiety about everyday things – if I am meant to do something, I will; I was attracted to black skin; I had no regrets about my split-up with Dave and whether my affair in Crete had played any part of it.

I was very fond of Alexander, not only his irreverent ways and ways of living, but the way he took care of his possessions – he carefully treated his little boat before stowing it away so it would be OK for the next year. He lived by protocols such as asking me to be careful with his tent and eating at the Big Bamboo restaurant in thanks for camping there.

The Big Bamboo restaurant on Anegada was a bit of a surprise – very shipshape, not at all bohemian or laid-back. The staff all wore the same colour-coded uniform T-shirt and they changed them each day for the next day's identical colour. Fancy, and Alexander looking so wild!

The restaurant had a good space for me to paint and enough tables so that I didn't have to move at lunch time – the only time it serves meals. I was however invited regularly to join other people for eating, though the menu was very limited for a vegetarian. Rice and peas and salad. Fortunately, there was a little camp kitchen by the beach for the staff to use, which I used. The campsite was totally informal (unlicensed) and the only people staying were staff who did not have housing on the island.

The strange thing was, I couldn't stop painting – I painted twenty-eight pictures in three days. I just had the appetite to keep going. And each picture was a success. How could that be? With silk painting you can't have a second go at it or rub it out – and I had never been good at figure drawing before. But somehow they all looked good. The work just flowed from me. I kept Sai Baba's picture on the table while I painted. I began to believe my relationship with Victor must be right if this work flowed so easily.

I needed to buy food on Tuesday, my first full day on Anegada, and so I walked the forty minutes into The Settlement. The landscape never changed, just low scrub and trees with cactus here and there. It was featureless, and that was its beauty for me. I could walk and think and never be drawn away by other sensations. A place where meditation could be a way of life – or a perfect discomfort if you did not want it.

The Settlement shopping was difficult. What they sold reminded me of 1950s general stores in the UK. Cream crackers and custard powder and tired vegetables. Back at the campsite, Kenny and Glen, the other campers, ate steak and macaroni. I just had sweet potatoes. To bed generally about 8 p.m. for me, leaving the men smoking and drinking and making wild and improbable plans for their futures.

Diary 7 May 2002

Up at 7.15 a.m., ran out into the sea. Little yoga and meditation. I asked for Plutonic energy for me to never feel anxious if plans seem to be going off course. To be able to discriminate between when I need to take action and when things aren't on my life path. So, I can plan, but not be concerned for the outcome when my plan gets put to the test of reality. It all feels good.

★

My painting set me apart from other people who just came to eat, but it never felt too solitary except perhaps at night with nothing to do except go to bed and wait for dawn to break. The sun came up over the sea so I would run out of the tent down the beach and throw myself in the water – shouting at the sun.

One day I lost my watch – not that it was going well, but better than nothing. I searched the tent. No. Now, I had hung up my sleeping bags to air, so when I took the thin silk inner bag off the clothes line (you may remember I bought silk at Eve's shop in Hawaii) there, hanging by a single loose thread was my watch. A little miracle, just to remind me that miracles were still part of my scene.

Every day seemed to have its 'discussion' moments for me. The next day I woke thinking about how I had met so many lovely people on my trip. Thinking of men and marriage, I could see that I could have happily chosen either Victor or Alexander. They both offered such different things, how could I be happy to choose? Jerry, Mike and Casanova John all seemed very distant now. Maybe in time Victor and Alexander would do too. I thought of my mother, and that, whoever I chose, they might never meet her. I decided to phone her when I re-entered the USVI – it was too expensive from the BVI, but, no, I caught my thoughts: money comes and goes and if I fear the loss maybe it will become my reality.

A little about Anegada. I really felt to have come home; the sea was the colour I had expected to find in Hawaii, but no. Neither was there anything so turquoise in Puerto Rico or the Virgin Islands so far. The turquoise on Anegada was just so bright and the sky so blue and clear. There's a total lack of pollution as the island stands a little apart, facing into the Atlantic. Funny to think of the UK being on the same ocean! The turquoise reminded me of the Balos Bay, near where I live in Crete, but it surpassed even that. And by being on my very doorstep – or at least by my tent, every day I could see it, no need for a journey.

The sea is so clear you can see the individual iridescent scales of the fish when you snorkel. You can see their eye sockets clearly and know in what direction they are looking. The white fish particularly just shine in the light. What was all this stuff about rip currents in *Frommer's* – it all seemed very calm, just a big lagoon framed by the reef that took the pounding of the waves, from all the way across the Atlantic.

I needed to speak to Victor about the arrangements we might make to be on St Croix together, but I had no number for him in Colorado Springs, and at the Big Bamboo they said they didn't take overseas incoming calls. However, I wished for it and it came. Diane came out of the kitchen and told me to go in and that I had a phone call. It was Victor. So, miracles are still happening. East of the line!

I told Victor that all I cared for on St Croix was that we would have a double bed together so I could sleep with him. The last illustration I painted for the book showed the iguana sleeping at the foot of the bed where the man and his wife slept, which gave the plot a certain unspoken twist. The book closed with the man waking from his dream about the iguana and his journey with it, but the iguana was at the bottom of the bed when he woke. I had always identified with the iguana in the story, but now I would be in the bed. He told me which hotel he would be staying in.

Then, having made such a bold step I worked on how I must be. I did not wish to fall back into old roles. My old self would have said, unconsciously, 'I want him to fall passionately in love with me and eat out of my hand.' Now, I needed a new focus. I decided that I needed to discuss with him what we would individually like to see and get out of the relationship, to enjoy a comfortable level of intimacy. And to ask Victor to help me to rediscover my own orgasm, not one based on male-type fantasy. Phew, that's got that one out of the woodwork! I understood that a lot of women use male fantasy as a turn on and I didn't wish this to remain so in my case. If I was going to be more of a woman, then this must change! Lastly I wanted the relationship not to be about success or failure, blame or whatever – just pure experimentation. I wanted us to be equal for each other. I look back now and see a very tall order.

After all of that, I slept on the beach on my last afternoon in Anegada. No more paintings, but really, I had enough unless Victor wanted some extra ones.

You know already from my email about my journey to St Croix. Now, I was way over weight with my luggage, so the bags went on the first flight to leave Anegada, then the plane returned to take me. While I was on Tortola I could have gone to visit another island, Virgin Gorda, which has a wonderful beach with huge rocks, called The Baths. But every time I asked myself if I should go, the answer was no. I persisted but still it was the same. So, with wry amusement the flight I got from Anegada carried one other passenger and we touched down at Virgin Gorda to drop him off. I got there in the end, after a fashion! I smiled to myself.

In retrospect, I wondered why Pluto had let me stay put at the Bamboo restaurant, but maybe the changes I achieved several times a day were by painting yet another illustration. How could I have otherwise been so prolific when usually just one or two paintings would constitute a day's work.

Chapter Fourteen

ST CROIX – THE HONEYMOON

St Croix is a bit away from the Pluto line, and west. In geographical terms, Anegada is at the north-east corner of the Virgin Islands and St Croix at the south-west corner. Poles apart, but Pluto was still going to be the only influence, as it was in Puerto Rico, though I expected it would feel diluted after Anegada. A bit of a break, although I was enjoying being able to make changes so comprehensively and quickly while on the line – or east of it. I found it hard to understand why the A★C★G book said it was a difficult area to remain in. I had never understood how I could change; I used to think I was me and that was that. With Pluto change just seemed to be in the wind. I could look at something, ask for it to change and it did. Pluto was much more of a regular companion than Venus ever was. A friend indeed!

So, I came to land in St Croix. There were fields flowing over softly rolling hills. After the sheer flatness of Anegada this seemed quite novel. At the airport taxi rank I asked to be taken to Rum Runners Hotel, the hotel Victor had told me to go to. Nobody had heard of it! I felt petulant – what was this game? They had all heard of a restaurant with that name, but I insisted it was a hotel. With something approaching bad grace, I got in a taxi and went to the Rum Runners – aha! The hotel was called the Caravelle and it had a bar called Rum Runners. So why had Victor remembered the name of the bar better than the hotel? I just noted it.

Funny how I kept noting these things about him. I just couldn't put my finger on it, he was a dark horse. I had no reason to feel suspicious about him. He had told me that he had seven children. The first was by a local woman now living in New York. His second partner was an Irish woman with whom he had had five children, and the most recent woman was an American, who had had his latest child, now nine years old. Their marriage had foundered and his wife had gone to live in the mainland USA but had returned, even though they were divorced. She had nowhere to live and he had the house, so she moved back in and they lived together so they could jointly parent, but that was all. They were not lovers.

Well, that might not seem totally plausible – was I gullible or what? But Victor had to put up with a story of me being with Dave for twenty-eight years and that in the summer we still lived together, but just as brother and sister – so how plausible was that?

Victor had not reserved a room, so I took a room at the front overlooking the bay with a sitting area inside as well as a bedroom. Enough space for yoga practice. I paid up front $100 for just one night. Victor was not due in yet, he was on a later flight, but I began to feel a sense of unease. He had also told me that the hotel had bath tubs instead of just a shower, but the hotel staff didn't know about that one. Was this going to work out? I was anxious to put my new Pluto-inspired changes to the test – as well as see how I felt about Victor after my dalliance with Alexander. Yes, that was a thing – how plausible did I look when I'd already had another partner since seeing him last?

I idled the day away, getting photos developed, getting my hair cut, having my first shower in a week. The hairdressing shop had little mascara-type wands to put colour in your hair. I had a blue one already but really I never knew how to use it to advantage, so it gathered dust at the bottom of my washbag. I asked the hairdresser how to use them to good effect and she said quietly that it only looked good on young hair. So, I went to the hotel room and made a strip of bright blue all along the edge of hair that formed my fringe. Smarting, I thought, if it's only good for young hair I'd better use it up! The haircut was awful too.

Looking back over the time I had known Victor, why was he at the Island Beachcomber where I met him? Did he go there regularly to meet single women like me? If I had had more time on St Thomas that day I would have called in at the hotel because I knew where the answer lay. Leanne, the bartender from Barnsley was a woman to call a spade a spade. She would be totally honest with me.

I picked out a Medicine Card – 'Abundance' came up, whew! I'll tell you a story about that card. Now, when my leg was broken I went to spend a few days with an old school friend and her family. On the day I arrived they were also expecting their elder child to return from London. My friend, her husband and the younger daughter all picked a card. Everyone picked Buffalo, the Abundance card. They didn't know why I was so surprised, but later, the husband had a look at the pack, turned to me and exclaimed, 'But there's only one Abundance card in the whole pack!' Yes, that was right and they had all picked it. Now, in turn, I had picked it. Auspicious, I felt!

At 10.50 p.m. when I was just starting to wonder if I was there on my own, the hotel phone rang and, yes, Victor had arrived. From my torpor I surged forwards like a delighted child. I even watched the change take place with such glee. I tried to leave the room to hide and then playfully pounce on him so as to surprise him, but he saw me – he must have leapt up the stairs! We still seemed surprised to see each other. I had a blue fringe and he was sporting a moustache – and I did not like it. It gave him a sardonic, almost cruel look. Or at least a look that gave him the potential to be cruel.

Diary 10 May 2002

We pet, play and chat. His socks are left on the carpet as if he just leapt straight out of them. Just two little white sock heaps. He looks beautiful, more than I remember – a week of wrestling has toned him up. Every bit of him looks sleek and tight, his skin a perfect shining fit – and such a small waist. Every bit of him is beautiful. I feel dowdy, spotty and dimpled. But then I come round. I am how I am and eating a bar of chocolate has aggravated my skin. I tell him about my desire to change around how I have seen men as sex objects and want to redefine my own sexuality and sexual imagery. Sex is off limits; I have a herpes sore and it is the day of the month when I'd be most likely to become pregnant. He has seven children already. No matter, I also tell him that I need holding and loving after sex – no turning off the light and to sleep! So, with the help of a condom and spermicide we make love. Very gentle, very quick, perfect for the occasion.

Both satisfied we lie together in candlelight all night. We fit together as easily as the iguana and the man in the story.

★

This chapter is called the Honeymoon, and it really had a honeymoon feel to it. Making love whenever we were at home in our hotel room and doing seaside holiday things, kissing and adoring each other wherever we went. I gave him a foot massage, the oils chosen to help him walk closer to God. I didn't rush to show him my illustrations. I knew he would be pleased with them and so one thing at a time. We needed to move from one delight to another, not be like children opening Christmas presents so fast that they get fatigued. We had a splash in the hotel pool, a late and leisurely breakfast, then piff – Victor was off to his meeting. He was on the local Olympic committee, preparing for the 2004 Olympics – in Athens!

We were staying in Christiansted, a delightful place with streets with vistas of the waterfront, green hills and beautiful Danish buildings with balconies with highly ornate but delicate iron work, all picked out in white against the colourful boards of the buildings. Alleyways are filled with palm trees – doubt you'd get that in Copenhagen!

After a walk around, I went to the hotel and dozed for a while, waking a little before Victor's return at 5.30 p.m. We were delighted to see each other again. We were gentle and passionate with each other. I was beginning to realise what a wonderful lover he was. No urgency in him, just a mature appreciation of sexual encounters. I think he could keep a woman happy for years. Was I able to do wonderful things for him too? I don't know, but I hoped so. But I was completely knocked out. Dinner and then back to bed, sleeping late.

We ate dinner in the hotel – at Rum Runners, in fact – and we were sitting at the bar waiting for a table. Suddenly, Victor asked for a brandy. Then he showed some interest in the varieties they had, but there was something in the tone of his voice that went with the cruel moustache. I just noted it and got him to clean shave later – a relief to get rid of this expression. He smiled his big smile at me. It all felt OK.

Next morning we took a boat ride – a tourist trip to nearby Buck Island for snorkelling. Well, we couldn't manage to make love all day. We kissed and cuddled incessantly and I could see people eyeing us up – particularly Victor with his blissful velvety body. We snorkelled together and held hands. Then I noticed a shark resting on the seabed. Unlike the little fish it wasn't pretty and gay. It lay like a grey battleship by a rock so I couldn't see all of it from any one vantage point. I pointed it out to Victor. We surfaced and he told me it was a nurse shark and no problem to us. I didn't feel nervous anyway; I've never seen the film *Jaws* so I'm not given to terror. Back on the boat, people discussed what they had seen and Victor told folk that I had found a shark. That was nice: some men would have said *we* had found a shark – but my part was fully recognised. And no one else had seen it.

Diary 12 May 2002

I am a little anxious about the amount of Guinness and brandy that Victor can put back. It's not that great, but it has a certain urgency – particularly for the Guinness. Maybe it's just his manner. Whenever I look at him, naked or in clothes, I am just spellbound by his beauty. He has straight, long, long legs, a short, strong back and is short from the waist to the thigh. When he stands he is six foot tall, but when he sits he is smaller than me! I'm five inches shorter than him so his legs must be about six inches longer than mine. He tells me he is a leg wrestler and this is no surprise.

When we get back to the hotel I give Victor a massage. He is asleep most of the time. We are both using drops of jasmine oil on our heart chakras. I haven't told him that it is Sai Baba's scent! For a man of the Episcopal Church that would be too much.

Dinner in the hotel again. We don't have the energy to go out, except to buy more condoms and some cheese to give me protein energy. Did we make love that night – I really can't remember. How could that be?

Diary 13 May 2002

At 4.45 a.m. Victor rang up his work at the post office to tell them he was sick. His start time is 5 a.m. I slept fitfully and in the morning we made arrangements to see a printer friend of Victor's on St Croix. Victor was very pleased with my artwork. And I wasn't coy about showing it. It looked good and unique. The shine of the silk and some of the paints really enhanced the feeling of flowing water and sparkles. Now the manuscript and the pictures were united we could go for a vanity print run. This seems to be the way things are done here. You pay for a short run and hope a bigger publisher sees it and takes it on. The printer on St Croix was rather pedestrian and the examples of his work didn't give either of us the feeling that he was right for the job. But, in any case, hadn't Victor said that he had a publisher who was just awaiting the illustrations? Hmm…

We got the hotel to extend our stay in the room till 1 p.m. so we could taste a last bite of each other and we both changed our flights to mid-afternoon.

That's it for St Croix. I've seen a little of Christiansted, a little of the island from the boat, a little of Buck Island and a shark and seen a lot of Victor, wonderful.

★

Email to Friends

Dear Friends

Well, full circle. I am back to where I started in the Virgin Islands, at St Thomas. Now with lots of new friends and Victor, the boyfriend from St Thomas too. I feel a familiar figure round these parts with places to go where I am known and a hotel where I am made welcome. It's low season now so I am not living so much beyond my means this time!

St Thomas with its jeweller's shops galore is sorting me out for a new watch. What better place to have my watch finally go wrong.

Today or tomorrow I have to bite the bullet and see travel agencies to head out. Still haven't decided just where I shall go, Dominica? Guadaloupe? St Kitts? Antigua?

Etc., etc. They are all here. Just a flight away.

My weekend with Victor in St Croix was a great success we really got on well and enjoyed each other so much. He's not handsome in the face particularly, but he carries a beautiful body, with a body the same length as mine but legs five inches longer. He is a leg wrestler and beats his stronger opponents by this and stealth.

We went on a boat together to go snorkelling (I spotted a six-foot-long shark). On the way everyone looks at Victor because no one has such a good figure. Just lightly clad in muscle, but that defines his shape entirely.

Really pleased to see the shark. It just lay on the seabed partly concealed by the coral. But I saw it, so that's a milestone in my snorkelling. It was just like a matt grey shadow. Quite still. A nurse or sand shark.

Victor also liked my illustrations for his book and we took time out to visit a printing friend of his on St Croix. Victor just knows so many people, but I suppose when you're Olympic class that's what happens. That's all for now, otherwise the computer will get paralysis again.

Love, Juliet

Back in St Thomas and back to the Island Beachcomber for two nights. I found Leanne straight away and popped the question. Does Victor often come here looking for women? She looked me clear in the face: No, never. She'd never known him pick up a woman before. So, that put that one to bed. Other doubts might bubble up, but not that one.

Victor came by in the second evening with my post. The new brochure for our Summer Holidays Crete 2002 – and I wouldn't be there. The brochure looked impressive and Victor was interested in it too. By now air tickets had been bought and I was going to be on my way. Poor Victor had to go home – but neither of us could bear it!

Next day at the airport he told me he would return to his celibate life. I had said that I knew life would change and that it couldn't continue like on St Croix – our honeymoon!

Email to friends 16 May 2002

Subject: Pluto update, bye-bye St Thomas

Dear Friends

This is for now goodbye to Victor. Still changes are taking place and I am learning to find new forms of relationships and more fun in my loving one. Pluto is burning and replanting the pastures. Still, it hasn't felt too dramatic here. Even the shark didn't feel like a life and death situation. The info says that east of the Pluto line is more powerful. That will happen from today. So I wait to see. And I can always come back if it's too much. And Pluto doesn't care which islands I go to! Free choice.

So, the next update will be from St Kitts/Nevis (Neevis), assuming they have Internet cafés, etc.

I now have a beautiful new watch from the jeweller's that provides me free Internet. All goes to show it's good business, and what better place in the world to find my watch no longer works than a town with probably over a hundred jewellery shops? You can't move for diamonds!

Lots of love, Juliet

Before leaving St Thomas, I sorted out my LIAT air tickets: flight to St Kitts and Nevis, on to Dominica where I could arrange trips to see Guadaloupe and Martinique too. Then to Grenada for Carriacou, later to Tobago, then Trinidad. With Victor, we got the illustrations put on to CDs, one for me and the other for a publisher in the USA mainland. All a lot of busy tidying up and tying up loose ends, ready to move out. But at one moment I couldn't bear it. I wailed tears and couldn't cope with our parting. Then I got a reprieve. The flights were full next day so I had to put off going another day. No problem! So we made love again, but I was coming to realise I did not have to make love physically to show my feelings, I just gave love anyway. I love him a lot but sometimes I felt as if I were a bystander, watching this love. Maybe it was my way of withdrawing from our relationship. For, whatever else, the answer is always that my journey must continue.

Diary 16 May 2002

So often Victor seems to be running behind schedule, off sick from work, just too busy trying to do his job, do the wrestling coaching in afternoons and evenings, seeing his family – and me. I talk to him about his scheduling: something has to go. I think it's the post office – it's on borrowed time. He agrees and sees that in his juggling act this must go. He tells me that he wants to be in service and he has the opportunity of becoming a tour operator/taxi driver. He suggests that this could employ both of us because he could promote my massage when taking people around the island. I'm not sure whether that would work, but it offers a glimmer for the future.

I give Victor a whole load of things to look after for me as I need to offload some weight – out goes the sleeping bag, travel iron, all manner of things. Victor says he will keep them for me. I have noticed that he keeps empty bottles of Guinness in brown paper bags in the back seat wells of his car. They're in paper bags because, Victor tells me, if the post office thinks you are drinking at work they assume you have a drink problem. So, their identity is masked. Interesting one…

★

Back to the hotel and instead of lovemaking we just got on with the business of tidying up loose ends, talking about the manuscript and the illustrations – which I had individually signed, and I had got an agreement from Victor that he could not use them without my permission and profits would be shared. I was excited at the thought of leaving; it was both wonderful and terrible.

Victor saw me away at the airport, me going through the last door that would finally divide us without realising it. Suddenly it was all over. We had no glimpse of the future and all that we had done suddenly felt a bit distant. My way of coping with the separation.

I slept on the flight, stopping first at St Maartens and then on to St Kitts.

Chapter Fifteen

GOING DOWN-ISLAND: ST KITTS AND NEVIS

I arrived in St Kitts and went to the accommodation I had booked – a villa near to town. Well, it was a pretty little villa, rather like a doll's house, but near town? I don't think so! I tried phoning Victor to tell him I had arrived – no answer – already in bed I supposed. Being at work for 5 a.m. made for early nights.

Diary 17 May 2002

I wake early in my new home. Lying there, I wonder what I will do with my time here. If I am not trying to start a new relationship – and the changes I particularly focused on with Pluto had related to men and relationships – what would I do here? I don't wish to engage in another relationship just to facilitate making Plutonic changes. That would be too much of a strain and out of keeping with my new femininity. I am not going to resume bed-hopping!

★

My life felt a bit like a desert. I decided to suggest to Victor that we tuned into each other and gave each other energy at fixed times of day so that we might build up a telepathy – or at least have some contact. Something we could both hang some warmth on to.

I examined the new shoots in the aftermath of the burning fields: the shoots were about living a creative life where sex and romance were less important. I decided I needed to make more female contacts. The feminist book I got in Malibu, *It's Our Turn Now*, favoured making female friends. Strengthening femininity by friendship instead of living in a man's world. The shoots were brightly coloured and beautiful. I asked that my life might reflect that change and diversity of colour. Oh! Pluto, keep me sane!

I went off towards town, and it was a long way. I almost got run down by an overtaking car and decided this was no fit place to walk, particularly after dark. So in town I looked for tourist information so I could move house.

Email, 25 May 2002

Subject: Pluto Update St Kitts and Nevis

Dear Friends

Love you all! This is a great couple of islands. I flew over from St Thomas, saying goodbye to Victor, but feeling as if he was travelling in my pocket. I have big pockets!

I arrived in the evening so I had booked ahead a reasonably priced accommodation. It turned out to be a beautiful villa with lovely gardens. But the next morning the nearby supermarket (from the guidebook) I couldn't find, so I walked into town – twenty minutes, not eleven. Hmm... Well, I had had to book two nights there because when I left in the morning I didn't realise how isolated it was, and what can you do, until you find somewhere else to stay?

Into town, Basseterre, and the tourist information office came up with a list of accommodation from $22 US a night (a bare tent site on St John had been $27.50!) So, I fell on my feet and got the wing of a house with full kitchen, laundry, choice of beds, bathroom, everything, and a really loving couple who used to live in Stevenage to look after me. My first villa had been $78 US per night. I speak of US dollars and EC (Eastern Caribbean) dollars because both are used in St Kitts.

Basseterre is a typical British development,

rather mean streets with few gardens and open grey-water sewers in the roads, running directly in to the sea. I saw the same in the British Virgin Islands, but here the town is austere too. 'Bastair', as it is pronounced, closes down on Sunday and bank holidays too, but on my first morning the schoolchildren had a demonstration march through town which I appreciated: 'No to TV Week – unplug the plug-in drug.' But I couldn't buy the sloganned T-shirt.

I liked my new home, Griffin Villa, so much that I decided just to travel to Nevis (Neevis) by ferry on a daily basis, so in the ten days I have been there three times. There's the lure of a hot water spring which has helped my back. It is almost better – I can run now! So, every day, ferry permitting, I now go over to Nevis to hot springs, beach and little walks in the rainforest. Charlestown (the capital) on Nevis is much nicer than Basseterre with gardens from the moment you come off the ferry (along with the smell of sewerage, but never mind that, it was fleeting). It has flower baskets hanging from lamp posts – looks like Britain in Bloom has arrived!

I travel around the islands on buses painted with slogans such as 'U Da Problem, Na Me' and 'Dem Say God is Good'.

People here eat goat water, pig tail, pig snout and salt fish. Wherever possible in the language the letter 's' at the end of the word is dropped, hence pig snout, not pigs' snouts. Not much food for me here but I make out. Johnny cakes are good, like a savoury donut. Guinness is sold as a power drink! Oh yes, Victor was Mr Power! And egg nog – now, whoever hears of that one in Britain these days. If you're asked, 'How ya doin?' the answer is, 'Doin' good.'

I am likely to see Victor in Dominica, God permitting. I just asked that we both pray for the finances and time resources so he can come and we can be together and if it's willed it will happen, yippeee!

Love, Juliet

I walked into town, Basseterre, and found it austere and rather mean and poor on drainage infrastructure. The pavements are two steps up from the road – probably to accommodate sewer runs without the expense of digging down deep. Most buildings are made of timber but some are more shanty-town-style corrugated-iron shacks. It was a bit run down. However, I came to a lovely circus of good proportions, with little shops all around, so it was not all bad!

At the tourist information, I got a list of places to stay for $22–25 a night. They weren't easy to find and some had gone out of business. In the end I walked for a huge long way through really poor housing and to find Griffin Villa on St George's Boulevard. The road and the house looked respectable at least. I was to live in half the house, the original part where the couple had first lived before extending. So, it was really like moving into a fully furnished cared-for house. Everything was there right down to an iron. Now, you might be surprised at my delight in the laundry arrangements, but my clothes hadn't really seen a machine since December – everything just got washed in a sink and hung out to dry. I had a choice of beds and fruit trees in the garden that I could pick from. Not only all this, but Theresa, my host, would drive me to the beach each day, because she worked at a resort. If I timed it right I would get a lift back too. Shouldn't be a problem!

Back in town and I had an argument with the telephone company about the card they sold me being beyond its expiry date and so not working. Yet more problems with phones. Perhaps I should have given that one to Pluto to sort!

Having been to the tourist information, I was armed with

literature and chose to catch the little minibus public transport service out to Road Town (yes, same name as on Tortola) to look at petroglyphs. Now I had seen some of these in Hawaii and was keen to see more. It took me some time to find them. They were in a yard next to some school buildings, completely out of scale with their surroundings. Just a few boulders with pictures on them, marked out in chalk or white paint to make them clearer. So, two minutes later I was back on the next bus – pounding with music – up to Brimstone Castle. The bus stopped on the coast road and you then had to walk – uphill. It proved to be rather distant, but just as I was flagging, a car stopped and picked me up.

We took a drink together in the Brimstone Castle café and watched a rainstorm. We had a quick peek around the castle between showers, then they took me all the way north, around the island, then to the southern end of the island where the beaches are and beyond to small bays only possible to reach by dirt roads. My new friends were from Bermuda and their accents were soft against the rather harsher West Indian voices.

At a far-flung bar with the slogan 'Live da Life', a statement that has always stayed with me, we stopped and they bantered with the staff. I'm always a bit on the edge of such scenes because I don't drink alcohol, so it sets me apart. Never mind, I was obviously friendly enough for them to invite me out to dinner. So, I went back to my old home and got changed, rang Victor and felt really close to him. I knew he had been giving me energy all day – he didn't need to tell me!

Judy, Nolan and I went for dinner at a nearby restaurant with good food and relaxed atmosphere. They were good company. However, they wanted to go on to a casino – another thing I don't do! So, I sat in the casino lounge while they divested themselves of money and found myself chatting to Cosimo, an Italian who was laying floors on the island. He was a bit pushy but amusing, so I toyed with him for a while until my friends were ready to go. They drove me home and I left them to go and paint the town, while I packed my bags for the move to Griffin Villa.

In the night I was woken by my neighbour playing loud music, but next thing my alarm clock was jumping and it was time for Theresa to call by and take me to her resort, Timothy

Bay. Half past eight and there she was. At her hotel I could use the Internet. Now there was a bonus for you. And a surprise: my good friend and cousin Lynne has a daughter and she had emailed me to say that she could meet me either in Miami or Barbados, depending on which was best. Well, Miami was weeks away probably, but Barbados… A talk with Pluto was required! Perhaps I was now getting female company, or couples like the people I would stay with and Judy and Nolan. The energy was certainly a bit different. Was this because I was not in quite the same position with regard to the line or was it because I had dealt with certain issues? Whichever, I needed to have a word with Pluto to decide where to meet Annie.

Diary 18 May 2002

Just thinking about how people used to save sex for when they got married. Maybe it's actually desirable – certainly the other end of the spectrum from recreational sex. It might put more emphasis on love and companionship rather than the physical in a relationship. And you learn the discipline to say no. Now, that's something that could be very valuable in reducing the number of extramarital relationships folks have! I must remember that one. If men are surprised that I don't want sex straight away – would they want a wife who just bed-hopped?

★

I met up with Theresa in the evening having snorkelled at her resort. The access to the sea is stony and the sea doesn't seem ultra clean there. But the trees make for a nice shady setting. I also walked out to the further beaches: Frigate and South Friar, difficult to reach but with better snorkelling and with no developments there, and much cleaner. Only problem, I forgot my snorkelling T-shirt so I got my back sunburnt, then lay on my back on the beach, fell asleep and got burnt on my front!

Met up with Theresa again and we went back to Griffin Villa and I moved in, meeting Pat, her husband. They are really nice to me. Pat tells me that while they have never had any problems, if I go into town at night would I please get a taxi back so he can be at ease. Well, normally I would have said it was my business and, as I have a thing about taxis, there would be no way I would have agreed to that. But I found myself saying yes. I agreed to get a taxi each night! Phew! I'm obviously not looking for confrontation.

My only confrontation was with my suitcase. This was the second suitcase of the holiday: the first had not stood up to the train and bus journey to San Diego, so I had replaced it at a street market with Maggie and ended up with a rather bigger case than before. Now, the retractable handle for the roll-along did not want to cooperate and the standing support would not retract either. I fixed the handle, broke a zip and couldn't do anything with the standing support so it stuck out all the time making it very prone to breaking off. I sat down in my own new home and felt really pleased. I just sat and smiled, quite still.

I now had a phone card that I could use with the phone in Pat and Theresa's house. This would be useful for phoning Victor. However, that night he was not in. I went to bed and woke at dawn, went outside, but it was cloudy, no sunrise. So I returned to bed and sent myself on a trip to St Thomas. I found Victor in bed and sneaked in next to him. We made love, this time no condom needed! Then I sent him energy because I was sure he was sending me energy. I had never before experienced so much psychic activity – I felt his presence next to me all the time.

Another nice thing about staying with Theresa was that the resort she worked at ran day trips, so I had arranged to go on 'A Crater Walk'. Dan and Linette from the resort did the walk too, with our guide Royston. I seemed to be doing things with couples now. The balance of male/female felt good. What a change from Hawaiian days! I was really pleased to do the walk with them. It was a long way to drive, up, away from the coast on dirt roads through the rolling fields of sugarcane.

The walk itself up the volcano was through luxuriant rainforest which had us sweating with the humidity. At one point, only the hem of my cotton dress was still dry, the whole front was otherwise drenched from the neck down. The walk went over the unsure footing of tree roots and we crossed fallen trees – not the sort of thing to do alone! At the top there was a pinnacle of rock to negotiate and Royston stood on it with a smile from ear to ear.

The pinnacle was sometimes clear and then shrouded in mist. The crater below us was never fully visible; one moment it looked to be full of white smoke, just the cloud, of course, and other times we got glimpses of the grassy bottom. Naturally, we all took photos of each other, then headed back.

Diary 19 May 2002

The Volcano trip was long and we were out from 8.30 a.m. to 5 p.m. Hmmm... Not much different from some people's working day. I really enjoyed the day, gave Royston a tip – not like me – and I wished him well. I felt almost maternal towards him – now there's a new emotion!

Some miracles just take time to see. I was looking back at my stay with Victor on St Croix – our honeymoon. I had told him I was looking to make a change from using male sexual imagery in achieving orgasms and he was totally there for me. He seems to have the ability to take everything in his stride. He had even said to me that he wanted me to be slower in coming anyway. That was such a lovely way of putting my mind to rest. I was not going to tax his patience by being slow. Fancy finding such a sympathetic man at the right moment! He *is* the perfect lover for me (at least right now) and he told me that I treat him like a prince. Isn't that just wonderful.

★

That evening (Sunday) I went into town. Everything was shut. One restaurant was taking a delivery, but they were otherwise closed. I was told quite firmly that they needed their day of rest too. Well, that's OK, but I needed to eat! I found a Chinese restaurant open. It was not great food but there was enough for me to bring away to eat the next day because it was to be a bank holiday. Got a taxi home!

Late in the night I wrote to Victor – eight pages. I had travelled in my head to St Thomas round about 10 p.m. and I could feel him near me at 2 a.m., which was why I had woken. In my letter I asked him if he was having similarly timed events. Also if he would like to set up times when we might link up and just see how far we could push this psychic stuff.

In the morning, Pat came to see me and hadn't slept because he hadn't heard me come home the night before. Bless him, how sweet! He and Theresa were happy for me to do as much laundry as I wanted and even supplied the soap powder. So I set about an orgy of washing and ironing absolutely all the clothes I had. I also put the final touches to all the painting work I had done on my travels: the Anaguna (the iguana) illustrations, as Victor called them, a scarf for Mary in Malibu and my diary scarf from Hawaii. The scenes I had painted were now bereft of all the passions I had once had. Pluto was said to reduce the sexual appetite (ahem… St Croix!). Maybe, but looking at the scarf didn't rekindle the passions for Jerry, Mike or John. Would I sometime feel like that about Victor?

I decided to draw a Medicine Card, but I looked at both sides of the cut: 'Turtle' and 'Turkey'. So, as this was a lazy bank holiday I decided to do exactly what they said. Turtle: Meditate to Mother Earth for her blessings, with fertility and manifestations to follow. So, I meditated; I let my etheric hands go inside my suitcase to put it right and hey presto the supporting stand now retracted! It felt like a Pluto miracle. Then, Turkey: let go of the past, give gifts and feel free. Well, the scarf for Mary was now complete and ready to post. I can be very practical in my use of cards – nothing too esoteric, thank you! I drifted into town, but the Botanic gardens were closed, the weather was too windy for the beach and so I had a siesta and just sat in my room. And I wrote my diary.

Diary 20 May 2002

St Kitts. They drive on the left in right-hand-drive cars – that makes sense. Electric sockets are English style, there are Quaker Oats and open drains. The last is just so British in the Caribbean. Just let it all run into the sea! There's black dust everywhere. When I first moved into Griffin Villa, it was spotless, except for the windowsills, which were speckled with black. I could never understand it. The explanation came from Theresa: the black dust comes from the sugar refinery. It is due to close next year because the British now don't need sugar from St Kitts any more. UK-produced sugar beet has taken over the British market. Theresa tells me all over the Caribbean sugar is finished. This is causing a great push for tourism – hence the Marriott development I have seen being built. But I do wonder who is going to employ the hard-working people I have seen in the fields and around town. They don't look like hotel reception material. The island-wide railway, now used to transport sugar, will be turned over to tourist use.

It all sounds very speculative and ambitious to me, having seen so much of a decline in tourism – wherever I have been there has been competition for tourism. I remembered in Kona reading a local newspaper proclaiming the return of a cruise ship to Big Island, only to find the following week the fanfare had turned into a despondent article saying the ship had found Kona's docking facilities too small and so it wouldn't be returning. Nowhere has been busy. Where are all the tourists supposed to come from?

What else about St Kitts? There are children everywhere, in the daytime all dressed in school uniforms reminiscent of my childhood. How do they wear them in this heat? The children are courteous and greet you in the street – 'Good morning'. And the streets just teem with this young life.

When I think of Hawaii and the Caribbean they both strike me as so different from places I have been on holiday before. Take the Blackpool of my childhood: the people who lived there were just like us in Burnley, my home town. I am used to the seaside being a little up- or downmarket, but basically the people providing the hotels, etc., or just living there, were no different from us, their visitors. They had the same sort of value system, thoughts about litter, cleanliness, whatever you cared to touch on. In both Hawaii and the Caribbean local people don't necessarily have the same value system as the tourists. In fact they can be quite hostile, or at least uninterested. Looking at the change that St Kitts is going to be making, I can see how that comes about. When there is no sugar, why should people embrace the change to tourism? And all because the English don't see it as their responsibility to support industries they have set up. 'We have enough sugar from our beet.' Why not use UK soil to produce other things and keep the St Kittians in business? I fear for their futures, with a casino here already.

People in Hawaii were often poor. They allowed junk to accumulate; they had no outward expression of making things nice for tourists. In fact, the changes in Hawaii that had taken place so quickly (in a lifetime) were causing all sorts of problems. Why otherwise were there drug and alcohol problems? Jerry came to mind – and his family saying to me that their New Year was a family affair i.e. not really for tourists like me!

People here are noisy; the music in the minibuses (driven at speed) can often be ear-splitting. They are colourful and friendly, or not friendly. They live on island time and services, shops, etc., work for the convenience of staff, not the public. They close early if trade is slack and often won't give you change. They allow queues to develop without feeling any pressure to stop conversing with each other. Chickens roam the streets even in town – here and in the Virgin Islands too!

★

In the evening I went to phone Victor, but he was not in. I went to a public phone box because I really didn't like to keep on asking Theresa and Pat for their phone, I felt I might be intruding. The streets had their share of undesirables who could be a bit harassing – perhaps there was something in Pat's concern for me. I even saw a man walking along with his thumb in his flies, letting his penis hang out. Well, that's a first.

I felt a bit lonely, so I sat still, then read, ate, ironed clothes and painted. I had decided the manuscript could do with nine more pictures so that the publishers had plenty to choose from. After this quiet day, I was off to Nevis the next day.

Email sent 25 May 2002

Dear friends

So, just a few snippets from St Kitts and Nevis.
Ferries between St Kitts and Nevis were interesting. There seemed to be three boats running the trip. Some days the boat left at 7 a.m. and others at 7.30 a.m. I just turned up

at 7 a.m. each time, just in case! Sometimes it's a car ferry where people sit on plastic garden chairs intermingled with the vehicles, while other people watch the telly on hard benches, under cover. Some people play dominoes and cards noisily. Sometimes it's a ferry with no cars and we all have to sit down all of the time, all inside. On Thursday I turned up as usual: no boat in, no problem. I sat and waited and lots of familiar faces were there. Oh, but at 7.40 a.m. someone told me that there are no ferries on Thursday, it is maintenance day (for all three!). So, why did people turn up at all that day?

St Kitts is full of sugar cane but next year that all comes to an end. It's losing money because Britain now grows so much sugar beet, so production stops next year! This means an end to black dust everywhere from the process. They hope tourism will fill the gap. Well, everywhere I have been in the Caribbean, except St Thomas, the lament has been how to attract tourists, whether it is to St Croix, St John, Tortola, Puerto Rico. Only Anegada doesn't seem to care. We will see, but I predict precarious times.

Both Nevis and St Kitts have great rainforest volcanoes and quite good beaches. You find a beach that's good for you, stick with it, no need to look further. There's not likely to be another that fills the bill. Hurricane damage, roofs off buildings, are still much in the picture and the reefs are not really good for snorkelling because they got damaged too. They're partially covered with sand.

Accents are fun with the vowels all over the place. It has changed as I have travelled. Corner becomes 'carner'; wrestling is 'resslan';

hall is 'harl'. In Nevis, I met a man called 'Anador', he wrote it down for me so I could send him a card – it turned out he is Arnold Dore.

On miracles: My suitcase decided to fall out with me. The handle wouldn't retract and the metal support for standing wouldn't close up too. So, I got the handle to go in eventually, but the metal support needed a more creative treatment. So I asked for angelic help and, just as if it was a person who was ill, I asked for my ethereal hands to go inside and put it right. Well, at the end of all that, I thought for a moment I could only wiggle it around as I had done loads of times before, but suddenly it swept in one smooth move. Mended!

Recreational sex or sex too soon has now stopped. I met a man in Nevis who would have liked me indeed! But no, I wouldn't. I just decided he had to respect me or he was dead, and if he was amorous I just told him I was uncomfortable.

That night I had a dream which seemed pretty significant. I'll tell you it, so you can see what you think.

My parents had organised some kind of con-ference that involved family and friends of mine. The family were unidentified, and as I try to remember the friends for you, they just seep away and so I don't think names were important. It's just symbolic of family and friends. During the event I managed to sleep with everyone's wife and just about everyone else too! Then it all came out in public and after that it was as if the ceiling had fallen in. When I was called to account I said that I couldn't possibly affirm or deny what had happened; each person I had slept with must be asked separately. But for all my seeking to pass on responsibility I could see the day of reckoning had come.

All of us are surrounded – and we are wearing black. I am asked to explain my actions in an almost courtroom-like setting. I can't look anyone in the face and just apologise profusely. I am told that I must pay back a 'loan' of 8,000 (pounds? dollars?) to someone.

I had spent it. My only retort was to say it was 6,000, not 8,000. It was a final indictment, but I could still challenge it. Even during my dream I realised this was the cost of my casual sex and how much harm it did.

Back to the dream: I knew I had completely disrupted my parents' conference by deviating everyone's attention away from the subject (whatever that was) to sex and the anguish that caused.

I woke in a sweat and looked at the dream. The court had a feeling of a funeral with everyone, including me, wearing black and it had the feeling of something being finished – it was all over and in the end I would pay highly for it. But I could challenge the amount. From my dream book I deduced that it represented the end of the casual sex and that I shouldn't judge myself too harshly. Looking back at the dream I suddenly remembered that in it I had actually felt a moment of relief that it was all in the open – and over.

My trips over to Nevis were as regular as the ferries would allow. Every time I walked out of the main town, Charlestown, to the Bath. The Bath was a hot spring which had been exploited by a hotel of the same name. But a hurricane had torn open the hotel years before and it still stood, large and broken, at the top of the field. Below, in the field, the small, warm stream flowed between two cracked concrete walls in a narrow valley. You could take your clothes off by the pool and go in almost naked. There were houses around, so full nakedness was not appropriate. I lay in the bath, which was not deep enough even to cover me, for about forty minutes each time I visited. Sometimes other people came there too. They praised God for giving them such a wonderful facility. By the end of the ten-day stay in St Kitts and Nevis my back was completely better. You may have noticed it hasn't been the subject of conversation recently. It was nearly better, but this warm bath put the finishing touches to it. Possibly it was the physical response to the end of casual sex. I just rejoiced; no need to navel gaze everything!

Nevis has a good bus service and so I was able to mix my daily bath with finding beaches. And I found a favourite one, palm trees fringing the quiet white sandy beach and with a view back to St Kitts's southern rocky peninsula across a turquoise sea. Just like the pictures of paradise, though not so bright turquoise as Anegada. That name alone causes my breath to slow and opens my chest.

Some of the beaches I visited on Nevis had hotels with fine dining and I remember one wonderful lunch where the waiter even spread the napkin across my lap for me. And me with bare knees! Mango and pineapple soup, fine local produce. Another time, on the recommendation of *Frommer's*, I approached staff at a Four Seasons Resort to find out about snorkelling trips to a Champagne Garden. Oh boy! It was so sumptuous and well mannered that the reception staff didn't bat an eyelid at the front desk where I stood in just a wet swimming costume while guests smoothed by me on their way to what would surely be a most elegant lunch. No, very sorry, they didn't know about a Champagne Garden – even when I was persistent. The guidebook said it was an underwater sulphur vent with escaping hot gases, causing bubbles to rise from the sea bed. I am sure they had their own version of a Champagne Garden though – and it wouldn't smell of sulphur! So, a glimpse of the high life. I remembered Chris, the cyclist in Hawaii, saying I was a low-maintenance woman; now here were the high-maintenance people. Glamour with polish, unlike me – at best I can manage glamour with a racy air.

Back to the mango and pineapple soup. I met a young man called Glenn at the restaurant. He was a bit pushy, but amused me – in fact he reminded me of Alexander and kept making me laugh. We went together to the Botanic Gardens, a real treat of palm trees and all manner of exotics. But he constantly wanted to touch me. As I enjoyed his company I decided that I just needed to think; he should respect my views and not be pushy. I knew he had been sent to me for a purpose so, despite his amusing ways, I kept to my plan. But I did feel tested by this cheeky young man!

While in the gardens I did a healing on a whiplash injury he had. It made me feel vulnerably close to him, watching him sleep afterwards. But it was OK; in fact, in that moment the word 'respect' came to me. He had to respect who I was. I also found the phrase 'I am uncomfortable when you do that' in that moment too. I had many opportunities to practise it, too! I continued to bump into him on my

Nevis forays but, thanks to my efforts, neutral it remained.

Next day, however, another Glenn came my way. I had been to catch the ferry as usual at 7 a.m. and a woman told me the first one would be 1 p.m. – that was too late for me because I could only be at the Bath in the morning. Otherwise it was too hot as there was no shade in the field. So, I had been sitting and waiting for forty minutes in vain. But I didn't care a bit. It had been good meditation time. I went back 'home' and then off to the Botanic Gardens in St Kitts. They were developed in the extensive gardens of a former sugar estate owner's house. It was a lovely walk around and as the place is home to a batik fabric craft centre and shop I bought a pretty, if expensive, cotton dress and matching shirt. All in sky blue and turquoise refreshed by white. While I was still at the craft centre, I threw away the pink dress I had been wearing; it had been left by a visitor on our holidays and had now seen better days. The second big purchase of the day; I had already bought a practical, multicoloured (won't show the dirt) dress in town while just strolling around.

After the Botanic Gardens, Glenn appeared and wanted to guide me on a walk. I acquiesced because I wanted to understand the workings of the sugar factory ruins. The batik producers gave a commercial emphasis to the gardens now rather than either the botanic details or the historic ruins. It was a helpful introduction, though I had to prompt him to tell me things as he didn't give me the really clear picture I was after. I was supposed to give him $27 EC, but I didn't have change – and of course neither did he! So, I gave him $40 EC and didn't begrudge it him. A change for me, who doesn't like a forced tip! And afterwards, I realised that I had had the change, so it must have been meant to be to give him more. I just smiled.

Back in Basseterre I bought a bikini too. It was a while since Hawaii and all my girly purchases, so it was nice to go home and show my new batik wear off to Theresa and Pat. They had warned me that batik clothes at the sugar plantation came with a high price tag, but I could see from their faces that my choice was right. And, if I was going to see Victor again, I wanted to look my best. None of the new clothes were pink – Venusian energy was over.

I spent the afternoon at the beach, meeting some women from a travel agency business. They would email some information about a meditation holiday in St Lucia. I checked it out and, yes, St Lucia was OK. If I wished to visit, I was allowed!

All for now, Juliet

Victor phoned and he told me how much he was missing me. I had the usual sort of reaction being on an Ascendant line. I was at a loss to know what to say. It was my needs that counted, not his! Pat was really excited for me, and loved to come to tell me that Victor was on the phone for me. He was a real sweetie.

I asked Victor about meeting me in Dominica and he was keen. He wanted to make a link with the Olympic committee and Ministry of Sport in Dominica. He told me that Dominica's wrestling was moribund and if it were improved could lead to the USVI team having a greater amount of local competition. Victor's team was very isolated. Would we rendezvous? – I didn't know. In a way, half of me wanted it, the other half shied away because it would lead to yet another goodbye, maybe even more difficult, as our relationship deepened. But as I shied away, the other half definitely took the upper hand; I would walk boldly towards our meeting – if it took place.

So, the days on St Kitts and Nevis were frittered away with beach trips, walks and the Baths. I had arrived on 16 May and now it was 26 May and time to go. There seemed to be a slowing down of the pace of change and the need for change. Yet the line still stretched out in front of me, right down to Trinidad.

Two last points about my stay there. In Nevis I went for a high rainforest walk on my own. The map I had acquired included a disclaimer about the directions and length and how difficult the walk could be. One moment I looked down into a deep ravine which I would have to negotiate by stepping steeply down, going up and down over tree roots and mud. The possibility of twisting an ankle overcame my desire to go on. I crouched down on the tree roots and looked into the distance, where I knew the walk would go. Then I heard a strange noise. I realised I was listening to humming birds and they were feeding off heliconia growing almost at my feet. I was spellbound. My first experience of humming birds – and I could so easily have missed it if I had gone on! A little miracle came to mind.

Second point: My host Theresa had seen my silk paintings and had asked me to do a portrait of her grandchild from a photograph. I did it with trepidation, because once I had accepted the commission I knew I would have to produce a good job. I hadn't done a portrait since I was thirteen and at school with a live model. Still, the work progressed well – and Theresa blessed me by asking me for another, this time of her granddaughter with both her daughter and son on it too! Oh, how would I possibly manage to do three portraits without a mistake? And she asked for a silk painting of the Griffin, for their villa. Whoa, steady on, that would keep me busy! I carried the commissions and Theresa's crinkled photographs of the family on with me when I left St Kitts. This was not a job to be rushed. I took my leave of Mr Patrick, as Victor called him, and Theresa. She had also confided in me that she was not happy about her weight and how she had used a fennel product that helped to lessen her appetite. This allowed me to work on something new. I had fennel oil in my box of aromatherapy products and decided, against all that I had ever been taught, to put a drop in a bottle of water and drink it. Well, I found it tasted wonderful, almost addictively so. It sweetened and refreshed the bottle of water I travelled with. It was a little 'cleansing' at first, but my need to go to the toilet quickly went and I returned to 'normal'. So, from then on I drank fennel-flavoured water – and recommended it to Theresa too, though with a disclaimer.

Chapter Sixteen

DOMINICA

Now I was definitely east of the line, said to be more intense, and yet as I was now further away from the line, surely it would be diminished in some way. How would that feel? My experience of being 'on the line' in Hawaii had been intense to the point of overwhelming – when I flew up the line in the four-seater, I was completely overcome. Then, moving away, just a sort distance, perhaps just ten miles away it, it had lost its grip. For me therefore I couldn't see how this would work. Maybe it didn't matter.

I made the journey away from St Kitts via St Maarten to Antigua; then changed for Dominica via Guadaloupe. That's the way LIAT operate – island hopping. So, it's not direct, but you get a view of other islands too. It's a bit like being nosy: poking your head out of the plane window, looking down. Oh! So that's what I'm missing!

A little miracle to start with: On the first flight I sat opposite a woman in bright red who turned out to be venting her spleen about the airline's service. Always bad, she said to me. I could see this being a bad journey so I put my hand on her arm, when she stopped gesticulating for a moment. I said that she was creating her own reality by believing it would always be a problem. I then said, 'Just accept what God sends you.' At that point her eyes lost their hatred and she sat back and made not another sound!

From the air, Antigua's beaches looked lovely and then Guadaloupe looked as if we were entering an exotic part of France. Everything was highly finished, roads broad and engineered – not just asphalt over the old donkey tracks – and there were stylish street lights. Fields were square, neat and orderly. Guadaloupe and Martinique are both departments of France, not colonies. Having experienced the British and Danish colonial stuff, you could tell the difference. This was France! Except that there were funny little hills over a large part of the island, steep-sided with perhaps just room for a cluster of six houses atop and then a steep road winding down in to the next valley – and up again to the next hill. It almost held the rhythm of music. Between the clusters of houses and roads the land was densely forested. There were also mangroves and coconut plantations and green pastures. So much of the surface was either cultivated or developed for housing. The overall effect was of verdant abundance with high-density development. There didn't seem much extensive nature left – hardly enough to get lost among.

I had no idea where I would stay in Dominica, but, no problem, it would only be 3 p.m. when I arrived and I was well fortified on sandwiches courtesy of Theresa. So, I would have time to solve that. I hoped to find a little guest house or a home-away-from-home as Griffin Villa was described. I mused about money. St Kitts had been described as expensive in *Frommer's* guide – well that wasn't my experience. Dominica, it said, would be cheap, but I didn't really trust it any more. Let's see for myself!

I arrived and the courteous, well-dressed man in tourist information office made some hotel suggestions. I could get a room for as little as $14 US, but I chose one at $20. My taxi driver, who took me to the accommodation, said that the man in the tourist office was dressed up because he'd just been to church – it was Sunday. I got the impression that that was a normal Sunday occupation. When I got to the hotel no one was there – just like at Brewer's Bay campsite! Anyway, he drove me to another, the Continental, in the main town Roseau, pronounced Roussou. Twenty-three dollars, shared bathroom – that would do.

I unpacked and went out on the town. I found the promenade and seafront. It was almost deserted and a bit run-down. It looked as if a new quay had just been built to accommodate a cruise ship, but really the quay was a miniature version of the ones in St Thomas – did they really expect a cruise ship? There was a posse of phone booths to welcome people ashore, still to be connected – that's a shame, I could have used one to tell Victor I'd arrived.

All the vagrants and beggars found me. Town and the

promenade were otherwise deserted. Just the vagrants resting up. They didn't have anything else to do and I was their only target. Sloughing them off, I walked out of town and as I pulled uphill a guy called out to me. He came over and I was on my guard awaiting another financial favour – relieve you of the weight of your wallet, miss? But no, he came over and sang to me! I was charmed. He was handsome, too, but I could resist the romance.

We walked together and as we passed a cemetery we stopped and he took a branch from the flamboyance tree – one stem made a whole bouquet of bright red flowers and he handed it to me. Oh, I forgot to mention, when he first called out to me across the road, there was a rainbow behind him. Now all of this seemed very sweet but I felt a bit ill at ease; why should he want to sing just for me? What would happen next? He showed me around a bit, going out into the open country beyond the main town. We bought ice creams of gooseberry and tamarind from a friend of his. The gooseberries were not what I knew from childhood: gooseberries and custard, mercifully their season was short! He told me he sought no physical contact and he hadn't touched a woman since his wife left him. As he was quite handsome – and if it were true – it must have been by choice.

So, I got back to the hotel with my bouquet after I had agreed to meet my new poet friend, Julian, around dinner time. He was poor and asked me to help him publish a book of his calypso songs. His day job was house painting and so that he could work the next day I gave him $25 EC (East Caribbean dollars) to buy a paintbrush. He was friendly and kindly, so it felt OK.

Until the evening I wandered around. Nothing much was open – it was a Sunday between afternoon and evening, a time of limbo. I went back along the front, beyond the quayside, in search of a phone box to tell Victor I had arrived. No boxes were working, or taking my money. When I did get one to work, he wasn't in. I felt a bit blank. However I had found the offices of the Ministry of Sport which were on the next street from the hotel. Victor had given me the name of a contact there so I could tell them to expect Victor to come. The Ministry was housed in little more than a two-storey shack – the office occupied the top floor. That was it!

I could see I was back where the English had been – open drains. Bet you don't get those in Guadaloupe! Well, I would find out because I had decided to visit both Guadeloupe and Martinique if possible by ferry from Dominica. Guadaloupe lies to the north, Martinique to the south. I would sort that out in the tourist office another day. I had eighteen days before my next planned flight date; I had noted that I tended to average about six days on each island. I could see the plan. Let me just settle in.

My first impression of Dominica was that it is colourful – people and town – but very poor. People here looked thin. I hadn't seen that before. In fact, American obesity had been de rigueur in Hawaii, Puerto Rico and the Virgin Islands. St Kitts and Nevis? Well, I hadn't really noticed whether folk were thin or fat. Here, they were definitely thin, particularly the men. Their cheekbones stood out, not only causing a hollow in the cheek, but one above, in the temple too. Cheekbones carried a shine as the skin was tightly drawn over. Male faces generally had a chiselled look, but more elegant than austere.

Housing generally was of timber boarding and corrugated iron fastened together as best possible in some cases. When I was out people (young men) latched on to me or just started to walk parallel to me, at a few feet's distance. I was getting really fed up with all this slinking up on me and they all wanted to know my name and where I was staying – I don't think so. I told them I was Jane and I was with friends. It felt a bit like being solicited by prostitutes – tiresome at best, threatening at worst. The men wanted to pick me up for my money. However, my new friend seemed genuine.

Diary 26 May 2002

I have the miracle of feeling as if Victor is always with me and we have both asked that if it is God's will he will join me in Dominica – this with him having little money and no holiday entitlement left. We will see, but it certainly revitalised things for us both. We both expect it to happen.

I feel freer than ever from money shortages. I feel certain that money can slide in and out of my hands and I shall always have enough. This does not mean I intend to throw caution to the wind, but I wonder just how far I could take it. This journey is certainly God-given and I am protected, even from penury.

My suitcase has taken another big knock. This time the extending handle has come out completely. It will take a big miracle to see that fixed, but I'm sure the town will have repair shops.

In the evening, the only restaurants open are Kentucky Fried Chicken and a pizza place opposite the hotel. I sit in the lounge area of the hotel, just outside my room and wait for Julian. I'm reading *Autobiography of a Yogi*. Then, just as I am slipping into sleep (often happens when I read) and I'm thinking of going to bed, it's been a long day, in walks Julian. He says he comes when the spirit moves him. Well, that's going to be a challenge! Maybe I should have listened when my watch went wrong and learnt that I don't need to know the time any more.

Julian says he's already eaten, but we share a couple of slices of pizza. Then he whispers that he would like a rum. Well, I am host, so I acquiesce and we go out on to the front; it feels quite shadowy and not quite safe. There's a sense of loneliness in the air. The street lighting is poor and people sit still, so you don't see them so easily. I have a distinct feeling that anyone abroad here is up to no good. Whereas in St Kitts I could walk around with my wallet in my hand, here, I wouldn't do that. My beach bag over my shoulder feels fine; pity it has no zip.

So, my calypso friend is called Julian Leonard, nickname Picky. I am quiet with him. We take a bus out of town. It feels quite a long way but eventually it pulls up by a bar and we get off. I have a Malt, which is a Caribbean non-alcoholic brew, and my friend has his rum. At 11 p.m., we walk back. It's not so far by foot because the bus made several diversions, it turns out, to avoid what Julian describes as sewerage pipe works, which look a bit long-term to me. Maybe work goes slowly. We stop at a friend's house and Julian introduces me fleetingly to his brother, who is leaving, but I'm tired so none of this makes much impact. Life here feels to be rather on the edge, with eating more of an optional extra than a life necessity. The choice seems to be: do you eat today, or drink or smoke?

Julian brings me back to the hotel. He has bought his paint-brush (here – on a Sunday!), but at 1 p.m. tomorrow he will take me out to visit the Emerald Pool and waterfall.

I climb into bed and fall into the same hole left by the count-less others and fall fast asleep.

Diary 27 May 2002

Ah! Life on the streets. Noisy from 5 a.m. Grinding and tooting traffic and high shouting voices – what a difference from Sunday. Life has returned after the torpor. I feel energised by it all: I shall do Internet, post, tourist info office this morning and maybe a bit of painting on the veranda. It's a limited space but it will do; there's a low table and chair. I notice my fingernails are still getting filthy from the black sugar dust of St Kitts.

So I do these little chores and find a repair shop for my suitcase. Town is busy and joyous. I find a shop selling veggie pasties, so that will be good. I also have the name of a contact picked up on my travels, Jean Louis, and so I go to visit. I find the house, on Hillsborough Street, but he's not in. His family tell me he is in Dominica, just not here right now, but it's nice to make a friendly contact. They all smile at me.

At the hotel, the veranda is now in full sunshine so I can't paint there, so I fall asleep in the chair outside my room while waiting for Julian.

Half of me says it would be better to use 'recognised excur-sions' run by the tourist board, the other half says what better than a local to show me around and be fed a rum from time to time!

No Julian, so at 2 p.m. I decide to take my suitcase in for repair and then to catch the Soufriere bus, with my snorkelling gear. There, as I board the bus, I meet Bernard, Julian's brother. I didn't remember him from the night before but he is the image of Julian so I know they are brothers. He has just arrived to tell me that Julian is ill – headache, fever – and he has come to town to find me and buy tablets for his brother. I take the piece of paper with the tablet name on it and buy the tablets, just $10 EC (the equivalent of $2.50 US). They're just paracetamol.

Bernard talks to a friend of his who tells him that his (Bernard's) car will be fixed by 3.30 p.m. He will take me to the Emerald Pool tomorrow. That's fine with me. We agree I'll go to Julian's with the tablets right away and I'll see if I can offer healing. Meanwhile, Bernard waits in town for the car. I give him $50 EC for petrol. That's still cheaper than $50 US for an 'authorised' guide. Bernard tells the bus driver where to drop me for Julian's house.

It's further out of town than I anticipated and the driver drops me by a bar. I'm in a small village – and no one had ever heard of Julian. Aha! They know him as Picky, but they still don't know where he lives. A guy in the bar sets out with me to try to find him, walking back towards town. This doesn't feel right – then I meet Julian's ice cream and juice-making friend, Ken. He's in his shack making juice. But he can't say where Julian lives either. It's so frustrating – everyone seems really doped up or drunk.

In the end, I head back to the bar and bus stop. I feel totally unprepared for all of this, and what am I going to do with these paracetamols now? So, I leave the paracetamol there at the bar, with a note for Julian, and head off for Soufriere – something must happen today!

Well, I wait ages for a bus and at 5 p.m., I realise it's too late to go all the way south to Soufriere so I get as far as Champagne Beach, the nearest beach. Well, that's OK. I meet other people on the beach and snorkel with them. Fortunately, it is a delight with little pockets of bubbles rising to the surface from vents in the seabed. So, this is what I had been looking for on Nevis! The bubbles shine as they come up to the surface, a real champagne garden – I must bring Victor here. The water is clear and the fish are lovely. The day has turned around!

I get a lift back into town in a joint taxi with a nice driver – but one of the obnoxious slinking characters from Sunday afternoon is in the taxi too, and he recognises me, and gets busy showing off – bad-mouthing about other people, swearing and so on. So that isn't too good. I talk to the driver in order to avoid him and the driver agrees with me that his native passenger is not at all nice – a freeloader, now trying out his inane French on two other people in the taxi. He is trying to persuade them to let him be their guide for other trips. I agree that sometime I might do a tour with the taxi driver – as long as he doesn't have Mr Loud Mouth with him! The taxi man says he will charge $40 US, if there are four people. But I'm on my own so I say if he can find three others I will make up the party.

Back at the hotel, I try my new phone card – it doesn't work – and I notice that it's past its expiry date. And I had bought it directly from the Cable & Wireless office. I decide to make a charged call to Victor – it costs me $59 EC. I get a receipt so I can make a fuss at the C&W office. This is too much! I get Victor, however, who is anxious about me and says he will be in Dominica the first or second week of June. So, I will leave Dominica for the French islands and then return.

I go out to dine at the Internet café. There the vegetarian food is good but not prepared with love, but by someone with something else on his/her mind. That's the nearest I've ever felt to a human energy in food, other than love or anger. This was indifference.

I walk home and sit outside my room where two people are playing crib. Then the proprietor comes to tell me I have a visitor. It's about 9 p.m. and up comes Julian.

He tells me he wasn't ill and didn't need paracetamol. His brother is very bad and has told me a pack of lies – and he doesn't have a car, so he can't take me to the Emerald Pool and the money was not for petrol! It turns out Julian has two brothers, so the one I met with Julian in the evening had not been Bernard. But then, if this was another brother – how did he recognise me at the bus stop? Oh! It's all so confusing and I feel duped.

Julian says he had just missed me earlier in the afternoon. My concern is not about the money people have had from me, just the sheer waste of my time; and landing me in the middle of nowhere was irresponsible. And I cannot make sense of why Julian hadn't come by to take me out at the right time. There seems to be so many loopholes in today's stories that I feel to have no confidence in anyone. The money I gave for petrol is not an issue (that's good, given my work on money). I feel totally duped, confused and out of my depth with the way of the world here.

So, then Julian wants $10 EC for some food. I don't want to

give him anything. I feel my heart harden towards Dominica. So much for the slogan about being the friendliest people in the Caribbean – all they want is money! Anyway I am in two minds whether to give him anything, so I split the difference and give him $5 EC. He knows that I am really fed up with all that has happened between us. He leaves and I go to bed.

★

That night I woke about 3 a.m. and felt so aggravated by the turn of events. I sat up, meditated and it all went quiet inside me. It took so little effort and just happened. Even when I lay down again I couldn't string a thought sentence together. I fell back to sleep quickly, sleeping through the first hour of the din of traffic and voices, waking at 6 a.m. I dreamt in the night that I had a large area of baldness on top of my head. My dream book says it may indicate a loss of power. It certainly didn't feel good, but wasn't awful either.

So, up and about. I got a refund on my phone card, then on to the travel agent for ferry information to Guadaloupe and Martinique. But I don't want to book yet. I could leave the next day. I would have left that very day, but my suitcase was still in for repair so I was grounded. Armed with the information that Victor would come to Dominica, I went to the Ministry of Sport and met Victor's contact: Ossie Savarin.

I found him in, but waited in an outer office for him: small and with mail baskets labelled for each different sport. Two desks were obviously unused and there was a secretary with typewriter. The office reminded me of the days when I had worked at the Recreation Department in Sheffield, part of the Sheffield City Council – both had trophies in a glass-fronted display case on the wall. So Dominica was about on par with my old city.

After a short while I was called in. With all the aggravation in the Cable & Wireless office, where I had fumed, and after the sloth I had dealt with at the travel agency, I found myself in front of a very nice man. I told him my business and that of Victor. We exchanged phone numbers so I could give Victor the Dominican telephone number and left – that was that.

Things seemed to free up a bit, so I was successful in making a call to my taxi driver of yesterday. The phones were becoming a barometer for how my life was.

Then as I walked back to the hotel the odious little man from the taxi of the previous day was outside telling me he would take me to the Emerald Pool. I gave him short shrift. He asked me what was wrong (so cheeky) and I just said that I didn't have to tell him anything and walked into the hotel. Dammit, this man even knew where I lived! However, I still felt that I had just got out of a bad loop. A little later, the taxi driver (Cabey) came round and said he had no tour for the day. I told him of my plan to leave, but that I would return. So, then it was back to holiday time and I left for the day. I checked and my suitcase was not ready. I saw it and the repair piece, but the two still had to be joined by something more substantial than the smile on the proprietor's face.

Sitting on the bus and I willed it to leave. 'When will it leave?' 'Will leave in a while, miss.' Me: 'How long is a while?' Impatience: 'In a while!' 'Have I time to go to the bank?' 'Oh! Yes.' It was 10.45 a.m. already; I could see the advantage in the organised trip starting at 9 a.m. Off to snorkel at Scotts Head, the most southern tip of the island, where the Caribbean Sea and Atlantic Ocean meet.

At Scotts Head (pronounced Scorsed) I walked from the main village cluster past corrugated shacks with working and obviously broken TV sets perched on their flat, corrugated roofs – I smiled, but it also looked really ramshackle. Then I took the shingle causeway/spit out to the Head, and, indeed, the sea on the Atlantic side of the spit to my left held waves and on the Caribbean side, just two metres away, on my right, the water was flat calm. As I reached the round bulk of the Head, I walked off on to the Caribbean side and along the beach. I snorkelled alone and felt a bit vulnerable particularly when two men individually came to the beach and just sat there, near my bag. I decided just to stay in the water. Then two children came along the beach – they must have been truanting from school, so although Sai Baba told me all was well, I got out.

One of the men approached me. Well, he would, wouldn't he?

It seemed to be the pattern. And, he turned out to be really nice. He told me where I should be snorkelling – out there, near a buoy where there was a sudden drop. But I found the water was too cold for me so far out – and maybe he had told me to go so far out so he could take my bag. That thought trickled into me as the water got a shade cooler and darker. I came back thinking how pleased that I was to be leaving Dominica soon with so much betrayal and anger around, everyone saying not to trust anyone else, bad mouthing each other and so on. I could do without all that sort of company. At least I had broken a loop with the guy this morning. But I was beginning to feel edgy at the very mention of Emerald Pool!

The guy on the beach told me he was the local guide for the area (stop me if you've heard this before!) and that he would take me to the sulphur springs by Soufriere, just back down the road, and I agreed. He felt benign – and he told me he had a fruit garden. So, I would have fruit with him at his house and go for a walk to the sulphur springs and hot and cold baths. We walked back from the beach via his house and the fruit, soursop, was wonderful. The house itself was without part of its roof and had no water or electricity supply. A hat in the room told me he was a construction worker with McAlpine. He told me he did sea defence work – when there was work.

We set off for Soufriere – and then I saw a house for rent, me thinking of when Victor came. It belonged to Big A, a friend of my guide. Big A was not in, but we got the key and I glanced it over. But it was very, very basic – spartan – and had not been lived in for a while. The bed looked tired, there was no lounge, but the area was quiet and it had a sea view. Quite a contrast from the palatial Griffin Villa; I would think about it.

Diary 28 May 2002

We left the village of Scotts Head and as we walked back along the coastal track to Soufriere, and to the springs, I realised that the view was just how I had expected the West Indies to look. Colourful boats moored up, a little village with a church tower nestling in palms which reached down to a rocky shore. There were high green mountains behind the village and turquoise and blue water in front. I was captivated and captured! In that moment of total happiness I decided I would stay for eighteen days in Dominica, no Guadaloupe, no Martinique! Oh! Pluto, about change!

★

The sulphur springs were through the little village of Soufriere, epitomising the West Indies and up into the hills. They were in an area made arid by the poisoning effect of the sulphur. The ground was cast in shades of yellow and white – sulphur banks. Then the hot pools were really a set of little pools formed by a trickle of a waterfall, shaded by the forest cover. My guide was careful and helped me through the terrain. I invited him to share the hot bathing pool with me. There wasn't much room and we had to lie side by side in the stream, but we both avoided physical contact, accepting that it was inevitable at times, so we were at ease. No sexy come-on. If anything I had a problem because I found him attractive. The body is lagging behind the spiritual decisions. I am not going to be tempted, and I am not going to play the temptress!

My guide (nicknamed Wespie) told me of a music festival to be held in Soufriere on Saturday. I would miss it if I kept my resolve to leave Dominica. But, back in the pool I had asked Sai Baba about staying for eighteen days – yes, it would be OK! It was OK either way – I was free to stay or go. So I decided to stay. Eighteen days in this place I vowed I would leave the next day – just three hours beforehand!

Wespie then took me to the cold pool, telling me to taste the water. It tasted of fruit, and… a slightly acidic flavour I could not quite put my finger on. I saw a woman there who was camping. Aha! Now that was a thought. Free camping was tolerated in Dominica. The thought receded at the prospect of leaving my diamonds to fend for themselves.

I told my guide to tell Big A that I would return on Thursday about the house, said goodbye and watched the bus leave Soufriere for Scotts Head, the end of the road and the terminus. I would have just a few minutes before it returned to take me back to town, so I phoned Victor – and I got him. I told him my news and about Ossie at the Ministry of Sport, giving him the phone number. He was impressed with the speed at which I work. For some reason Victor thought I would be in Antigua. Why should he think that? Never mind, he was relieved that I was not. He said it was unsafe.

Even on the phone I was conscious of how I looked for Victor and found that I looked a picture in my new batik dress and matching shirt. So smart and fresh. The journey back to Roseau by bus was fast and dangerous.

Back at the hotel, I fell asleep in the chair outside my door and dreamt an unfortunate dream where I felt I couldn't understand how Victor was not going to be tempted by a pretty woman who had come to live in his house. I woke up feeling weak and anxious. I nearly rang Victor about it till I realised it was just a dream. Maybe it reflected the temptation I was under at the pool that day. Also, the previous day when I phoned him, I heard him kiss someone who was probably either entering or leaving the house. It could have been a child, but I noticed it. But Victor was so nice to me and when I said I was going out for the evening he didn't ask about it – he never did. It felt very trusting and mature. I loved it!

Diary 28 May 2002 (continued)

So, it's 8 p.m. and I am waiting for Julian to show for dinner. I only have $42 EC on me so I can't afford very much. Maybe he feels that the fountain has run dry, but I know the Internet café is open till 9.30 p.m. so there's no sweat. It's hot and I've eaten so much fruit today: four bananas, one soursop, half a papaya and some cashew nut fruits. The papaya was gorgeous, and the same bright orange all over – perfection. The cashew fruits are a surprise. They are red and juicy, a bit like plums, but they don't encase the nut. The cashew nut just clings to the bottom of the fruit. The fruit and nut resemble a fleshy semicolon: a large full stop (fruit), with a comma below it (the nut).

While I wait I reflect on my life here. I am back to having men as companions, so why? What is Pluto about – haven't I closed on this one? Or is it for me to test out and learn how to respond in new and different ways? It certainly feels a challenge to find an appropriate way of being. First Julian, and now Wespie, both while waiting for Victor to come in June. But how different from Hawaii. The door may still be revolving but the flow doesn't pass through my bedroom. A period of innocence.

★

I felt that I was not so pretty when I looked in the mirror and I was desperate to get my hair cut again. I had thought to get it cut while I was in 'France' but that was not likely now – unless I got another turn of events. Pluto is, after all, about change and here I was perhaps feeling it at its most intense. I did agree with all the changes though, so perhaps that was why I didn't feel in danger. My dream book failed to come up with an explanation of the dream about Victor with the temptress, but I think it reflected what was happening in my life regarding Wespie and as Victor did not concern himself about my meeting someone else then neither should I be anxious/jealous if I heard him kiss someone else.

Still no Julian, so off I went to the Internet café. I felt confident in the streets now. I knew where I was going and no one pestered me. It seemed that in telling the undesirable man that morning that I did not want anything to do with him, the world had caught on. There was no more harassment. My new guide had accepted $70 EC for the walk in Soufriere and I had set the price. And I did enjoy the walk better for his company.

Diary 29 May 2002

It was a hot night and I slept with the fan on. That's a change for me! I was up by 7.15 a.m. because of the street noise. Normally, I am a late riser: 10 a.m. would be quite respectable. I'm getting ready to go to the northern beaches on the island because once I move south to Big A's they'll be too far for me to travel to. My suitcase has been repaired. I went to the ATM. At least they work for me here – don't speak too soon!

★

So first of all I took the bus up the west coast to Portsmouth, got dropped on the edge of town where I could take a bus to the eastern Atlantic side of the island to see Woodford Hill beach. It looked lovely in a brochure I had picked up. The beach was golden and surrounded by low cliffs completely covered in wind-sculpted greenery. The sea had a swell and there was not a hotel in sight. To be honest, so far in Dominica I had not seen a single tourist hotel anywhere. The Continental where I was staying was more of a commercial travellers' hotel.

The bus came along – and it was actually a car with bus plates. Well, I supposed, not many travellers in these parts. The first beach we reached had a very rough sea. This was the part the guidebook showed. But the driver took me around the corner slightly and the sea was quieter and women were washing their clothes in a river that entered the sea there. Perfect. I stopped and as I was his only passenger the driver said he would wait for me. And I had a new experience. I looked for a shady place to sit, because even here the sea was too rough to stay in long, and it was approaching midday. I checked the direction of the sun by looking at my shadow – I was standing on it! I laughed because I actually stood back in surprise, but of course my shadow went with me! The sun was virtually overhead.

Because I was interested in other beaches, I asked the driver if we could stop at Anse de Mai beach where I had heard that there were fishing boats that went to Guadaloupe. Maybe a day trip…

It was incredibly quiet at Anse, just boats moored up in the still inlet, and you could see right to the bottom. The sand was dark golden and rich black. The driver, Charlie, stopped and took a drink at the shack there while I swam and waded between the boats. Yes, fishing boats did go from there to Guadaloupe. It seemed a bit informal. I almost wondered whether I would need my passport. It seemed a long way to go in a little boat, too. I took the telephone number of a contact there, but, really, I felt I'd rather go on a ferry than a rowing boat with an outboard on it. There were some houses for rent here. I just noted it – it would be a long way to the nearest shop.

So, that fulfilled my plans and we headed back to Portsmouth. He would take me to Picard Beach – the town beach – or to

Coconut Beach, whichever I liked, for swimming. At Coconut Beach Charlie decided to swim with me. I supposed by then he was off duty. At least I would not be using his services further. I would be heading off down the coast again to Roseau by bus. I was on my guard, but in a very gentle way he just kept an eye on me. So, I suppose I must have relaxed a bit because all of a sudden I found I had let him kiss me. And, oh boy! Could that man kiss! He kissed me so adorably that I couldn't leave it at just one. So we lay on the beach next to each other kissing.

I was very upset with myself because I really wanted not to be doing this – I wanted Victor, not a taxi-car driver. I tried to keep my cool but my body let me down – I had an orgasm just by being kissed, and, worse still, Charlie knew it! However, even with that amount of provocation I stuck to my resolve: I would not make love!

I was so upset with myself. Why hadn't I thought to ask Sai Baba for help? Why was my body lagging behind my spiritual processes? I had imagined Victor holding me tight all day and then this happened! I still had to pay my bus driver and it felt as if I was paying for his sexual services. I looked to Pluto and saw a blackened field. Charlie wanted to see me again – of course! Half of me hoped to see him again. Kisses like that are dangerous, and when would I find a kiss like that again? I had lived for forty-eight years before finding it! But a kiss isn't everything – and at least I had experienced it that day.

Back to Roseau, feeling all disturbed. I recalled a French film I'd seen once where a woman travels by bus to meet her husband who is returning from military service. She has made herself and her child look all neat and presentable for the occasion. However, on the bus, she gets seduced by two men and arrives looking totally dishevelled, with shirt buttons still agape, into the waiting arms of her aghast uniformed husband. No, my case is not as bad as that! However, the desire to be with one man could certainly be deflected on to another.

Back at Roseau, I decided to call Big A to say I would come the next day to take the house. In coinage, I only had a quarter and Big A's answer phone was on (run by my bête noire; C&W) and it wouldn't take my message. The operator service was obliterated each time with beeps. Frustrated and nearly in tears I went back to the hotel – to be met by Julian. He had come to tell me that it was not his brother who had duped me. But I was sure it was – they were almost identical in face. So, I told him I was sick of the pair of them and didn't want any more to do with either of them and, no, I wouldn't go to the Emerald Pool with either of them. He really got it in the neck!

Half of me thought they'd rigged the whole thing up. Anyway, I didn't want to be in that loop so I cleared off out of it. Once inside the hotel I asked the receptionist to get me the C&W operator and tore her off a strip for my experience with the public phone box system – I felt close to tears (again!). The hotel switchboard then smoothed it all out for me and I left Big A a message to say I would be on the bus to Scotts Head from Roseau about 10.30 a.m.

I sat on my bed and cried. Being east of the Pluto line was really hard work. But I was told to stick it out. I was sure it would be good for me in the end. Why had I got a plague of men? Why couldn't I get women friends? Phone cards did not work, public phone booths swallowed all my change and – I got cut off. I had been in three Cable and Wireless offices in the Caribbean and told them their service stinks! I just listened to myself saying the words. Pluto was about rejection and hostility towards authority. Well, telephone companies got it in the neck. And, that night I could not even complete the arrangement to move into the house at Scotts Head.

So, a Pluto miracle occurred. I willed Victor to ring me (I had no phone card and I was not going to feed $7 US of change into a public box, to get connected and then feed the box with an everlasting stream that would lead to even more frustration of being cut off). Within ten minutes of my arriving at the hotel (just enough time for me to dry my tears and compose myself) the receptionist called me to the phone and of course it was Victor, who had suddenly thought: Why don't I ring Juliet? He didn't get it in the neck!

I stayed in for a while, packed a bit and sat still. Pulled a Medicine Card: 'Snake' – transmute all poisons, let go. OK, let's do it!

Tomorrow would be a new day; I would move to Scotts Head

on spec and hope to meet Big A and secure the accommodation. I hoped my life would turn around a bit.

And just two days ago I was writing this:

Email from Dominica, 27 May 2002

Now about Pluto. The effect is still not awful, it's fun and ever-changing (that last is as it should be). It's not lonely as predicted. I always have had company; this is giving me plenty of opportunities to try out new relationships without a sexual flavour. So, that is what I am doing. I shall meet my new calypso friend today (day two in Dominica) and go visiting waterfalls. There's supposed to be lots of danger on Pluto too, perhaps death, but I feel so safe.

So I am just going to see how Pluto has moved me on, and my calypso friend will be the next stage in that! I now feel that the discipline of saying no could lead to a much better long-term relationship, where we respect each other and live in innocence. I could almost see the benefit of saving sex for marriage! Me talking?

My back is now better, or so nearly so that I only feel it now and then. The hot bath in Nevis and my spiritual movement onwards finished all of that.

Oh, and in Dominica, when you say hello to people they reply 'OK!' instead of saying hello back to you and when they get on the bus they say good morning, but repeat it, so it's: 'Good morning, morning.'

Love Juliet

Snake: let go, and it was time to go out for dinner. On the way a man called out to me. I didn't respond immediately, but then I stopped and he said he was a friend of Julian's and was aware of some of the things that had been happening. He said that he couldn't vouch for Julian but that he found him to be a good guy. I hoped that I thought so too. But as Frankie, alias Balance, alias Hard to Kill (or Heart to Kill?) said: I could do without all this shit on my holiday. That felt very level. He told me of some music going on that night and on Thursday. Then he wanted some money too – just $10 EC. I gave it to him – I was glad to talk to him.

At the Internet café it was quiz night run by an American living locally and whom I had met at Champagne Beach. I felt I was beginning to get to know people and places. So fortified by dinner I decided to go to the music that I'd heard about.

I made it there about 10.15 p.m. and got entry OK. It was a nightclub called The Cellars, so it was subterranean.

I sat on a bar stool. The music was OK, but I felt preoccupied. Then the bar filled up with people from the quiz. I met Patricia again, the American. She was a real poised live wire. Her boyfriend had a restaurant and rooms in Soufriere. It sounded nicer than Big A's place. The boyfriend was called Larry Love and weighed some pounds. I arranged for him to pick me up in the morning to show me the rooms. Then I was surrounded by men, including Martin, who wasn't a turn-on for me – but I was to him. I had started to wish I didn't have a nice figure for my age. That was awful – when I was younger, everyone had more curves than me and at last I had come into my own, with a slender waist and breasts that were not large enough to sag. I looked pretty and young in the little batik outfit with its short skirt length. Anyway, Martin told me that he had seen my legs in the street – the nightclub has high level windows at street level – and wanted to meet me. Well, as I was not attracted to Martin, I was on safe ground so soon after midnight we left and went to Soufriere to the hot sulphur baths – not where Wespie took me, but to a more formal baths where you would have to pay in the day time. There we were both naked in the pool and it was pitch-black. Martin wanted me, but I had set out my terms for the trip and it felt OK. For him sex, could be both for procreation and for fun. For me, it was off the menu. At 2 a.m. I was back at the hotel, saying that if he wanted, I would see him again – then I was let into the hotel by the night security man. I had a slight headache and I was tired – are you surprised!

Diary 30 May 2002

Woke at 5 a.m., up at 7 a.m., and I'm packing. I am all addled and finding it difficult not to just keep shuffling things around. The suitcase repair is good, but I realise that the other handle could do with some attention. It's just held by the fabric of the bag, not the hard inner casing. I'm out by 8 a.m., pay for the repair job to the case (when I collected it they couldn't tell me the price) and then back to the hotel waiting for Larry Love. The man on reception is really nice and I thank him for his patience with me and the phone.

Larry has sent a taxi for me so off I go. I get to Soufriere and meet Larry. He shows me two houses, one on the front and one under his parents' house. This latter has a wonderful outdoor area ideal for painting. The other views the sea perfectly. I choose the painting one. It's $20 US. I had taken to keeping a financial record again in Dominica – time to stop that one – I was within my budget here all right.

I have two bedrooms, bathroom, kitchen, settee and television. The other house had a music centre to play cassettes. Never mind – but I do mind. It's a bit quiet here.

I unpack, wash clothes, it's raining hard on and off. I sleep from late morning to early afternoon. Then read a book I bought in town on Creole culture, or rather I decided not to read it – it manages to be pretentious, banal and totally incomprehensible all at the same time. I sit outside and write my diary. Larry comes around and I talk to him about the need for provisions. Yes, all right, he can help. I need to go and see him later. I pay him for two nights' stay. The shops here in Soufriere are just shacks – it's difficult even to make out which shack is a shop. I had a walk around in the morning so I could ring Big A and tell him my plans have changed. I apologised profusely, but he was OK. And I managed to buy a few things, but there's no butter, cheese (a strong favourite for me) or fresh vegetables, other than roots. What happened to Hawaii's macadamia nuts – I never give them a thought.

Thinking of Big A's place compared to my new home – I couldn't have taken Victor there! I feel like a difficult, changeable person, not at all like the usual dependable person who keeps her word.

Larry tells me he does group trips each day, so I can go with him and thus get out of the loop of dodgy guides. I don't know what the price tag is, but sanity is worth a lot of EC dollars!

Roseau was often described as hot, but here today in Soufriere it's almost cold, as well as raining. So, I'm hungry. I'm emotional too – before my midday nap I could have burst into tears again. With the rain holding me in the mood is slow to lift. Grey sky, low cloud, waiting for my washing to dry.

I went upstairs to meet Gloria and Andrew, Larry's parents. Larry had said I could use their phone and their computer – that was wonderful! These things that we take so much for granted at home become an issue when you're away long-term. His parents were not in so I left a note for them. By about 5 p.m. I was agitated that I had not been able to contact Victor. I willed them to find my note and felt the typical front of head opening that often accompanies people telling me that part of their healing is complete, or, in this case, that I am making a request that has not been stonewalled.

Within a moment I heard stirrings above. Two minutes later Gloria came down with the phone. Unfortunately, Victor was out. Today's card said 'Touch the invisible'. OK, so I touch Victor.

Normally, when I am offering healing, I come back from this state of openness quickly to attend to my client, but today I can let the feeling deepen and the top of my head opens to the sky, and I have a light in my third eye area. Victor is my guardian angel, my Archangel Gabriel in a black skin. I ask or hear a voice saying, 'I will love him for ever.'

★

Larry came in and told me he would fetch me to his restaurant if it continued to rain. I felt in a different loop now. Victor was in when I phoned and all of a sudden I was getting that open feeling when I asked for him to be there for me and I knew he was. We discussed plans and it may be that I have to go and visit him, not vice versa. I may or may not be able to do that. We had a really lovely chat. I paid Gloria (Larry's mother) for the call and she was so nice – she invited me to go to church with her on Sunday. Now, normally I keep my distance from churches, but I agreed to go almost without thinking. The service would be at 9 a.m. and would be Catholic. As the church in Soufriere was part of the view that caused me to stay on Dominica, I felt comfortable to go. I told Victor about the top of my head stuff and he warned me of the devil, so I told him we must both respect each other's beliefs. He agrees; that's nice. Everything seemed so much more relaxed now that I had moved out of town.

I walked to Larry's restaurant. The Sea Bird was on the track that runs along the shore from Soufriere to Scotts Head – I must have passed it before with Wespie. It was not busy, so I met Robert, the chef, his girlfriend, Elie, and a couple from French Guiana. The food, particularly Larry's salad, was prepared with love.

On my way home I lost my way among the houses, so I headed back to the restaurant and ended up going into town with Larry and his staff to listen to jazz. All of sudden going into Roseau was a pleasure, even exciting. The combos were good and I met Julian and Frankie (Heart to Kill) again. All was about OK again with Julian, though they both tried to touch me for a drink. I acquiesced for Frankie because his actions got me started on my path to living in Soufriere. Got back in the early hours.

To bed. The room smelt a bit musty. I would have to remember to leave the bedroom door open. I looked to Pluto and found fields of green shoots. As I looked they turned black and then green again even as I thought. I asked about health work: we are all energy, I move misplaced energy/stagnant energy which is causing pain, disease, etc., from where it is stuck (areas of shock / injury) to areas that need it, but the area needing energy can be anything physical, mental, emotional, or spiritual. My work is holistic because although it often focuses on a body part it moves energy to any of the four aspects of being. I wanted more spiritual energy!

My back pain was now so much better I could lie straight in

the bed, but I was not sure I could do that yet on a hard floor.

What I had enjoyed was that I could move to Soufriere, without knowing where I was going, without getting a bad back. Compare that with Hawaii!

So I lay on the floor next morning to see how I was. My right calf hurt a bit, so I put all my energies into getting rid of the pain. I felt a balloon of energy coming away from me: Roseau, Charlie, all the pestering blokes, all things past and gone. The balloon was so heavy it wouldn't lift away. Then I injected love into it and away it all went. It became like a mesh basket and I could see one of the chief pests trying to climb out – but he was caught! Away they went to Mother/Father God. Archangels Michael and Gabriel sent new energy. The fields for a few moments were covered in green shoots, but then returned to black, but they had not been on fire for a while.

The air in Soufriere had a smell of fruit, like the cold water bath with Wespie, and a little of sulphur too. Not a rotten eggs smell, something else – like something hot.

Elie, the chef's girlfriend, was from England and she would give me a list of contacts for other islands and places to visit in the southern Caribbean. She had a dilemma in her life: to stay or to study. I resolved to tell her that there is a time for all things that are on her life path. A further meditation to Pluto indicated that Pluto wanted change and more of it – in all areas of my life. I asked for more miracles, but was told that this might lead to life being even harder. I looked at the fields – they were ablaze again – so quickly! I asked if it would be OK to go to St Thomas if Victor could not get to Dominica. Yes, but it might mean that I had to forgo another island, Grenada.

So, my trip might go like this: Dominica, St Lucia, Barbados (for my cousin's daughter), Tobago, Trinidad, then a re-visit to St Thomas before heading back to Miami. Trinidad represented the point where I would resume travel on my round-the-world ticket, so I would have to check whether I could break my journey to re-visit St Thomas on the way to Miami. Whatever, I would have to contact the airline offices to tell them I had changes. I was unlikely to find any boats going north. It was against the flow of yacht traffic as people moved south in the summer to avoid hurricanes, so no chance of riding the seas.

265

Diary 31 May 2002

I have decided to stop eating. The shops here are decidedly iffy on food and Roseau is miles away – twenty minutes by bus – so I'm giving that one a miss. Anyway, I only ever saw market stalls there and that just in the morning, and I don't want to carry food around all day if I buy it in the morning. Also my yoga book mentions how the plants struggle and get 'pain'. For the second day running I get the Medicine Card: 'Dolphin' – touch the invisible. Last time that was Victor, this time it's food. But – I'll do breakfast first! The change can't be a complete immediate withdrawal – unless it can.

★

Gloria came to see me; I was painting. I finished the piece of work and felt hungry. Painting always does that, except in Anegada! So, I had a couple of cheese sandwiches – no point in wasting food, anyway. I'd run out of fennel oil to put in my water bottle so I asked what I should use to calm hunger and to taste nice – camomile, not a favourite taste!

I ventured out to the post office down near the church. It was closed. Well, it was lunchtime. Next time I went it was open. The post worker had lived in the UK for twenty years and he knew I was from Yorkshire by my accent.

In the afternoon I went to the hot spring and lay down in it. I analysed the smell: sharp, acid fruit, ripe fruit giving sweetness and fermenting fruit giving earthiness, almost a sourness. I returned at dusk and went to Larry's Sea Bird restaurant again and had a double helping of his salads. Before I went Victor called – I willed it and there he was! He still had not found a way of getting to visit me. I told him that if I came to him it would be in at least three weeks' time. He was still very concerned for me so I did not tell him I was going to start fasting. The salad was nice. One salad had taro, a root vegetable, in it so it wasn't entirely raw 'rabbit' food. I met Elie again and she gave me a list of places and people in St Lucia and Grenada. I helped her to prepare for leaving Robert and returning to the UK – her dilemma.

I walked home. Oh, I nearly forgot, on the way to the restaurant I saw fireflies. As I walked along the unlit coast track the sea was on my right and a steep bank of green shrubbery and trees was on my left. I kept seeing little lights winking on and off, and moving around in the greenery. When I first started to take proper note of them, I thought that it must be children having a game – then I realised there was no noise from them. It felt a bit spooky so I stopped to have a better look. Fireflies popped into my mind. I had never seen then before. Larry confirmed their existence. I was so excited to have seen them and later Gloria showed me one close to in the eaves of the house. It was so bright that its glow was reflected in the white paintwork.

On my way home I stopped to listen to some music flowing out from a building, and got touched for money and then saw it used on cigarettes – bah!

Diary 1 June 2002

The first of the month – always a moment of celebration in Crete: *kalo mina*, I wish you a good month! I'm up at 7 a.m. and painting. I am doing a few more illustrations I promised for Victor when I saw him in St Croix. Better get on with them. He's due here soon – if he comes. Anyway, it's good to do them because I won't necessarily have such good painting conditions when I leave here. By 9 a.m. I had walked to Scotts Head and gone snorkelling. This time I saw the drop off in the bay quite clearly. The water was fabulously calm but I might have got stung by some floating lantern-like things because I had a bit of stinging and a rash to follow. While I snorkelled, I noticed a man arrive on the beach, but I only had $50 EC with me, so I couldn't work up a sweat about it. I just waved at him.

When I got out he told me I was the first white person he had ever met who didn't get out of the sea immediately he got there. I told him that the guidebooks tell you not to leave bags unattended on the beach, so people coming out of the water was not something he should take personally. Then, Wespie appeared, alias Keef. Can't remember what his real name was – if I ever knew. Everyone here has nicknames. Larry Love is a nickname. His parents' last name is not Love.

I told Wespie how apologetic I felt about Big A and letting him down, so we both went to see him. He asked me if I wanted to see another house he had – I felt I needed to say yes. The location was perfect, just where the Atlantic and Caribbean meet, but it was not well appointed, except for having a bath tub. The advantage of being out there would be that I wouldn't be in the middle of a village. The noise at the house in Soufriere could be quite deafening. How come it was so quiet when I had moved in? Everyone has their windows wide open and televisions compete with reggae, heavy metal and shouting people with shrill voices. I sometimes wonder how I can bear it for another moment. If this were England…

I agree to see Wespie later and walk back home armed with lots of fruit, stopping briefly by the Sea Bird – and there I meet a woman who does fasts. She said that I should have high enemas to stop toxins from being reabsorbed and causing headaches. Otherwise her advice sounded OK.

I go home and paint, then Gloria comes down with the telephone and Victor tells me he still isn't certain to come. I tell him about the fasting – I suppose I was fortified by the woman who had endorsed it – and surprisingly Victor is enthusiastic about it. He tells me he fasts part of every day to help his contact with God and to keep slim.

I told him about the music festival in Soufriere and he just said to be careful. That's a surprise, he usually doesn't say that. I plan to go with Wespie. I take the phone back to Gloria and, being careful, I tell her of my plan to go that afternoon to the hot springs and later to the music with Wespie. She says he is the touching type – well, I don't know whether she meant for money or sex. She tells me he has been in jail for theft. Hmm… and a few minutes later both she and husband Andrew come down to see me. They both look very serious. Both have come to tell me that they had forgotten for a moment that he had also raped a sixty-year-old woman while at a carnival about two years ago. They tell me to have nothing more to do with him.

Now, and this about a guy who has seemed very nice to me. I said I couldn't cut him off because my experience of him had been good, but, thank you I'll be careful and thanks for the warning. They do not want him at their house. Well, that's OK, I haven't invited him. Next news he is there at my front door – carrying more fruit. He comes in but I have put all valuables away and we went off in a trice to the springs.

At the springs, he became a bit amorous, but 'no' seemed to take care of that. We would meet that evening or the following morning when he would have a fire on the beach and roast cashew nuts.

So, Pluto is about rape, the book had informed me.

I had agreed to go on a walk to the Boiling Lake with Wespie. This is a six-hour walk starting some distance from Soufriere. I had been really looking forward to doing it. I feel the answer must be that I shouldn't go, and yet it feels mean to judge him by words told of him, not how I have found him. On the other hand I don't want to spend all day on my mettle in case I am attacked on the walk. It feels an awkward situation.

When I get back from the Springs I meet Gloria's sister, who was visiting and I tell them that I am back safe. They like to keep an eye on me, just like Theresa and Pat. They give me guava juice but I am feeling a bit hungry so I eat more bread and cheese, resolving again to fast for just part of the day and eat supplies up. Everyone is saying be careful tonight – folk will be here from all over the island for the music.

I take a nap and then head out about 10.30 p.m. – why do all these things start so late? I meet up with Keef/Wespie nearly straight away. The music is powerful and we dance together. Wespie wants to go inside a building with more music playing inside. I am happy outside but go along with it. We pay to get in – and we are the only ones there – just us and loud speakers delivering sound from outside. Wespie tries to dance close, but I won't even hold hands with him. Somehow the environment doesn't feel all that safe – there's safety in numbers, but now we are alone. With so much attention at the house about being careful I am beginning to feel edgy. No one can feel romantic and edgy at the same time. It's just not a chemistry that works!

I talk of the pleasure of innocence and he asked how long he should wait – five months? I leave him. I don't want that sort of pressure. So I am home by 1.45 a.m. It's late enough if I'm going to church with Gloria at 9 a.m! There certainly weren't the thousands expected at the music event – maybe 1,000. Seeing

Keef without his shades for the first time makes me realise he has strange eyes that somehow you can never quite see. I'm not sure why, they just don't seem to pick up any light.

★

I didn't sleep very well that night. I had acid indigestion – probably too little to eat and too much fruit. But I drank some camomile water and it did the trick, just like that! I lay in bed and devised a method for fasting:

1. Visualise a cheese sandwich on a plate – or anything else that takes my fancy – and then imagine taking bites from it and then physically swallowing after each bite and seeing the sandwich growing smaller. Eventually it would be gone.
2. Hold the knowledge that God will sustain me.
3. Take Herbalife supplement in the morning.
4. Eat fruit – because I have plenty!
5. Drink camomile water.
6. Breathe in energy, breathe toxins out.
7. Anything else I feel I need, like iron, can come to me as infusions – etheric substances.
8. Sing the Gayatri Mantra.

The purpose of the fast: to stop killing vegetables, to be closer to God, to do miracles, to live without eating food.

It was then time to go to church. It was a very pretty church, lightly decorated and very much built to human scale. I hadn't been to a Catholic church before so I would have to take my cue from Gloria. I also couldn't compare it with services in the UK – except that I was sure that in Britain would be no gospel-singing choir! The service lasted about two hours and was run by a dashing young priest with a stunning pale cream cloak with two stripes of predominantly red and blue and other colours down one shoulder and arm. Gloria whispered to me that Victor had telephoned the night before, about 11 p.m. The sermon was about man needing more than bread alone to live on and the Corpus Christi as the flesh and blood of Jesus. Funny old world, I felt it gave sanction to my fast.

I'll tell you an amazing thing about the village: after all the revelry of the night before – with lots of stalls selling food and drink – there was not a spot of litter anywhere! It had all been cleared away by morning. Now, that's something I haven't told you about Dominica: there's no litter. You can be imprisoned for littering and it doesn't matter how awkward places might be to sweep – they're swept, even in and out of the corrugation of metal buildings and fences, whether there is asphalt or weeds. It's all clean. To my shame, on one occasion, I threw a banana skin out of a bus window and the bus screeched to a halt and I had to get off the bus and pick it up from the grass at the roadside!

After the service there was a little parade, but I extricated myself from it as soon as I could.

I called Victor and found him still in bed; he talked of contacting Ossie Savarin at the Ministry of Sport. I told him that when he talked to Ossie he should say that he doesn't need any accommodation or hospitality – he will have that with me. This was a very poor country and to expect hospitality would not do. I had been told that civil servants were not being paid at that moment. The country had run out of money. People were still working – what else could they do? – and hoped to get back pay later. It would not be right to stay at the government's expense. He asked if I could set up a written invitation from Ossie (without expenses) so that it might oil the wheels with his employers. I said I'd go and see.

After all this, I was late in meeting Wespie for roasting cashew nuts on the beach.

I had been thinking what I might do about the Boiling Lake trip. It was troubling me a little. I still couldn't say that Wespie had behaved badly with me. Is it not natural at a dance to want to hold hands and have a kiss?

Problem solved: I got to Scotts Head and there was a honeymoon couple there. We snorkelled together. I told them about the Boiling Lake trip. They ate cashew nuts and stated that they would like Wespie to be their guide too. So, we would all go together – what a relief! I noticed that Steve (honeymoon husband) snorkelled without a T-shirt. Now that's a recipe for sunburn if ever I saw one.

There was a woman from Roseau at the beach too; she told me a strange story. At first she told me that Dominica used to have good beaches, but they had been destroyed by a hurricane so tourism had declined. The hurricane had exposed all the rock under the sand. The movement of sand had also exposed a rock on the beach which had been sculpted in ancient times into a head and body with dead souls on it. She could see a boy's bottom, with older people behind, then the very old at the back. The rock she pointed to just looked like a rock to me with the faces that we can fashion in our mind's eye. She said that other rocks had come up with faces chiselled on them too. I was both intrigued and sceptical. But she was an educated woman who visited Scotts Head daily from Roseau.

I finished off the remaining pictures for Victor's book that day – great. I sat and had the feeling that I hadn't done much while I had been in Dominica. Looking back, how could I possibly feel that? It seemed an action-packed time. But I hadn't gone to the Emerald Pool, I'd not got to the many waterfalls that were promoted and I hadn't yet been to the Boiling Lake. All I had done was to go to Scotts Head and the sulphur springs. Probably because I was no longer cooking food I had time on my hands. Food shopping and cooking do take time – and I had given all that up. I had now been on a partial fast for two days.

I decided before the next day's Boiling Lake trip I had better eat. If I fainted away, someone would ask, When did you last eat? And they would roll their eyes if I said three days ago. Better not risk that one. I had felt tired on my way back from snorkelling – a bit short of breath. A feeling that I had to breathe just to support my walking. However, the air was not only filled with the smell of sulphur, fruit and flowers but all the time there was the beat of reggae (most prominently) at high volume – in a residential area! I had stood up from 10.30 p.m. to 1.30 a.m. the previous night at the festival, wearing platform-soled shoes (no one can stand on your toes then), and still my back had been OK, but I was tired.

I heard that the music festivals were a way of giving hope to villages, taking people's minds off drugs. They took place at different villages all over the island. I was made aware of how poor people were too by bread depots. They are small outlets selling just bread baked in town and brought out to the villages. Maybe there's a ration book system too, I never found out about that. One baker advertised itself as 'Ah fu ah we!' which I read as: How full we are! The voices of children with full bellies! A testament to hunger.

Diary 2 June 2002

Life and death are so tightly linked. Energy exchange holds us alive: breathing, eating, sunshine, love, gadgetry, beholding beauty. It is so easy to cross the line to death if energy is denied. Death is even more casual and easy than I had ever thought.

I wish so much I could be omnipresent as described by the *Autobiography of a Yogi* – which I am still reading. To see the world and understand people's thoughts and difficulties would be so helpful in healing. To be able to change people's energy and illnesses just by saying a word. How I long for these things!

When Victor comes, we will kiss each other's souls, not our base chakras.

★

I told Gloria of my plan to go to the Boiling Lake as a group of four. I couldn't have dreamt of a better outcome to the problem, but I had a nagging doubt it wouldn't work so sweetly.

Sure enough, next day I got to the honeymoon couple's hotel, Fort Young, on the edge of Roseau, and they could not go to the Boiling Lake because Steve was too sunburnt. For a moment I panicked, but I gave a little healing to ease the sunburn and then Wespie came in and we all agreed to put off the trip to Wednesday.

As it was early and I was already in Roseau I decided to head out north to Portsmouth to the Indian River and Cabrits National Park. I couldn't find the bus stop and I didn't want to walk back to the bus terminus. As I looked around I was approached by a young man – Thomas – who would be my guide for free. All I had to do was to pay for the boat at Indian River. I said, OK, as long as there was no come-on from him. OK. So, we waited for the bus, got off at the right place, just before Portsmouth, and he directed me to where there were boats and we sailed upstream away from the coast. The scenery was lovely, quite exotic, with lots of lovely birds and plants. The river was smooth and held a perfect reflection of this natural richness, just tiny ripples from the oars. It was as rich as the people are poor. We stopped at a bar with a garden. I was obviously supposed to disembark there and buy drinks, but I just walked upstream so that I could take a swim.

Thomas came upstream after me and started a continuous barrage of how beautiful I was, and he kept trying to get hold of me. So, there I was in this lovely place unable to relax and just enjoy it. Oh, just a kiss and a hug! No, thank you. He even had the cheek to say the whole thing came as a package: guiding and lovemaking. I felt so cross I could have wrung his neck!

So, back at the bar I bought drinks for the three of us: boatman, guide and me. It seemed to be that without doing this I might not get such a genial return boat trip. The price of the drinks was eye-watering – not a lot in other currencies, but still I felt cheated.

Thomas and I walked through Portsmouth so I could get to Cabrits. Nowhere are there directions, and local people just don't seem to be able to tell you where anything is – just in case you're wondering why I had a guide!

At Cabrits I got an entry ticket and it came with a map. I didn't need a guide, thank goodness, but Thomas was sticking to me like glue – and sometimes it's more fun to have company than be alone, so I acquiesced. Once we were alone he was all amorous again. I felt so oppressed I thought I might do something I would regret. I told him that I regarded him as my guide only, not a groper or potential lover. He was nothing else, except for being an ambassador for his country – make him see the big picture! He kept telling me he had never met anyone with views like me before and he made judgements on my lifestyle: 'You can't do that, man,' – seemed to be his standard phrase. He told me he would cook Rasta food for me. I didn't bother to tell him I was fasting. I felt I hardly saw anything of Cabrits for warding off this idiot.

On the bus back to Roseau I felt pretty sore about the whole thing. Thomas would expect a tip so I told him that Dominica had lovely countryside but the men were awful and untrustworthy. I almost spat the words at him.

Elie had told me that the men in Grenada were even worse than in Dominica, so I decided there and then I would not visit that island. The next day I would go out with Larry Love or with Cabey. They had self-respect and so respect for others.

Back at the house my hosts were out. I felt drained of energy and lay down to sleep. My hosts being out meant that I couldn't make any arrangements for a tour the next day, unless I chanced the public phone box. I really didn't have the strength.

I woke up later feeling weak, thin and dizzy. I talked to Sai Baba and I was directed to sit. I found myself singing the Gayatri Mantra and had enough energy to get up, shower and generally take interest in the world. But I looked a bit pale and my ribs showed a bit. Where was all this going?

Diary 4 June 2002

Up at 7 a.m. and I phone Cabey. I want to go to the Emerald Pool. Yes, he will take me. I caught the bus up to Roseau – 'Morning, morning', on the busy bus taking people to work. I put my suitcase in to have its other handle strengthened and found Cabey. The Emerald Pool was really beautiful. I was so glad I had come – and so pleased it was Cabey who took me. It is the pool of a delightful waterfall and perfect for swimming. Now, if this were the UK a pool of this nature would be freezing cold. Here, it is just fresh and soothing to my spirit. I was totally on my own in the water and just able to immerse myself in nature. I could breathe deeply, it felt quiet and Godsent. If I had come with a tourist information guide, I would have had to share this. No thank you!

★

My stomach was a bit upset and Cabey suggested Angostura bitters and water – it seemed much harder breaking a fast than entering it. I munched a few peanuts. I had never really felt enduring hunger but now digesting food seemed to rob me of energy. Cabey then had me eat lemongrass and that made me feel much fresher. I suppose in a country that boasts that it can feed all its people but where somehow that doesn't happen, cures for digestive complaints and hunger must be commonplace. Cabey relaxed and smiled at me gently. As I am enthusiastic about water he decided to take me to Layou River. He told me there was a hot spring there. It was not so far to drive but when we got there we had to push our way through the bushes to get to the water's edge. Then he pointed out to me a little area, just lined out with cemented stones on the far side of the river, slightly downstream. He said if I got in the river there, the current would take me downstream slightly as I swam across and I would be able to reach the pool from there.

The plan worked, though it felt a bit disconcerting to be swept gently downstream – what if I overshot the pool? But it went to Cabey's plan. It was just so wonderful to lie in hot, still water watching the green, sparkling water of the river rush past just beyond my feet, under a lofty canopy of trees. The bath was just for one person and I was it! One of those lifetime pleasurable moments. I didn't need to stay long, just long enough to take in all the exquisiteness of life without my mind drifting – then swam back a little strongly as I was headed upstream and landed back next to Cabey.

On to a further water experience. Cabey took me to a black sand beach, but I was not so keen. There was a smell of fish and pollution. I would give it a miss. I felt so cleansed by the hot bath. Had a Malt to drink and a Johnny cake – like a donut. Then headed back to town. Did some little chores and looked for a hairdresser. I still had my awful St Croix haircut. That would not do, but I needed a hairdresser who would cut non-Afro hair. They all say they do European hair, but when you ask to see a book of styles they have only Afro books. Had a sticky coconut cake. Nearly delicious.

Caught the bus back to Soufriere mid-afternoon, had a quick

shower to cool off and went straight to bed. But then Gloria was calling me with the phone. It looked, for the first time, as if it could not fail: Victor would come.

Then Larry came by and we talked hairdressers and rent cars – I had decided that when Victor came I would get a car – I wanted to show him things and not be hanging around for buses and risking guides. On Friday Larry would take me on a trip to Titou Gorge and waterfalls in the forest.

So far, I wanted to take Victor to Champagne Beach, Scotts Head, Emerald Pool, Layou River and the hot pool and the sulphur area and hot pools above Soufriere. Perhaps to the Indian River too. Oh! And Woodford Hill Beach and Anse de Mai. And how long would Victor be staying? I didn't know!

I had a salad at Larry's restaurant and came home to bed again. It might be early but who cared! The beauty about being alone is having precious moments of living unobserved.

Boiling Lake Walk – at last! I caught an early bus into town – 'morning, morning' – and headed first for the pasty shop, but they didn't have veggie ones that day. I made do with a grotty but welcome cheese sandwich – not ethereal! The honeymoon couple, Steve and Jennifer, were ready and when we were about to give up on Wespie, he arrived. So, off we all went in their rent car to the epic Boiling Lake.

We parked in a village and found many people coming out to greet us and tout their guiding services, but we already had Wespie. Thank goodness for that. I could see us getting killed in the rush to be of service to us otherwise, because there were no other tourists around. There were protest signs about a proposal which was explained to us by Wespie. An entrepreneur wanted to erect a cable car to the Boiling Lake and local people were dead set against it. There was a pile of metal parts in a locked compound that looked like the beginnings of such a project. Weeds were starting to grow. It all felt very hostile. The guides were too numerous for the number of visitors and have the demeanour of people who could easily turn into lynch mob if a construction worker walked by. I was incredibly pleased not to be alone with Wespie. And incredibly pleased not to have to choose a guide there.

The walk was good, but very hard going. There were, in all, about twenty paces on the flat. Otherwise it was up and down all the time. Sometimes there were wooden ladders and rickety steps to help us up and down, with slippery yellow mud between them. There was one very treacherous descent (and later ascent), I remember, where most of the ladder rungs were broken away. It led into the Valley of Desolation and I did wonder how we would ever get back out of it. All the time we were accompanied by a bird whose call went: seee seee; up an octave: peee; down: eeee. It sounded like a metal gate, swinging open: see-see, and closed: pee-eee.

Sulphur hung in the air and then we were down in the Valley of Desolation, meeting with yellow sulphur banks, sparse vegetation and all manner of water rivulets: sometimes black, sometimes cloudy white, leaving behind a variety of coloured residues on their stream beds. Most of them were steaming hot.

Ahead, now, we could see that other people were making this arduous journey. Three hours there and three hours back. Over a slight rise and then the first sighting of the crater, with steam blowing off it. We looked back and Wespie wanted to see if we could work out where we had come from. I had no problem finding it, to his surprise. I was wondering how I would have felt if I had come alone with him – and not been able to see the way back! I was so glad to have Steve and Jennifer's company. It just made the trip highly enjoyable.

We reached the crater's edge and looked down into the boiling pool of dull grey-yellow viscous mud going flop-flop like a pulse as heat and steam rose from it. It seemed impossible to gauge how big it is, how deep down it is – there was just nothing to scale against, except the tiny people sitting on the far side. Some people were struggling with the fumes and had handkerchiefs in front of their faces but I just revelled in it. I really couldn't get enough of the smell... the view... the energy. The information said it was the second largest boiling lake in the world. The biggest one is in New Zealand – and I'm going there! I felt to have a link to the future and back to Pele, the goddess of volcanoes in Hawaii. I could have sat there for ever. In fact the thought ran through my mind how much I would like to stay and sleep there witnessing this chaotic spectacle. Could you imagine coming by cable car? I couldn't. You needed the walk to prepare you, sort of soften you up. Arriving in heels and hairdos you either wouldn't feel the immensity of it or you'd be totally bowled over by it. Walking was the way – though I suspected that the protest campaign we heard about had more to do with jobs for guides.

We stayed for perhaps an hour looking down into the crater, totally transfixed. Then started the long journey back. At the end of the long walk back there was a small hot pool so we stayed for a dip. There was a sign mentioning Titou Gorge. I mentioned it to Wespie but he didn't go for the idea of adding it into our visit. I took his advice. I had seen enough for one day. Anyway, I would come another day. Just as we were leaving, a dog bit my hand – hah! Dogs and flies were mentioned as among the animals in the Pluto arena. I was really shocked and that showed itself in an uncharacteristic fit of temper. I told the girl (owner) that it should be leashed. And that it was not funny – she stood there inanely smiling. In the end, the fracas involved a black man too, who was with the girl. I was glad to move away and get back to town. Ah! I was just too late to pick my suitcase up: the shop had closed. But on my way back to the bus stop I met Julian again. He introduced me to a friend who was with him. Julian told me he was a hairdresser – and his name was Caprice! Well, this was just the man that Larry Love had recommended to me. So, we went straight back to his salon and he cut my hair. He cut it really well, but really short. It suited me, but nowhere was it more than two inches long!

Back to Soufriere, not to go home, but to go onwards to the Sea Bird for dinner – salad and garlic bread. In the restaurant the phone rang and it was Larry's parents worrying about me. And they said Victor had phoned twice. I suspected they had passed on to Victor their anxiety for me.

I got him later that evening – and, yes, he was waiting up for me. Then home, where it suddenly occurred to me I had just had loads of energy all day. I mean, fancy going to get your hair cut after a six-hour walk and a mind-blowing view; fancy going out to dinner without a wash and change. I was like dynamite. So, this comes of fasting! All I had eaten that day was the Herbalife supplement, a cheese sandwich, a small piece of bread, a salad and garlic bread. It felt great.

In the night I had a dream of death. I dreamt that a friend of mine (Richard) was going to die in three days' time, although I was the one who was limping in the dream. Now Richard has diabetes (yes, he does), was I limping with a diabetic ulcer? I didn't know. But he did die in my dream and so did other people (not known to me), according to a prophecy. Then I dreamt that, in front of an audience, I did a yoga pose in the air, held by Victor's hand and a vertical rope. It was very acrobatic and felt very beautiful.

I called in Sai Baba and decided to go back on full fast – this time no Herbalife or anything. Baba will sustain me! I need to put a bit of weight back on my ribs.

Diary 6 June 2002

I look at my hair. In the ordinary light of the day, it looks very brown, all the golden blonde has gone. This won't do! I paint it blue at the front with the mascara wand – only looks good on young hair!

Into town, to Caprice and he's busy. He has a mauve wig in the window. I decide to try it on. That's OK, so I shall have my hair golden yellow everywhere, except for a purple piece at the front. Now, Caprice has a photo dating (from the clothes) back to the sixties in London where he had a salon, so I have confidence, all will be well. He asks me if I want to walk about with the purple wig on to see if I like it. No, no – just do it. He agrees an asymmetric shape with me and the colours. It's a big step.

Go round town, get chores done, email to friends. Back for my hair appointment. After that, most people's eyes lift to my hairline as I pass, but no one takes offence. But I can see it's a challenge. I just love it. I have often toyed with having my hair an unnatural colour, but I like – and wear – so many different colours. Which to choose? So, I never have done it. Now, I don't have any purple clothes – so it's the obvious choice!

★

I emailed friends to say I was having my hair dyed purple, and I received an email back saying succinctly: 'Purple is good.' Of course – the crown chakra!

I seemed to be in town all day one way and another and arrived back at Soufriere at 5 p.m. not having eaten all day. I settled to half a papaya, a little rice and beans, giving the rest away with my old bread to the chickens down the road. I ate without a thought to my proposed fasting.

Victor had phoned. He could only come to Dominica for a short time because his ex-wife, Grace, had made some plans for the weekend and so he would be child-minding. I suggested bringing the child, but Victor said his mother wouldn't allow that. And Victor wants me to be his focus, not the child. We remain ever hopeful that something might turn up. At least he is coming!

Next morning I was up and about getting ready to go with Larry to Titou Gorge and Trafalgar Falls. But, when I saw Larry, he looked harassed and overworked. He said he had lots to do and the ferry strike was exacerbating things. He passed me over to another taxi driver. So, I would be the only person going after all, no company.

We arrived at the start of the Boiling Lake walk and there was the little hot pool I'd been to before that had the signs to Titou Gorge. I changed and got into the water. Then I asked my guide – now what? Well, you swim to the end of the pool, just a few strokes away, then turn a corner – and you're in the gorge. As easy as that. I swam towards the further edge of the pool where it appeared to end in a wall of vegetation. I had previously thought that the pool just stopped there, but no, indeed, there was a corner! I turned it and found myself in a narrow corridor of deep, dark water with sheer sides riven into magnificent pothole shapes by water cascading through it. The sky above was a mere slit between the two formidable grey stone walls. Luxuriant growth at the top edges cut the light further.

The water instantly became cold and I was aware that I had to swim against the current. There was scarcely room to turn around, there were no handholds and I had no idea how deep it was. Certainly I couldn't feel the bottom. My fasting made me acutely aware of the change in energy in my environment. I felt that I confronted death in this dark passage. All alone. There was not a string of life to grasp. As I moved forward a little in this grey rock passage I became aware of the noise of fast-running water. Had it been there all the time, or was this a new threat to my life? I couldn't tell. Then I could see slightly that, at the end of the gorge, just to one side, was a waterfall. I wanted to swim closer but the cold and the current forced me back. In a pothole-wide opening I turned round and was back out so quickly to the corner I was almost blinded by the daylight.

Like a child who has just been on a scary funfair ride I wanted to go again, straight away, but I was also dizzy with tiredness. Thank goodness I didn't try this one after the Boiling Lake – it would blow your mind to experience the two in one day. I felt you could not survive both in one day. Death again!

I recovered in the warm water for a while and got my temperature back up. My guide asked me if I'd like him to go with me this time. Yes please – I wanted to see if I could make it to the waterfall. So, Vincent got in and we went so far, then he motioned that at that point there were some underwater rocks, where I could stand down. I got my breath there, knowing that if I ran out of energy/breath there's not a single handhold or other resting place. Then I swam on to have a better look at the waterfall, but I was beaten by the current and the cold once more.

So, that was it: Titou Gorge. A place where I confronted mortality. How near to death I felt, and how small and vulnerable in that mighty sculpted enclosure, with nowhere to grasp if the torrent of water that had created those majestic curves came surging down while I was there.

This was another place I wanted to share with Victor. With the magnitude of all this playing through my mind I was silent and then realised that my guide wanted to caress me. I was so totally unresponsive I couldn't imagine why he persisted. Vincent told me how he would like to be with me and be my lover. Whereas I had nearly killed my Indian River guide for less, this time I just remained poised and forced him out of my mind and life. I felt as if I just closed down. I am not my body. It was raining hard.

Next was Trafalgar Falls, with a difficult walk requiring a guide. I would have had no idea how to get there or back without one. The walk criss-crossed slippery muddy tree roots negotiating steep slopes – to get to a lookout point. Then down again to the where the water drops into a deep pool where Vincent got in the water uninvited. When I wanted to look around and enjoy the place I found his rough hands trying to massage me. I felt so upset – yet another opportunity to commune with nature dashed by stupidity. I got dressed and then slipped on the rocks and fell into a pool of water, getting soaked and muddy. I fell on my coccyx so my back was jarred. I took time to give healing to myself and then put on a long T-shirt I had brought with me – the only dry garment I had. We went to some hot springs and I just wanted to relax my back, but again I was harassed by him. But at least I had found that I could control my anger and just go within. I had hoped to leave Vincent in town, but after picking up my newly repaired suitcase I didn't feel I could do more in my poor state of dress – just a T-shirt – and with the purple hair too! What a sketch!

He drove me home and I agreed to pay Larry, not him, and then washed all my clothes. Chatting with Gloria soothed my nerves. I was hungry and ate guava jelly and grilled plantains and finished the few beans I hadn't given to the chickens.

I wanted to complain to Larry about Vincent. Women here tend to say to take no notice, but I can't bear it. At least I didn't kill my guide today. I certainly couldn't recommend a singles holiday here. As part of a couple you probably get a completely different impression of the place and people. For me the island is beautiful and the men ogres. I felt that my exuberance and sense of fun were misinterpreted.

In the night I became angry because I did not feel that I could just enjoy myself. Either I was on my own and a bit lonely or I had a guide and had to be persistently on my guard. I felt as if I could be very violent with the next person who tried it on with me. My reaction would probably be out of proportion, it would be the straw that broke the camel's back. I was even transferring my anger to Victor because I really didn't want to stay in Dominica till Tuesday when he was due to come, in this climate.

Also seeing Victor for what amounted to just one whole day and two parts would not give me time to relax and really enjoy him. I had not spent all these times phoning (and writing to) him, just for thirty hours! I would be anticipating his departure from the moment he arrived, trying to fit everything in I wanted us to do together. I could go to 'France', till Tuesday but with the ferries on strike I might go and then not get back. I felt trapped and oppressed – even by Victor's visit!

Because the Ascendant is about my needs, half of me felt impatient to get out of both Dominica and the relationship with Victor which held me there. I did not know whether I even wanted to see him, given how much anger I held just then. I did want to see him face to face to ask him about seeing him in St Thomas at the end of June. I could engineer a change in my round-the-world ticket, flying from Trinidad to Miami via St Thomas instead of direct. I could manage about ten days without compromising greatly my schedule and leave St Thomas on a Wednesday – Victor's day off, and the day after my birthday. If I was to end the relationship, all this would just come to a close.

I decided on the practicalities: in the morning I would check out ferries and air tickets and leave by the next afternoon, one way or another. But, did I want to run away or stay and confront the problems I had with men? I might get a resolution by staying.

I meditated: Sai Baba guided me to fast for longer so as to reduce the number of sensations I had. I was told not to give in to the whims and fancies of the tongue.

Then it was all change. Victor would come that day, just for the day and I would rent a car. Could I really believe he would come and would my doubt increase the chances that he would not come?

The car was UK style driving on the right and a manual gear-box. It seemed a bit strange – I hadn't driven that way round for ages! The insurance was basic, by my request – if I damaged the rent car, I would pay in full.

Diary 8 June 2002

I drive back from town. Things keep playing on my mind – the anger at being bitten by the dog, the anger at men here. I get home and phone Victor. Spitefully, I tell him I don't see much point in his coming to see me if it is just for a day. In any case I want to leave if he is not to be here. Time to leave. He rings back to say he has cancelled his ticket. OK and not OK. In a sense, just to see him for five minutes would seem wonderful – and now I won't see him at all! I had had such a deep impression that he would pull it off and come today – and stay, hence my renting the car. I felt very disappointed. I was all over the place, like a sea swell of emotions, conflicting. I don't know what is worse: not seeing him at all or hanging around here for the next four days, for just thirty hours' of pleasure. Anyway, the ticket is cancelled now.

★

I decided to go out for a drive, visit some places which I had liked and pick up on things I hadn't yet done. A trip around the island. I went north to the Layou River and did the hot bath bit again, then over to the east coast to Woodford Hill beach. Then, time to go. The sandflies had started to bite – almost as bad as the men! Aha! My sense of proportion and humour were returning. Women were washing clothes in the river again. I told them to do it for ever, to resist the temptation of a washing machine if it came their way. Picked up the Hampstead River. Now, that is one lovely river, not so much for the water (there's not a lot of it) but for the massive buttress roots of trees either side feeding from the stream. There was a silent dignity about them. I hoped to go to Anse de Mai again, but I overshot it. The roads are so badly signposted it's a tricky one.

I drove around the very north of the island, giving lifts to people as I went: a boy from St Thomas, a teenage girl and a woman carrying a full Calor gas bottle on her head. I wouldn't even look at a man who might want a lift – forget it mate! Gave a final lift to a youth who advised me that the road I wanted (and shown on only one of my maps) hadn't yet been built and that I would have to go back! Now, that was a bit embarrassing because I really had only enough petrol to make it along the north coast to Portsmouth in the west, not for driving back along the north coast, which had also proved a tricky one to drive: potholes, steep corners, etc. I would have to face them all over again without much daylight left.

I had seen a gas station, hours ago. Could I make it? Worse still, would it still be open? Well, the gas held till Blenheim and the gas station was open. Saturday night – now, if it had been closed it might not have opened till Monday. It's funny how we can feel anxiety when really we are quite safe, and if I had not got petrol the end of the world would not have come, but somehow anxiety had driven a wedge into me.

In the falling light I followed a petrol tanker, blaring its horn at every bend and taking up the whole of the road. With that in front of me driving was easy and I didn't have to concentrate as twilight turned to night. All I had consumed so far that day was a tamarind juice. I decided if I were to drive safely it was time for a bite at a Chinese restaurant in Roseau. A party at one table all turned around to look. Yes, I had purple hair!

My meal came all very quickly; then the bill was slow. This seemed to be a pattern of dining alone, maybe they want you out as quickly as possible, but then find they've not made much money on a vegetarian (fasting now) and so they can't be bothered to collect the coins. My fast has now lasted more than a week, I calculated – broken only for the Boiling Lake walk and dinner that night. Though I had never gone completely without food.

I called Gloria from the restaurant on a whim. I was so glad I had. They were really anxious for me – it was 10.30 p.m. I decided I would take them out for dinner tomorrow as a thank you. But...

Diary 8 June 2002 (continued)

I'm still feeling sad at not seeing Victor, and I can't bear being here much longer on my own. A new island will be good for me. If anyone else tries fondling me it could spell murder – can I afford to stay? Men's behaviour has really marred the beauty of the island for me. In the night I devise a plan: I'll get out of here at the earliest, take a ferry to Martinique. I have seen something of Guadaloupe from the air – that will suffice. I can get a ferry on Monday morning, come back Wednesday or Thursday and then fly out to St Lucia. Oh! How my plans change.

★

If you feel you're having trouble keeping a pace, you should try living with it! Pluto is a line where everything is up for grabs, and instead of some thoughts being discounted before they really take shape, here everything surfaces and must be analysed, challenged, or acted on – whatever it may be. I'm not normally given to mood swings, but maybe I was experiencing just that.

I've also been looking at how I dealt with my guide Vincent at Titou and Trafalgar Falls – why did I decide just to put up with being fondled? OK so it wasn't particularly erotic stuff, but why did I just get out of body? I had felt the spell of Titou would be damaged by anger and debate (Why can't I touch you?) but it still left a bad taste. Titou Gorge had made me feel powerless.

My anger with Victor for not managing to come for a 'reasonable' length of time was because I would have liked to see Dominica through new eyes. Through the eyes of a couple sharing the experience. Coming for just one day – how could that exorcise all the ghosts of the guides? Maybe in the future I could revisit Dominica with Victor, or another lover, and recharge each special place with new energy. No, I could not use Victor to turn around my experience of Dominica. I must do it myself – or not. I have to change in order to love it. In Puerto Rico I had to stay till I liked it. So, I must see something new here too, not necessarily by staying, but to keep my focus on Dominica so that as I travel its joy comes to me.

The next morning was Sunday. I had asked Gloria if I could go to church with her again. Yes, she was delighted; she hadn't asked me because her husband, Andrew, had said I might feel obliged and had counselled her not to ask me. This time the service had no appeal and I found myself quietly clock-watching. I found myself criticising the service and sermon for being judgmental!

I had asked my hosts if they would like a ride out in my rent car and a restaurant meal for their kindnesses. They chose their son's restaurant. I was a bit disappointed at first because this was not new to me, but then glad because I hadn't been there for a while. They were busy in the afternoon so I took myself off to Middleham Falls, Fresh Water Lake, with a quick dip at Champagne Beach. Gloria's sister Alice and her small niece came with me, but Alice said they wouldn't walk to the Falls. So, we went to Champagne first and there she got chatting to a French couple who wanted to see my 'home-away-from-home' at Soufriere. But they also wanted to travel around with us because they had no car. So, we all went to the Falls.

The usual pattern: walking up and down and over tree roots and fallen trunks with birdsong to accompany us. This time the path was waymarked, no need for a guide. The Falls were great and we climbed down to swim in the waterfall pool. It was a delight, and, oh to have non-invasive company! This freedom allowed me to swim nude in the water, although my concern at leaving Alice and the little girl stranded for some hours caused us to return a little quicker than I might have done. Is it reasonable to expect total perfection?

Back in the car we got a bit lost on the return and this really panicked Alice, though to me the island is small, so you can't go far wrong. Island perspectives.

I led the party back to the house in Soufriere and the French couple were impressed but happy to stay in Roseau for a day or two more. I was a bit disappointed because I would have liked to have found new tenants for Gloria and Andrew as I then proposed to leave slightly earlier than previously arranged. Our conversation turned to ideas of taking a trip to some reservoirs together the next day. They were pleased and I was overjoyed. This turned Dominica around for me, I would have company and no more guides. So I phoned Victor and told him to come after all and I cancelled my ideas of leaving for Martinique or St Lucia. I had really only one more day to go and Victor could be here! I took Gloria, Andrew and Alice out for dinner. It cost me the same as six nights' stay! But, globally, it was not that expensive and the food was nice – and there was plenty.

Back home I was all excited and Victor could still make the trip. So, I was up in the night making plans of where to go. He was arriving at Melville Hall airport, which was a good distance away, not Canefield airport where I had arrived. Never mind – that was what the car was for!

My purple hair was fading fast with the bathing and sun, but what a change round a good day can make – without guides!

Diary 10 June 2002

It's my mother's birthday today. She's eighty-four. At Roseau my new friends have gathered two other people who want to walk to the reservoirs. This is great – a car full! The first lake we go to is Freshwater. I swim, the others don't. Then a more arduous walk to Boeri where we spent a lot of time, swimming, sitting, eating, just perfect. I commune with nature.

Afterwards we went to Titou Gorge – what a finale! They loved it, though for me, it was too busy (there were other people and shouting, excited children in the narrow part) for me to conjure up that initial, awesome response. But they were happy and of course I saw it through new eyes. Tomorrow we will go together to the Carib Community. When I dropped everyone in Roseau I arranged to get my hair revamped ready for Victor – can't have half measures, it's got to be full purple!

I am really looking forward to seeing Victor. Why? I don't know fully. He is kindly and I have a great feeling for him. Not sure it's love, but I feel comfortable when I tell him I love him.

★

Next day, I washed the bedding and towels ready for Victor. I went into town early for the hairdo, food, getting films developed from my throwaway cameras. I was still awaiting the camera to be repaired and returned. Then the Internet.

Email 11 June 2002

Subject: About Dominica.

Dear Friends

The countryside is exceptionally beautiful, and volcanic so it is steep. Walks consist of trails with steps up and down and no flat. Everywhere is heavily forested (what else can you do with steep land?). The most beautiful thing is the total absence of litter (or litter bins) in town or country. That's so refreshing. A fine of $150 or a month in prison is the enforcement.

The people are slender, particularly the men. I have never seen so few obese people, in fact I haven't seen any. Housing is poor in some areas with corrugated iron and wooden boards being the chief materials in use. Many houses are without water or power and so in the streets there are Public Conveniences, which means there are showers and sinks too. It is common to see people with a towel round their neck and toothbrush in hand in the streets. Many people wash clothes at the taps at the roadside or in streams leaving their clothes to dry on bushes.

Largely the kids go to school and, as in all the Caribbean, they are in uniform.

Travel is exciting by minivan buses and they go fast and frequently. They have right of way on the road, so get out of their way. Roads are narrow, steep and full of potholes. Driving is on the left with right-hand-drive cars, like UK.

I now have a rent car. It's interesting that people think I am brave – they don't know I haven't even taken out more than the basic insurance; in other words, if I have a crash and it's my fault I pay for the damage to the rent car in full.

Language is great. A hotel that I heard as Fortian, and decided was probably called Fortune, turned out to be Fort Young! Reflecting poverty, a bakery (selling bread at bread depots) has a slogan AH FUH AH WE, which I assume translates as How Full Are We. Still on language, the response to hello here is yes, all right, OK. Goodnight is a greeting. Patois is commonly spoken.

Music is everywhere. There's no personal space away from it. The only time I haven't woken to the sounds of telly and reggae was when there was a power cut. The light didn't come on, so I listened and realised it was village wide. No one ever tells anyone to turn down the volume. My hosts have the radio and telly on at the same time. Music on the buses too, loud but often really great, fast, upbeat and lively Soca music – Sounds of Celebration!

Back to the countryside. The volcanic stuff is still active and so there are sulphur springs, hot water springs and a boiling lake, with a three-hour gruelling walk to it. But it was mind-blowing and the photos don't tell you it's noisy too! A big grey-yellow crater full of boiling muddy water with sulphur in the steam. I could have watched it for a week.

There's also a little hidden gorge that you can swim in. It is totally hidden. My guide (yes, another groper) just said, 'You swim through there.' So, I entered a passage, leaving the sunlit pool behind, turned the corner and found myself swimming in a one-swimmer-wide channel with high, high walls cut smoothly into undulating shapes by the water. The water was deep, black and cool. There was nothing to hold on to. All that was possible was to swim between these curtains of rock. High above, the rainforest cut out any sky that might have given light. The air was full of the rush of water from a fall at the far end. The whole thing is about a five-minute experience, but it brought me strangely close to my own mortality.

The chief crop here is bananas, but the US is now getting them from Central and South America so the market is depressed. Just as

Britain seems to be causing the closure of the sugar industry next year in St Kitts, so, I hear, the Americans are ditching Dominica. Funding here comes from Canada and Taiwan.

Victor comes today for just thirty hours, but just to see him for five minutes would be great. He couldn't get away at the weekend because of childcare arrangements not working out. But in the end that has been perfect. Next update from St Lucia or Barbados. I haven't decided. Life here is so changeable for me!

Love Juliet

A mad rush back, made the bed, put out fresh towels. Back to town for the hair colour because Caprice was late into work that morning and couldn't do it. Got purple nail varnish too. Then to the hotel where I was to pick up Mary-Lynn and boyfriend and off to the Carib Community. We passed the Emerald Pool without stopping, but the Community was a bit disappointing. Local people had stalls at the roadside selling products which didn't interest me either to look at or buy. A nearby place called the Steps had no more interest for me, it was just a dyke running out to sea and a rock that looked like a dog's head. My friends were happy to be dropped off at Marigot and I reached the airport at 5 p.m. Good timing to fix my face or whatever one does while waiting for a loved one to arrive! I had not made us a picnic – I just ran out of time. But I did get Victor a Guinness.

The plane touched down and I waited in a press of friends and relations at the exit swing door, while taxi drivers lounged and smoked nearby. The crowd thinned. Eventually only me and a few drivers. 'Everyone's through', someone ventured. 'Who are you waiting for?' said another. I began to wonder! One taxi driver tried his chances at picking me up, grr… I stood awkwardly, not knowing quite what to do, when out Victor shot. 'Hi guys, how you doing?' to the taxi men, and then he saw me and smiled. He looked very elegant in a black blazer and rather larger than life. As I had just started to make contingency plans for his non-arrival, some of the gloss had started to come off. I found myself partly enjoying the reunion and partly watching myself acting out a role.

I drove Victor to a beach and we sat on some logs, but I was very quiet. I felt a bit let down – why had he been the last out? He told me he had helped a woman with a child and then got in the wrong line at the passport control, but nothing he said could refuel the joy I had expected to feel. You know, the sink-into-his-arms feeling. I just felt distant, asking myself, is this what I want? I ached to feel differently.

However, sitting quietly calmed me and I began to relax and felt gradually more able to enjoy him. I explained it to myself that I had just been so caught up with preparations – will it happen or not? – and closing down emotionally with the guide, Vincent, that opening myself up to Victor was difficult.

We decided to eat locally at an acclaimed restaurant, Floral Gardens. I told Victor quietly about my experience with Charlie, the 'bus' driver, and the spontaneous orgasm and how upset I was. Victor took it in his stride – although later he did say that it had taxed him rather. The food was OK, the ambience lovely and the bill cheaper than the Sea Bird! I told him I would pay for everything on Dominica – he was my guest. We drove home and in the dark I could tell that the roads would be so pretty, but Victor had fallen asleep anyway.

I nudged him awake – we were home. Andrew and Gloria were in bed. Victor loved the house. He did some stretches and then we went to bed. We made love tenderly and then I cried with delight at having him so near to me. Physically, he is just so beautiful: a gentle sheen over his almost hairless skin, so slender, like a young man who hasn't yet filled out. I could not take my eyes off him.

Diary 12 June 2002

I wake and find we are touching from head to toe and I am a little underneath his shoulder. He wakes, turns and smiles at me, his big grin. He asks me if we can make love without a condom. No, I don't want him to have a nasty parting gift. In the future, if we are together, it would be different.

We go to Titou Gorge, to get there before anyone else. He is enthralled and says he will include it in the next part of the book.

The iguana tale that I have illustrated is the first book in a trilogy, held loosely together. Then into town. Caprice had wanted to meet Victor, but he was out; Ossie Savarin was in. I introduced Victor to Ossie and Victor spoke of promoting wrestling in Dominica and what actions Ossie would have to make to get the necessary funding. No one made notes so I wasn't sure whether anything would come of it or not. However, it was done.

We went on to have a bite to eat and I saw Julian in the restaurant having an altercation. None of it made any sense – what was the man on? I wanted to get a Hotmail account set up for Victor, but the Internet café computers were down. So we went to Champagne Beach. Victor hadn't brought his snorkel. Why on earth not? So I lent him mine, otherwise he could not have seen a thing. But it was not the same as sharing the magic of it together.

Somehow I felt frustrated with the day. I couldn't pot balls at pool, couldn't skim stones at Champagne, couldn't introduce Victor to Caprice, couldn't get him an Internet account and Ossie had seemed a little preoccupied. I got indigestion from the lunch – now that is unusual – so we went home. Victor liked Champagne Beach, so that was good. At home Victor gave me loads of little gifts. So we put fragrant shower gel on each other and enjoyed swilling it off. Later to the Sea Bird, and Victor still had to tell his employers that he would not be coming in to work the next day. We tried phones this way and that and then a collect call to Elmo, Victor's nice cousin who also works at the post office. He'll tell them. Good, that means no getting up before 5 a.m. to try to phone.

We came home and I packed. It felt a very turbulent time. Great with Victor, but changing islands added to the frustrations and challenges of the day. I needed my own quiet space to pack, and that conflicted totally with my wanting to give all my attention to Victor. But I did not want to stay on Dominica after Victor had gone. That felt very firmly fixed. He would leave early in the morning, I would take the car back and then sit on the beach till my afternoon flight.

We caressed, fondled and made love. It all just felt wonderful. He was my black knight. He said that he would give up smoking in the future, as part of a package of changes he will make with God. I was concerned about the amount of Guinness he could consume, but I'd said my piece about smoking, so that would do! I told him I might like to marry him in the future. Was that bold? It certainly surprised him a little, I think. But the longer this mini-holiday lasted the more I felt for him.

I asked him if, when I came to St Thomas I could live with him in his house. He felt not, because it would be hurtful to his ex-wife, and his older sons might have difficulty with it. That was all OK with me, just thought I'd ask, and it's often nice to give people the chance to rise to an unusual occasion rather than behave stereotypically.

Diary 13 June 2002

I love Victor dearly. We get up early, and I finish packing and before seven o'clock we're gone. We chat on the journey to the airport and it feels as if it won't be long before I see him again. I will make the stop over in St Thomas if it's not too expensive to add it into my itinerary. We have breakfast at the airport and off he goes. I am fortunate; I can leave my luggage at the airport for my afternoon flight. It's raining hard.

I leave the rent car behind, no damage (!), and walk out to the main Marigot road. A car stops – it is Charlie of orgasm fame. He takes me to Woodford Hill Beach but I refuse to let him join me on the beach. I sleep on the beach (it's stopped raining) and then swim. I feel advised to leave by 1 p.m. I see a most beautiful river I hadn't ever noticed before, catch a bus and I'm back at the airport. In the end it's time to go.

What a strange time this has been. I feel rather like a cat being swung around by the tail – the tail doesn't move much, but by the time you get to the head end it feels like a whirlwind is in charge. Dominica – a place of hurricanes. I certainly wasn't in the quiet eye of the storm. How much more of this can I manage? And yet, for change, this is where it is easiest – I want to change, I sure can have it! And now to St Lucia.

Chapter Seventeen

ST LUCIA

I slept on the short flight to St Lucia. Refreshed, I arrived at the airport and went to tourist information. Yet again, really helpful. They could tell me there was room at Alexander's, which Elie had recommended. I had a precious scrap of paper from her giving accounts of Good Places and tips for St Lucia and Tobago.

Alexander's was one road back from the beach and just perfect. It was just a room in a boarding house in a terrace of housing. By early evening I was on the beach and looking around. There were lots of people jogging and exercising on the white sand – now that was all new. Pollution and litter were present but not enough to be off-putting. When I walked along the streets people sitting out by their doors shouted to tell me that they loved my hair! They seemed open, joyous and enthusiastic; I felt very welcome and pleased to be there. It just felt much more relaxed. I realised that Rouseau was menacing – that's the word!

I phoned Victor to tell him I'd arrived and for the first time ever I caught fully what he said as he picked up the phone – I'd never fully heard it before: 'Praise the Lord, good evening!' Spent $40 EC on the call – money well spent!

Came home and fell asleep – woke at 5 a.m. to find both the fan and light still on. I could hardly say that the short flight the previous day had exhausted me, but perhaps the journey through life in Dominica had.

Next morning my host gave me a lift to Rodney Marina for a trip out. The trip was on a replica tall ship (later used in the *Pirates of the Caribbean* film). Sharon, the captain's wife, and I had a chat – she had a bad back. Both husband and wife talked to me about the negative energy their partner held! The husband agreed to massage my back.

There were mainly British tourists on the boat. I was acutely aware of English accents; I had become so used to American and Caribbean English that this was a real surprise. Do I sound like that too? I supposed I must! Another new thing: they all carried frowns on their faces. If for nothing else, because of the glare of the sun. But they looked a sad, unhealthy bunch and very insular – did they see beyond their navels? I suspected it was a cheap package holiday that was being promoted in the UK since Americans were not travelling anywhere.

The boat sailed along the coast with a crew of men agilely attending to the sails, then stopped so we could disembark at Soufriere and go to 'a drive-in volcano'. The town looked interesting – a large, open-sided market building dominated the square with lots of local people just sitting around. It had a lovely, colourful feel to it. The coach headed out of town to the volcano. Well, I like volcanic stuff – but drive-in? It all seemed a bit tame, with handrails and notices not to get too near, but the sulphur banks were impressive and the smell of sulphur was liberal and there were boiling ponds and a guide. After that, the insatiable crowd was taken to the Botanic Gardens and waterfalls, but there was a mineral pool and so I chose to do that instead. I could see other people pulling away from the group to do the same, but the flock mentality took over and I had the mineral water bath to myself. Back on the ship. Lunch, snorkel, swim, souvenir photo keyring – mine was the only one with purple hair. Good trip, but I certainly felt aloof and distant. Maybe the bit about Pluto making people feel uneasy with you made them wary – and my being alone. Most were families. I still missed Hawaii's youth hostels that help you to tag along with someone else. But then Pluto isn't about easy friendship. Loneliness could be experienced, the book had said.

Later, I returned to Gros Islet and to Alexander's Guest House, my home. I washed my clothes and watched a lovely sunset. Had a couple of hours in bed because there was a 'jump up' that night – music and dancing. Right there, on my doorstep! At 10 p.m. the crowd had yet to swell, so I walked around and got the measure of it. There was a makeshift stage for live bands, lots of stalls already trading their food successfully. I stood around and felt a bit peripheral when Janet and Theresa befriended me and we all warded off men together and had an amusing time. They were friends from Milton Keynes and in their twenties. We told the men we were married, which was nice because the girls could have said I was their mother! The crowd was a mixture of young white tourists and local people all mingling together and having a good time. But on the edge was a darker scene of young men lounging in the shadow, beyond the festive lights, listening to very heavy bass-noted techno. Not everyone seemed in festive spirits. Janet and Theresa left about 2 a.m. and so I did too. We exchanged email addresses. They wanted to know how I got on.

The next phone call I made to Victor. Grace answered: she's Victor's ex-wife. She had answered before but I was always quite quick at asking to speak to Victor. After all, these were international calls. This time she stayed on the line. She sounded really American and told me effusively how much she liked the paintings I had made for Victor's book. I had given Victor the finished set while he was in Dominica. She was very impressed by the consistency of my work – well, I was limited in techniques so they all did have the same character. I felt a bit uneasy about her generous words, not being sure what she would think if she knew all! Maybe she did, maybe she did not, I didn't know. Living with a divorced partner can't be easy, even though there is childcare to consider.

As I wanted to go to St Thomas before heading off to my next line I had hoped to stay with him. Although Victor had given the word no to that, he might have compromised if I agreed to stay as a guest – and did not sleep with him. We would see! I believe in rocking the boat sometimes!

I remember hearing – years later – of a mistress telephoning her lover's wife and saying, 'May I borrow your husband, for a while?' It led to divorce, but I was always captivated by the audacity of the mistress, when mistresses are expected to be discreet. When I heard of this break with tradition my only thoughts were: Wow, now that takes panache! 'Borrow', and just 'for a while'. I would never have thought of doing that!

I really wanted to see Victor as far away as possible from holiday mode. In 'real life' he might be boring and mundane – but I did not know. We'd had our honeymoon (St Croix) but I still hadn't met the 'everyday' man. I had to know, or at least that was how I felt then.

The next day, I walked up the coast to Pigeon Island, linked by a causeway to St Lucia. Nice walk, with lots of flowering trees, nice snorkel, nice expensive breakfast. I phoned the airline – not Victor this time. I changed my LIAT flight to the Sunday evening so I got another full day in St Lucia. It was not really the best solution for me because I like to arrive early in the day with relaxed time for finding accommodation. I've always had a thing about getting settled before nightfall. But seeing the St Lucia sights on Elie's list and also having seen Victor out of Dominica would mean that some comforts must go – and daylight arrival was it. I tried to change my main ticket too – to include the stop in St Thomas – but that would have to wait till I got to the American Airlines office in Barbados. No problem, it could wait. I wanted to fly from Trinidad, then to San Juan and on to St Thomas and stay there, moving to Miami a few days later, all flying American Eagle. By phone, they weren't sure what excess I must pay. It almost felt as if it were a discretionary system so I was hoping they would be lenient with me. But money grows on trees, and so if they charge highly, they do! (My mother used to caution me that money doesn't grow on trees, but then I went to live in Crete where olive trees give the cash crop.)

After that, I was on the bus to Castries and to Soufriere with its market square. My hosts were not sure that at midday I would have time to go all the way to Soufriere, but we would see. Well, I did it, nearly! It was a long hot journey and I kept falling asleep on the bus. I got off the bus before Soufriere to visit Anse Chastanet. It looked a steep and tricky road down to the beach, but then I was informed that there was a water taxi. I was shown lots of small boats in a rocky crevice and off I went to Chastanet. Lots of barracudas, and the water was lovely and clear with lots of fish and corals – it was a real joy. A gentle swell just added to the fun. A guy came up to me at the end and said he loved my hair, nothing more. Then I was back out on the road to catch the bus back at 4.30 p.m. The last bus connection at Castries to Gros Islet was 3.30 p.m., so I knew I had missed that one. Something would turn up. Well, it was actually after 6 p.m. before a bus did come to take me back to Castries and then it broke down – but a spark plug did the trick and away we went again. We got to Castries at 7.30 p.m. and I headed straight to the Cultural Arts Centre. I had seen a calypso evening advertised.

The calypso was due to start at 8 p.m. except it did not. It said 8.30 p.m. on the ticket, then it was late, so another wait! This was island speed, and my being there for just a few days trying to pack things in jarred against that. Well, that was OK. I still did not know how I would get back at the end of the evening, but never mind – something would show.

I sat on my own in the auditorium. It was not packed. There were many more women than men. Women came together; men came only with their wives. The music was good and the evening was star-studded with a raunchy, busty and comical lady MC. Every song featured a new artiste until 10.45 p.m. when there was intermission. I decided that I'd be pushing it to stay longer, so I left and yes, I found a bus stop. Lots of folk waiting – great! There could be no loneliness in that crowd. We all seemed to be exuberant.

Home to bed: a cockroach landed on me at 5 a.m. I got up and put it outside.

Diary 16 June 2002

My last day. I had ticked off the things that Elie had suggested on St Lucia and might have even slept in the same bed as her! I shook out all my belongings. No cockroaches would travel free. Instead I had ants in my case. By 9.15 a.m. I was out, leaving my bags till later and going off with Sam (the captain of the tall ship) and Sharon. We went to the beach at the very south end of Rodney Bay. I snorkelled for ages. It was an informal little spot, with just an empty shack for shade and the sea was clear and calm and the fish profuse. All in all, a good place to be!

★

I gave Sharon healing to her back in a beach shack where we were snorkelling. She visualised other colours than the colours I was directed to give from the angels. Don't know what that meant. It might have been a fear-based response. I gave her green/blue for her lower back strength and a feeling of peace for her upper back. She was tired.

I went to a restaurant – all that fasting was over – and Sam and Sharon went home. After I had eaten Sam returned and he did some work on my back – it was hugely better but always appreciated a bit of attention. Then Sam suggested we went to his ship where he had oils and could give me a proper massage. Well, he had been a perfect gentleman so I agreed. The massage, however, was a little intimate and I had to warn him off, but it was nice that I didn't get roused. I never feel I can blame a man for trying, as long as 'no' is heeded.

I got home and had time to kill. I was uneasy about getting to Barbados so late, yet I was glad I'd stayed for the treatment. So, at 5 p.m., I was sitting on the beach with reggae music blaring out from local vans parked up by the beach. I was sick of it blasting out everywhere. It was like graffiti – unwanted and unasked for, just imposed. I mused over something Sam said he could do: astral travel. By that he meant that he would read a book and find (like me) that he would fall asleep. The instructions were to be on the edge of sleep and go quickly to bed and imagine turning to the side and propping yourself up on one elbow. Next, look down at yourself as if you were tied to your body by a mere cord and then go to visit someone. Just go!

I thought I might try it sometime, but for the time being I cast it to memory. At that moment I was still so full of lunch that I would be grounded! Island time and I was hanging around.

I hoped the Barbados tourist information office would be open when I arrived. I wanted somewhere cheap near Fitts Village, where my cousin's daughter would be staying with her émigré father and family. Back to snorkelling and I was looking for sea horses, but I did not find any. I'm told that they live on one piece of sea grass all their lives – I hope they do astral travel. Some children came up – they were bored so they decided to beg. It was a form of entertainment and you could tell that by their approach. No, said I, but they were really quite pushy – another sign that it was a form of entertainment.

Eventually, I made it to the airport – I was off!

So, how about Pluto on St Lucia? I always felt confident that all would work out, as if I have had so much life experience that nothing could worry me any more. I had been touring around so fast that Pluto seemed to have given me full rein to move around the island at top pace. Constant change. Other than that Pluto seemed to have gone behind a cloud, a little out of sight. I could, of course, expect to find that Pluto could be changeable too.

Chapter Eighteen

BARBADOS THE PLUTO PLUS

One of the features about A★C★G that I may not have mentioned to you is that the lines of planets on the Midheaven and Imum Coeli are straight, going pole to pole, whereas lines on the Ascendant and Descendant are curving, so there are places where lines cross. These intersections have an effect all around the world at the precise latitude where the cross occurs. So, for example, say your Venus Ascendant (curving) crossed your Mars Midheaven at a point on the Equator you would feel the effect of that all along the Equator. So, the guidebook describes what effects the various crossing lines have. When I was back in Miami and planning which islands to visit I had noted that there were other lines intersecting and had pencilled them in on the map of the Caribbean Islands in my *Frommer's* guide. Then I forgot all about them.

The flight out of St Lucia was quiet and I arrived in Barbados looking forward to seeing my cousin's daughter and possibly other family members on her father's side whom I had never met before.

I arrived at the airport in Barbados and at Immigration Control I could already see the tourist information office – great! So, when the uniformed official asked where I would be staying, I pointed to the office and said, 'If you give me a moment I'll go and get somewhere to stay and then come back.' As she was allowing me through Immigration Control I had to leave my passport with her. That was OK, quite normal. Yes, I got accommodation, inland, not too far from Fitts Village, and, smiling, I returned to the desk. It was all going so well. The immigration officer immediately pointed at me. 'You,' she glowered; 'Go to the immigration office over there.' A large finger swung around and jerked to a halt in front of a glass-fronted office. OK, so where was my passport? In the office. What was going on? There was my luggage with its thirty-eight diamonds and other assorted stones going around on the carousel and I couldn't get to it! (Why do I never think to pack my jewellery in my handbag?).

Once in the office I could see my passport on the desk. A trim, moustached man in khakis was behind the desk, engaged in casual conversation. No one else off my flight was here – just me. I strode up to take the passport – that stops the casual conversation dead. I now had the passport in my hand. I was told to sit down. 'No,' I said, 'I don't want to, I want to get my luggage and get to my accommodation.' I also had a small backpack on my shoulders which I would have had to take off in order to sit. I remained standing. The order was repeated and I burst out laughing. The khakis moved to one side and told another official to lock the door. I turned round and all eyes were on me, full of suspicion. I was not getting this right. 'Why was I in Barbados?' asked khakis. 'I'm on holiday!' I smiled. 'You're not on holiday!' roared khakis.

This was getting beyond a joke, but I was doing my best. Many other questions followed at which I became a little nettled, but if they wanted to take so much interest in me I would put up with it. But my luggage would by then have been vulnerable: the only case on the carousel, or by then in the boot of someone's car! How much money had I, what did I propose to do there, where was my onward ticket? Well… if you let me get my suitcase, I tittered. I think mine must have been the last plane in for the night because I noticed the man at the door glance at his watch. That seemed to decide for them it was time to let me go. I was a total mixture of indignation at their impertinence, vulnerability because they were in charge, anxiety about my suitcase and hilarity at the officiousness I had just had to contend with. At least I had found somewhere to stay, so that was all that mattered. They unlocked the door and I went back to the immigration official, who then without a word but with a look that could kill, let me pass. Oh good! My suitcase was still there!

I got a taxi, with a lovely driver, and felt to have arrived. My home-away-from-home was a room in a family house where I was introduced to all the family who were present: Brenda, Arthur, with children Camille, Johanna, Frances and Herbie, all living at Clearview Heights.

I slept well between sheets with religious slogans mixed with a sky of pretty pastel shades, clouds and rainbows. 'The Lord is my shepherd.' All was well.

The following morning I wrote to Victor and sent him one of the two photo souvenir key rings from the tall ship in St Lucia. I looked at it critically: my smile and my purple hair were keenly evident. My neck would have looked better ten years before, not helped by my losing weight in Dominica.

Brenda, my host, gave me a lift into Bridgetown so that I could go to the American Airlines office and enquire about the change in my ticket so I could return to St Thomas before plunging off to Rio and out of the Caribbean altogether. I felt a little keyed up. How would it go?

American Airlines told me they could not help me because one of my later flights was run by LanChile, so they sent me off to phone LanChile to see if that were possible. Well, you know me with telephones. Cable & Wireless got it in the neck again. I wasted $60 Barbados and still hadn't managed the transaction. I was pretty sore by then. No amount of telling myself it was all OK could compete with the edginess I felt. I heard myself virtually screaming at the staff in the telephone office and at the same time I felt pretty close to tears and, finally, I was slightly relishing the fiasco. I did find out that the LanChile flight was a joint flight with American Airlines and so there had been no need for them to tell me that they did not know what availability there was.

I headed back to the American Airlines office rather indignantly, but by then all their computers were down. I really was champing at the bit to tear a strip off them for causing me so much of a problem with LanChile. But I knew that they worked in offices, lived in houses with phones, and for them making a phone call was easy. They'd think me mad if I made a scene. And I had started to realise what I wanted might have a discretionary ruling – people just don't seem to make big changes to their round-the-world tickets – and I did not want to find I was getting a punitive deal in order to get a troublemaker out of their office. I had to sit sweetly while tears of frustration welled up in my eyes. Oh, why couldn't I just behave sensibly like everyone else? Why did I feel as if I had been pulled through a prickly bush? My body inexplicably hurt all over. I fidgeted and kept asking the staff if they had any news. I felt my finances and my ability to see Victor again rested with them, not me. I could hardly breathe; I was on the edge of tears. At the same time, the financial tension should really have been no worse than you might feel listening to lottery numbers being drawn – have I won this week? But my stomach kept knotting.

I looked back over the time I had been there: the immigration office, telephone office, LanChile, post office (massive queue to post Victor's letter and memento), American Airlines. Computers down, the throwaway camera had a light leak and I had lost a load of pictures – not for the first time. I had arrived in town at 8.30 a.m. and by 1.30 p.m. I had achieved nothing that mattered. I had been abrupt with anyone who wanted my attention. Want a taxi? I gritted my teeth. But some things had gone all right since I arrived: tourist information, a good taxi driver and finding a new home. So I went for a light lunch and got a headache. Not surprising, the way I felt that day! I took a walk around town. It was quite nice but I had no appetite for it and no desire to take photos with yet another disposable camera. When I asked about vegetarian food at the little shacks, no one understood what I wanted and I got frustrated. I decided a hunger strike was called for.

Eventually, things got sorted in the American Airlines offices and I could stop over in St Thomas between Trinidad and Miami – and it would not cost me an arm and a leg! I was truly grateful to them, but I could not wait to get away and out of town – away from all the frustration and a whirlwind of mixed feelings and torment.

By 5 p.m. I was on my way home on the bus, where I met Camille, one of the daughters of the household. She was quiet but at least her presence made sure that I would get off the bus at the right stop and get between the bus stop and the house without mishap.

I sat on the bed and could not wait to get out the A★C★G information. Whatever was the matter? I noticed immediately that there were some intersecting lines at about the latitude I was on:

Mars and Saturn and Mars and Mercury. Where was the book, what did it say? Oh, it's impossible to live there! Of Mars and Saturn: one of the least desirable places to live with suppression of the masculine which leaves you open for victimisation, violence, cruelty and sadism. Others take their frustrations out on you. In turn you seek out others lower than yourself to vent your rage. Well, that explained a lot! Mars and Mercury: there is rudeness, coarseness, some maliciousness and a tendency to sarcasm and cutting wit. Nervousness maybe extreme, painful sensitivity – and yet effective (yes, I did get the ticket). You criticise and are criticised. This area is best avoided by those not already calm and self-possessed. And here was I coming into this with Pluto and Dominica still on my tail!

I closed the book and sat on my bed, quiet and small. Maybe if I did not move nothing would happen, but in fact I realised that it was only with authority that I had a problem. All the casual one-to-one arrangements had gone smoothly. So, I lifted off the bed and went in to see the family. They had a computer and I could do my email update, but not before spending time with Brenda's friend Sybil (also my mother's name) who said that she found me fun to be with. Not many people would have agreed with that around those parts!

Email to friends 17 June

Dear Friends

Firstly, I am forty-nine next 3 July and I have an address for an actual birthday card, if you wish to send one! I shall be back in St Thomas USVI by then. I go there 24 June and leave 4 July, if I can get away!

Well, lots of little things about Dominica still.

The countryside: Volcanic hills, so walking is very steep and if there are no trails it's not possible to walk because of dense vegetation. Other aspects of the volcano: a boiling lake with clouds of sulphur fumes, hot and cold springs and little baths in the village of

Soufriere that I made my home. The cold water spring tasted of fruit. The whole village smelt of sulphur and fruit – fresh and acidic fruit, ripe fruit and decaying earthy fruit smells, like wine fermenting. It's pretty heady stuff. There are so many waterfalls all with neat swimming areas below, with water thundering down. Titou was another great find. This is a narrow gorge, just wide enough for one person to swim through, which caused me to have life and death feelings. At the end is a strong gushing waterfall and the water is deep, dark and cold. I took four other people there because otherwise they would have visited it on the same day as seeing the boiling lake. The two are not possible in the same day. Both blow your mind and you would never recover from a joint trip. I took Victor there too and it has cemented a new book for him to write. Other volcanic activity is in Champagne Bay where gas bubbles escape from the seabed in steady streams. So, so beautiful. I took Victor there too!

People: Well, other than the near daily sexual harassment which ruined the countryside for me, I stayed with Gloria and Andrew, two great people whom I met through their son, Larry Love. A nickname of course. Larry uses one of the local sayings that I find slightly disconcerting: What's happening? What's going on? Meaning: How're things going? People carry things on their heads here. I gave a lift to a woman carrying a gas cylinder for the stove on her head. You know, the size you can't even lift. Absolutely neck crushing.

Money: Folk are poor. Civil servants aren't being paid at the moment: the government has no money, I hear.

Victor's visit: Well, I had told him not to come because I was so fed up with Dominican men that I would leave. Then I rented a car and found two people to share with and the whole experience turned round. Victor came for only thirty-six hours, but it was wonderful to see him. He had to leave from the distant airport and at a different time of day from me. I decided once I had waved goodbye to Victor to remain at a beach by the airport until my flight left. On the way, a taxi driver picked me up – and I knew him! This time I warded him off with ease and felt I had closed the door on the bad experiences.

Hair: It is now short and purple.

I left and went for a three day visit to St Lucia. Very built up, more like St Thomas with shopping malls and so on. Very wealthy after Dominica. There are even white lines in the roads! A little manicured for my taste, however. The wilds of Dominica did so suit me. Got lots done in St Lucia in the way of sight-seeing, mainly by going on a boat trip and then making friends with its skipper, and I did some healing on his wife. I, in turn, got a massage from him. So, volcanoes again, great snorkelling, hot baths, calypso music and a nice hotel. Cheap and cheerful, if in need of a lick of paint.

Barbados, where I am now – well it is another story!

Photos soon.

Love, Juliet

Diary 18 June 2002

On top of it all, my period started today – a week early. Wonder why, but at least it might clear the way for a period-free time with Victor in St Thomas, hopefully.

Off to town to send photos out to friends, phoned Annie – my cousin's daughter – no avail. Phoned Victor – short but sweet. He was in a meeting.

Caught a bus to Bottom Bay, a very lovely little bay with rocks (cliffs even) enclosing it. White sand, turquoise water, palm trees, but sea too rough for me to swim. A man came by touting coconuts, but I told him they were too expensive. But we sat and talked and he didn't try it on with me. He's a proper Rastaman and we talked of doing good and forgiving ourselves. He said he'd give me a coconut for being so nice so I stayed his hand and paid him what he'd first asked for. I tell you; outside of authority I can handle things!

Back in town and I bought things to make a nut roast for the family tonight. They'll eat it tomorrow, but I'll eat a piece myself today.

I enjoyed cooking and the nut roast was quite nice, not star but eating helped to clear away my period headache. Victor phoned and told me how much I had helped him with the Dominica wrestling connection. He's so generous in his praise of me. Still no word from Annie. It seems as if I have lost touch with her. I've phoned and emailed her, but nothing happens. And I only came here to see her! Tomorrow is my last day here.

Diary 19 June 2002

At 6 a.m. I'm up and packing. Need to watch the clock – it's a leaving day! All done by 8 a.m. – a little breakfast, then off to Mullins Beach. The bus journey is nice along a lovely road behind the beachfront villas with verdant gardens. Exotic trees overhanging the road. Though for me, it's a bit manicured. The beach is nice, though so early in the morning (9 a.m.) the snorkelling is only fair. Midday is always best because the sunlight does not filter through the water at an angle. The low sun filters through sand particles in the sea like sun through pub windows, picking up the blue cloud from smokers and airborne dust particles. So visibility isn't what *Frommer's* said. How I ache for the clear conditions of Anegada – a place almost totally ignored by *Frommer's*!

Worse still, by 11 a.m water sports have started. Jet skis roam and zoom this way and that. There's skiing and paragliding. Time to leave. How can one snorkel and swim safely with all of that? I walk into Speightstown, a small seaside town, part of the coastal ribbon development. Still no news from Annie, though I now notice that I had a sketch of an address, but I would still want to know that she would be in before going. I telephone Victor, not in, but I leave a lovely message – can't wait to see him! No other person touches the sides [this is a metaphor for when you take a drink and gulp it down in thirst, rather than relishing the taste – it doesn't touch the sides]. Victor is it. He touches the sides.

Looking for lunch and food is the usual problem. Found a veggie café eventually, but too late. I've already eaten some nonsense elsewhere. Starting to rain. I head for a library and Internet café – one last chance to see if Annie has written. No. Well, that's that. Three days in Barbados have been enough to last me a lifetime. 'One of the least desirable places to be' – yes, I would agree. And without A★C★G I could choose somewhere like this for a holiday!

Bus back to Clearview Heights and Brenda is in. She talks to me, confiding that she does all the work and her husband hasn't worked since an illness years ago, even though he's fully recovered. She's really not happy about it. What can I do? Well, get a taxi, say goodbye to her and my lovely religious sheets and head off. Get on the plane and as I board I see the moon – always a good omen I feel!

★

Annie, I found out later had changed her telephone number, but I was glad not to have seen her, with me in such a state. Really, I was a bag of nerves. Not exactly a holiday asset! At my leisure, later, I looked even more carefully at the A★C★G information. Not only did I have Pluto with changes, miracles, life-death issues, intolerance of authority – and incidentally, loneliness, which would exacerbate sexual needs (a possible explanation for my spontaneous orgasm on the beach in Dominica) I also had the two crossings specific to Barbados, and there was also Venus to contend with. Venus, my old friend from Hawaii. This time

Venus on the Midheaven, not the Ascendant. The Midheaven has only a few strands that I could see as having influenced me in Barbados: I would be rather passive, have a pre-occupation with money, be identified by how I get what I want, and other people would see me as I would like to be seen – and Sybil had thought I was fun. How charming!

Chapter Nineteen

TRINIDAD AND TOBAGO

On to Tobago: still with Venus in Midheaven nestling next to Pluto. But the two intersecting lines were gone. What a difference from Barbados! Immigration wished me a pleasant stay, no one searched my bags and it was sweet. Outside the airport and away in a taxi to the guest house I had been recommended, by Elie, but it was inexplicably closed. The second was a little expensive. My taxi driver suggested a third (called Surfside, though the way the driver pronounced it I thought it was Suicide!) and in the foyer there was a photo of Sathya Sai Baba, the holy man in India I go to see! I was in clover. The hotel is a Sai Baba centre and I enjoyed singing sacred songs with a group of devotees there and giving a talk on my experience of India. None of them had been, but the aura of Baba was so present!

I went on a glass-bottom boat trip and snorkelled and did a walk to a waterfall with an English guide. The waterfall was not a patch on anything in Dominica, not helped by heavy rain that had turned the waterfall pool to an unappetising brown colour. My guide amused me. I told him of the problems I had encountered in Dominica and added that I had cancelled my visit to Grenada because that was said to be even worse. My guide told me he had taken two young women out on a trip and their comment about Grenada had been, 'We get out of bed in the morning, open the door and find two black men ready to put us back.' Glad I avoided that one!

We called at a patisserie and the accent of the French owner was so fabulously French that I was truly charmed. Only social constraints stopped me from begging for at least a kiss – if not a lifetime with this (married) man! A touch of Venus.

Dear Friends

Tobago. The island is pretty. There are some built-up areas, some really nice mountainous zones and reasonable snorkelling. The main town, Scarborough, however, is the ugliest place I have ever seen. They say that the money for refurbishment after hurricane damage went missing, leaving the town a monstrosity of crumbling, unfinished concrete structures and cobbled-together wrecks from a hurricane. Buildings have no-go danger zones around them for fear of falling masonry. They are partially fenced and weed-strewn. This, combined with broken masonry mixed with corrugated sheeting to hold the whole (hole?) together, does not make for a pretty sight. In fact, it was pretty depressing. However it furnished me with a pair of pink shoes to replace the pair that were nearly falling apart on my feet.

Bus services are diabolical and timetabling incomprehensible. One choice of beach excursion was made purely on the basis of which bus was available in the ever-so-grey bus station. There were the usual frustrations over phones. I'm now well travelled in this area, but it still gets to me!

My hosts at Surfside looked after me so well, feeding me a wonderful Indian dinner because I couldn't get vegetarian food locally and taking me into Scarborough to buy shoes. In the end, they paid for them too! Two-for-the-price-of-one, but I needed only one pair so I asked my host to choose a pair too – but then she insisted on paying for them!

I made more female friends than male and had less harassment than usual.

The ride wasn't smooth here, but neither was it rough either, just another slightly difficult holiday location for me. For example, on a glass-bottom boat trip we were issued with plastic sandals and asked to wade across the reef to see fish and coral. Our guide turned over broken coral to release detritus which the fish then greedily consumed. Everywhere else in the Caribbean there had been notices to say don't touch/damage the coral, and here we were given shoes to walk on it! I had my fins and mask so I was able to avoid joining in, but I was heartbroken to see damage so thoughtlessly done to the corals. It made me feel a loner in the company of heedless tourists.

Bye for now, Juliet

On the last day and feeling a bit beached out, I met Anne and we had a lovely day at her brother's house, out of the sun and humidity and often very grey sky (a feature of Tobago that June was the grey sky). I was even able to practise my massage. I wished I'd met them before.

I was trying to find a way of getting more time in Trinidad. I wanted to see the asphalt lake I had been told about years before. But my flight got in at 7.30 p.m. (from Tobago) and left at 7 a.m. No matter how I tried to perm it nothing could be done, without huge changes that meant flying to Miami to get to St Thomas. I began to feel it must be OK and intended that I only did an overnight stay. My hosts at Surfside gave me a contact in Trinidad and Anne and her brother took me to the airport. I left Tobago airport with the shine of a near full moon, always a good omen!

To Trinidad and just an overnight stay ending my mad dash to make room for a sojourn to St Thomas to be in the bosom of my loved one before heading out of the area altogether – or not!

I arrived in Trinidad, thanking LIAT for their good handling of me down the Caribbean and with the moon still shining, to find a six-foot-eight-tall man, Alston Griffiths, waiting for me with a big old romantic yellow-and-white convertible Cadillac. What else would it be with Venus involved? He was the tallest man I'd ever seen! Maybe the tall dark stranger of fairy tales. He took me off to a guest house which was a real haven, Alicia's Guest House, a green oasis of tropical trees with swimming pool, jacuzzi and intimate gardens in the middle of a built-up area. I had no idea where I was in the island and had no desire to venture out and leave this idyll. Above the gently lit garden tree canopy I raised my eyes and saw grey, featureless buildings ascending in the gloom to the sky. They seemed just a negative to the positive of this garden.

I sat on the pool side and read my book, *Autobiography of a Yogi*. The chapter covered his leaving India for the USA and what a wrench that was. Tears filled my eyes and I cried quietly because I felt this was a preparation for me to leave St Thomas (and Victor) to travel to South America. My journey felt inevitable. There was still no feeling within me that it would be right to stay. In fact the very thought of staying caused me almost to panic, even though at another level I would have rejoiced to give up the travel, throw in the A★C★G towel and to have seen what life with Victor would bring. It would be December before I could see him again in Cape Town – a long time away and without any guarantees! A phone call to Victor caused a change in my emotions to show a secret smile of knowing that I would see him in less than twenty-four hours now. But still I was wistful.

I felt very still and continued to marvel at the beauty of the space I had come to. The hotel continually delighted me by its beautiful intimate little garden spaces: secluded and charming – and filled with the sounds of gently running water. It felt a wonderful, peaceful time and space. This haven of boundless beauty felt almost as if I had been given the stillness and poise of someone about to make an Olympic-class dive off the very top board. Inside my head, you could have heard a pin drop.

The whirlwind tour down the islands came to an end and at 4 a.m. I was up and whisked away by my tall driver, leaving Trinidad as I had arrived: under cover of darkness.

Later I discovered that my Venus on the Midheaven line runs really close to Trinidad, even closer than the Pluto line. The A★C★G book says of the line: 'Other people come to see you as you like to see yourself. Lifestyle is crucial here and you enjoy more, and more obviously than most people.'

I did enjoy more, and more obviously, than most people would. Even as I sat being nourished by the gardens I had been aware that my response was extreme.

Diary 24 June 2002

Awoke a little before the alarm. Showered – all excited. Pack. Taxi comes: Alston Griffiths again, all six-foot-eight of him. He is really nice and the journey goes easily. I buy lots of duty free – brandy (Victor's request) and perfume for both of us. Is that a lot? And I buy *Conversations with God Book One* and a full copy of *Autobiography of a Yogi* – mine had some pages missing.

I'm so pleased to be seeing Victor again and I shall stay with him till 10 July by the looks of things, but then I must go. But I shall ask Victor to come to South Africa. Cape Town, Venus on the Descendent – the most likely place to find a man to marry! I had thought to end my trip there when I was planning. After all, what better way to finish your travels than to settle down with someone? And I didn't want to get there too soon otherwise, hey, why have a year-long ticket and travel plan?

The flight to San Juan was very cold: a slow turbo prop flight, so slow, about two and a half hours. No food on the flight. Landed in San Juan – to a row in immigration. Lots of questions and a private interview for which I had to wait – or was expected to wait. However, I spied a box of complaints forms and started to fill one in. All of a sudden I was at the head of the queue and ushered into a private office. There I was asked why I had certain slips of paper that the immigration officer had found tucked into the plastic cover to my passport. It appeared that you're supposed to hand in these slips of paper, given to you on entry to US territory, when you leave. I had just collected them. No one ever asked for them so they accumulated. It was spelled out to me very clearly that it was my responsibility to hand them in, even if they weren't asked for. It all seemed petty and ridiculous, but I agreed to do so in the future – and off I went. What a difference to my immigration fracas in Barbados. Although I still thought it was heavy-handed, none of the really difficult stuff repeated itself now I was away from the Mars/Sun and Mars/Mercury crossing points. I was quite grateful for the event to just point up the difference.

Chapter Twenty

ST THOMAS RE-VISITED

Diary 24 June 2002 (continued)

Got to St Thomas. No Victor until I had cleared baggage and I was looking for him – but the flight had arrived a little early, so forgiveness was in the air. Then I found him with his arms around the necks of two shorter guys, approaching the bar. They were garrulous, animated and laughing. I made to surprise Victor, but at the last moment he turned and spotted me. I was so pleased to see him – dizzy and delirious. So happy.

We went immediately by car to a guest house. I thought he had been looking for a more permanent home for himself since he had said he would like to move away from his ex-wife. We'll address that one later. Went out to Lindbergh Bay for lunch. A full circle as I had first met him there. Then back to the guest house room with a view overlooking all of the town of Charlotte Amalie – without being a part of it.

We made love, took a shower, talked and showed our total affection for each other. I told him I would still go on my travels, though I couldn't conceive of it at that moment. But by the tenth of July I must go – though my ticket I had changed to fly out on the fourth, not the tenth.

Eventually things had to be done so we went out: a phone call to Victor's daughter's boyfriend, buy food and go to ATM to pay for the room.

Back to bed and each time we made love I cried with happiness and anguish at the thought of leaving and the past stresses of waiting through the grey sky days and Barbados difficulties to see him.

Victor got up at 3 a.m. to take his daughter's boyfriend to work. I expected him back about fourish and lay there warm and waiting.

Diary 25 June 2002

Time flows by – so far through June already! I feel I have no idea how that happens, how time passes. Do I live enough in the now?

I decide that as it's Victor's day off today I'll stay in bed till late rather than try to live to his early work hours and get up so early. Victor's day off is precious to me. I wake out of a deep sleep and it's 6 a.m. No Victor. I drift in and out of sleep. I have felt uncomfortable that he hasn't told his family what he is doing but he called them last night, so at least they will not worry for his safety.

★

Eventually I got up and about, had breakfast, paid for the room and started to feel fed up that I didn't know where Victor was. I started to feel sore, so I decided to go to St John for the day to have a look at a shop to buy binoculars and a camera. I knew this meant that I would not see him all day. I felt bruised.

At 9.15 a.m. I pulled a Medicine Card. It said be patient, live in the now. I sat and wrote my diary and waited because, of course, I wanted to spend my day with Victor, but I don't like waiting. If he was going to have a secretive nature, this relationship was going to be pretty short-lived, that was for sure!

Maybe he went home, I did not know, but by 11 a.m. I was on the ferry to St John wondering why I had just spent $500 US for seven days bed and breakfast. The living beyond my means idea still called for Victor to pay his half, but I had noticed the only things in the room that were his were the presents I gave him and a toothbrush. Would he come back at all? I left a note for him in the room to say: 'I might go to St John. Back later. J X.' Then I added in little letters: 'Never ever do this again.' I wasn't sure that this was a good idea, but it was done! I knew that evening he coached a wrestling team and I did not know what time that finished.

When I got to St John I phoned his home number and Grace said he was out, but I also heard his young son shout 'Dad', in summons, as Grace spoke to me. So, I suspected that he went home and maybe the balloon went up because he had deceitfully not told them anything and they had found out in the worst possible way. So Grace was upset and wasn't giving me a friendly reception. He probably had it in the neck from them – and he would from me too – if he came back. Maybe he would decide to call the whole thing off, leaving me free to travel immediately to Rio de Janeiro. Maybe he just went to work on an impulse. What ever it was, it would not do! I would not have it happen again. I didn't want to spend my time thinking things over in this way, double guessing!

Was it fear that made him like this? He was an Aries and so could be a bit selfish and thoughtless to others – but this much thoughtless? My eye spanned the horizon. Pluto on the Ascendant makes me selfish too. Would it have been better to stay in St Thomas that day? Had I cut off my nose to spite my face by going somewhere where we would not meet? However, if I'd stayed in St Thomas I would have been too miserable to paint. I had come to St John and injured both my legs on corals but at least I had a new camera and binoculars, and done little chores. But still I felt let down. Live in the now – I was getting sunburnt!

I was one person on Honeymoon Beach having a day of torment. By 5 p.m. I was heading out and my film had been developed and printed. I would send the prints to my mother, as always. I picked up my new camera and binoculars and headed out on the 6 p.m. ferry to Red Hook. As I walked up the hill to Island View Guest House some kind soul gave me a lift.

Note from Victor of apology. Yes, it said: Never again. He would be in about 8 p.m. Well, 8.25 p.m. to be precise. I had been packing. We were moving hotel room and if necessary I was packing in case I moved out altogether, if I stayed in this mood.

I felt wretched. My feelings of love had totally evaporated, leaving just a feeling of disappointment because a romantic moment (his day off) had been swept away. Victor came in and got it in the neck. I just couldn't free myself from the cloud that had come over me. I felt overwhelmed by the yoke of disappointment: I was not for forgiving. So, we had a monosyllabic dinner.

Back home I went immediately to bed and woke in the night to a feeling of total oppression. I got up and walked out on to the balcony and then came back in and lay down on the carpet.

Victor woke up and I told him that it was all over. I would complete the writing of the contract about how he could use the pictures I had painted, in total eleven clauses, and then leave. Eventually, I got back into bed – but not too close. In the morning we made it up a bit and I cried and cried and that made him cry too. Part of me had died inside. My romantic child within felt dashed and broken.

I told Victor that I found him deceitful and cowardly for not telling his ex-wife and family and that not telling them would only compound problems for himself, his family and me. Grace had been uncharacteristically short with me on the phone the day before.

What had happened was that after he had given Lucien a lift to work he had gone home, felt tired and gone to bed. He had not talked to Grace, but had headed back to the guest house at midday. He had gone to Red Hook to see if I was going to catch the noon or one o'clock boat and then went to Lindbergh Bay, in case I had gone there. That was his story. But I had already left the island.

Diary 26 June 2002

Decided to stay. Felt wretched and tired because of my change-able nature and because my love for Victor has changed. I lay in bed; he worked at the manuscript of the book I had illustrated. We have scanned the paintings and they look really lustrous and wonderful – even better than the originals. They have a depth of colour that enriches them. We make love and it feels a bit better, but why do I feel imprisoned in this reproachfulness? Why can't I just 'snap out of it'? I doze, he types, till we go for an evening meal at the marina. I look around at other men. They are mainly yachties, gnarled and boring, sitting drinking while flirtatious women hang around in a tawdry glamour. What a life!

Back home we make love, but my romantic inside still feels battered. I have asked Victor at dinner to tell his wife and he has agreed, but wants to do it in his own time. I tell him to tell me when he has told his family. He feels he is not deceitful – just cowardly. I long to go to the house and just tell them!

At 3 a.m., Victor phones Lucien. No, he doesn't need a lift today. Victor gets up for his 5 a.m. shift and although I intend to get up too it's suddenly 8 a.m.

Diary 27 June 2002

I have breakfast and change rooms, paint a shark picture that Victor has asked for to supplement my work. I go out and do little chores, and find a hairdresser of some repute. But she doesn't speak English and, no, she doesn't have purple hair colour. My purple patch has gone to a rather dingy colour, near to the dreaded brown. Eventually she understands that I am happy to wait for her to buy the dye for me and she says it will be a permanent colour – good! Then, as if back on holiday, I go to Coki Beach where I haven't been before. I think they feed the fish because there are masses of them – 'they' being Coral World, home of a glass shaft going down into the sea so that you can get underwater views without getting wet. Now, why would you want to do that? To me, Coral World is an eyesore and makes the beach next to it busy with folk visiting the monstrosity. It even cuts off the view of the open sea – the horizon that's so important to me! It's funny, I get a sense of ennui about beach and island life, but when I actually sit on a beach it's different. It's OK once I get there.

★

I had discussed with Victor over dinner the previous night how I could see my life. Five to six months in the Caribbean running yoga holidays in the upper 'conference' room at the Island Beachcomber Hotel with Victor running a taxi service (his thoughts of what he might do after finishing with the post office). He would do island tours, and also promote my services as a masseur; six to seven months in Crete where he could work at the American military base, teaching wrestling and helping Dave and me with our holiday business. This would mean that he would still see his family in the winter. So, with that mapped out, life was possible. We also discussed again his coming to South Africa to see me on my Venus descendent line – and we could marry!

But after our roller coaster times, his secrecy and cowardice we would have to see: the bottom no longer dropped out of my stomach so much when I saw him. Needing to have my romantic side nurtured seems so difficult for people to comprehend. Dave, my long-term lover, had once fallen foul of the same thing for a whole week, and more, after he had failed to go swimming in the sea with me on a full moon night when we were on holiday together in Corsica. I had been so excited about a moonlit swim I could barely eat dinner. He could never understand how I could just throw away the whole of our relationship because of his reluctance to swim with me. It was a terrible holiday. In fact as I write this book I've just had a look at Corsica astrologically: Mars and Neptune lines cross over at about the latitude where we had our big row.

The book says, paraphrasing: All things considered, this may be the most undesirable place to be as Mars's aggression gets mixed up with Neptune's uncertainty. It is possible to feel victimisation partly because aspirations are out of proportion to reality.

Well, my aspirations were certainly not met on that occasion and my reaction was certainly out of proportion.

That was another story, so back to the now! I knew I could not have shown myself in a good light to Victor, being out of sorts to the point of feeling like a victim and seeking petty ways of getting my own back. Even though he had agreed never to do it again I just couldn't let it drop. I thought back to the fact he had been late seeing me off from St Thomas before, that he was last off the plane in Dominica, how he was not focused on my arrival when I returned to St Thomas. He was just never in the right place at the right time. And Dave always was.

On a wall in the guest house was a framed photo which Victor told me is from a calendar in which he featured – and sure enough I could recognise the younger Victor in the picture. The small ear and shape of the forearm gave it away. So, he had been a model. At least some things he told me were true.

Diary 27 June 2002 (continued)

I must ask Victor why he is a coward. What does he fear? Because generally he is not fearful.

Now I'm at Nisky Complex having my hair done purple. Everyone says this is the place to come, but they don't seem to have a clue how to arrange artistically a patch of purple. In the end another customer who is watching me wrestle with the hairdresser comes over and directs the proceedings. She tells the hairdresser where to apply the paintbrush. It's not perfect but at least the atmosphere calms down a bit after the tension of a possible bodged job.

I cannot stop thinking about Victor. I feel he has done well to put up with me being so changeable, telling him it's all over one minute and then it's not. Not exactly exemplary behaviour! I have asked Sai Baba to take away from me this problem of not coping when dreams are dashed. It has helped me feel sanguine all day, but I am not sure that Victor is the man for me now, even so. The tricky part of this relationship is not being able to see each other regularly and just letting our relationship develop in a relaxed 'normal' fashion – it's either all or nothing and I can't seem to find a way of minimising that. And it shouldn't be about big decisions all the time. It could be relaxed. It could be without Pluto!

The secrecy, cowardice and not facing things before they escalate remain serious issues. After all, I know his wife wants to talk to him – hardly surprising – so how can he just walk out of the house without telling them what is happening, particularly as it's school holidays so childcare must be at a premium? I feel a loss of confidence. Why have I come back here – to this?

I get home at 8.15 p.m., purple hair done. Victor follows me in at 8.25 p.m. and I tell him how I think he has done well to put up with me. We go out for dinner and immediately I become limp and distant with him again. What a change from last time we were here at this restaurant when I couldn't stop kissing him. Now we feel very apart. The constant unhappiness at staying high and dry in a hotel away from his family, his not telling his family, make me feel so estranged. We keep up a miserable conversation, but that's all.

Back at the hotel I feel he is yesterday's man and decide that I shall leave once we have finalised the terms for his using my pictures. I really can't stand much more of this. Or of myself? In

Hawaii men were always leaving me. This time I shall do the leaving. In a way, I see a shadow of his beauty and try to chase it, but it's hard.

I cannot even paint the pictures for Pat and Theresa in St Kitts, I am too unhappy.

Diary 28 June 2002

Awake at 4 a.m. and I can hardly bring myself to look at Victor. I feel ten years older than on Monday when I skipped into the restaurant at Lindbergh Beach just after meeting him at the airport. I doze and then get up and finish writing the agreement about the pictures. I feel really out of sorts and I can't stand being like this: really unhappy, but aware that just a few things (Victor telling his family) would really change my mind. I must not depend on the activities of others for my moods!

I want a shoulder to cry on and I think of Leanne at the Island Beachcomber hotel. Ha! She's off till Sunday, so no respite there. I decide to see Victor at his morning break. He's meeting someone over his break to do with a land deal so he can't see me for long. OK, so he tells me about an idea of his and his cousin Elmo to build a house out of a lorry container. I ask if he has permission for this on his land. He smiles and says that when they see it they'll agree. I want to cast a doubt over it, to give his confidence a knock – why is he always so sure of himself and me so unsure? He doesn't seem concerned so I try throwing another spanner into his confidence: I tell him I am most unhappy being stuck in a hotel. I feel so oppressed and all I am doing is moaning! He asks me how I cope when something big goes wrong. No problem, I say and I know it's true.

I go to a beach, but the whole thing is still eating me up. I want to leave, but I have said I will be here to receive my birthday cards on the third of July – my forty-ninth birthday. My mind still runs over the details: Victor says he is concerned what effect his family knowing about me will have on his sons. I wonder what effect it is having not telling them. I had threatened Victor that I would tell Grace myself and he asked me today if I have done that. He almost smiled as he asked me. Perhaps he would like me to. I can't bear the fact that Grace was so generous in her admiration of my pictures – real heartfelt praise.

Did a few errands and got back to the hotel feeling better, distracted from my unhappiness. But the prospect of seeing Victor put me back into a loop of despondency, floppiness and oppression. I feel I can hardly breathe, let alone be civil. His manner assumes that if life is going OK for him, it must be for me too. No!

I need to get out of this oppression – after all, I create my own reality. I could stay in St Thomas but move out of the hotel, perhaps see if I can find a family to stay with, like I did in St Kitts or Barbados.

Victor comes in and I tell him how I feel (again!) and he tells me that it would make life too complicated for him if he told his family now. I believe it. He says he can spend more time at the hotel, but it will be spent on the manuscript – I have no problem with that! I suddenly remember that this floppiness occurs when my fire (Aries moon) is extinguished and my cool, damp Cancer sun leaves me feeling a victim and I just withdraw. Why hadn't I remembered that before? At least it explains it to me. Why had I forgotten it? We are suddenly back to being lovers and all playful.

Diary 29 June 2002

Victor up early to go to work. We will be together again at 1.30 p.m. I go into town and write the agreement for Victor's use of my pictures on the computer and do emails. Lots of birthday emails. Time passes quickly and I meet Victor and we go to eat lunch near the beach. Life feels good with him. Not quite as good as it did, but good. Then he takes me to see where he lives. I sit in the car while he goes in and I wonder what the neighbours think. A white woman sitting in Victor's car outside his house! Not that I care about neighbours, but it was an interesting moment. We go back to the hotel for Victor to work on the manuscript, but we make love and then he sleeps all night through. So we are in bed from 4 p.m. to 8 a.m.!

Diary 30 June 2002

I got to see Victor's piece of land today and I think I might have a look at designing the trailer idea for a house. We went to the beach – Linquist. It's beautiful. Then to buy me a little food so we have food in the room instead of eating out all the time. Though that evening we eat out. Victor wears a formal shirt but open to the chest. As he leans forward at the bar I see the deep curve of his chest. Oh, it does turn me on, so he buttons it closed. At the restaurant there are people he knows so he asks me to cool it a bit. I sit on my hands a bit and do as I am told – most of the time.

We go home and make love most exquisitely. Next thing we know, it's 4 a.m. and time for work. A new day and month!

Diary 1 July 2002

Victor leaves for work and I sit and read *Autobiography of a Yogi*. As usual, it puts me to sleep as soon as I have read enough to assimilate and have a new take on life. I rise at 7 a.m. and do some more paintings. Victor's changes to the script mean that there are now some paintings which aren't correct and others are needed. I am also finishing off the paintings for Theresa. I have no idea how I will feel about painting when I reach Rio, my next adventure, so it's important to do all I can now. I book the de luxe suite at the guest house, as Victor wishes, and we'll move in this afternoon. No rush, slowly, slowly as Victor says when we make love. Room 13.

Into town so that I can put the agreement about the use of the pictures on to disc. I feel good about this. All's well. I go off to Lindbergh Beach and see Leanne at the Island Beachcomber. Great – she's there! But now I don't need a shoulder to cry on. She's had her hair tightly braided. It looks painfully tight. My purple hair looks good, but not as bright as in Dominica – a bit too dark. I have come to realise what an excellent safety feature it is. If I'm lost: Seen a woman with purple hair? There could be no maybe, it's yes or no.

I talk to Blare, the stressed-out manager who says he's laid-back. He tells me to put my idea of yoga holidays in writing to the owner. Blare tells me that October and November are quieter months so those would probably work. We might not have to pay for rooms before knowing whether we have people to fill them. Not all winter though, as they are busy after Thanksgiving. Well, that gives me some thought for the future.

Today I could become pregnant by Victor. I like the idea, but I haven't put it to him yet. It's a bit scary but I'll put it to him and see what he thinks – after all it's a physical risk to him of getting herpes, and he may not want to be a father again. Just been watching a beach wedding. All romantic: couple, priestess, two photographers and two impromptu guests.

I'm much more confident about snorkelling than when I was here last. I went out for forty-five minutes, then rang Victor and agree to meet him at the Internet café when he's finished work at 2 p.m. Oh! Every time the café door opened I looked up to see if it's him. Eventually it was. Went home together to our new room.

Proposed over dinner the idea of making me pregnant. Victor wanted to think about it, but smiled. Went to bed and just fell asleep without a thought to anything. Woke up at 2.30 a.m. and set the alarm for 4 a.m.

Diary 2 July 2002

I moved the clock hands to 4 a.m. but forgot to set the alarm button so Victor was late for work. I finished *Autobiography of a Yogi* and sent that and my *Frommer's* travel guide off to Dave with a note saying read the book – not *Frommer's*! The day ran late for me too. I was supposed to meet Victor at his 11 a.m. break but got talking to someone I had met the time before when I was on St Thomas and then went to the hairdresser – the purple is fading too fast! The bus to the Sugar Estate post office eventually came, then went a more circuitous route than usual and even got stopped by the police. So, I was a bit late. That still can make me anxious – speed up, speed up, a voice keeps saying inside me. I don't like my being late, given how I feel about Victor's time-keeping.

We came back to the guest house together and Victor paid for the new room. Then he returned to his shift and I went to get the purple done again – so much for permanent colour.

I tried to get all the pictures scanned to disc at a nearby computer shop, but no, not possible. I didn't want to send the portraits to St Kitts without keeping a record of my work. I just beat Victor back to the house. He had called at the hairdressers, but I had just left. Never in the right place at the right time… hmm.

Out for lunch, made love, time for dinner. We often go to the Mill for dinner, its food suits me. But oh, if we were living in a house, we could cook. Cheaper and more natural. This half-life of hotel/living together just doesn't suit me. It doesn't feel as if we are quite living together, just being together with work and holiday elements mixed up. Home again to lovemaking and tomorrow is Wednesday, Victor's day off – no alarm needed. Used a condom, so that's the answer about pregnancy. I feel momentarily a bit let down, but it's a fleeting feeling.

So, why all the detail, day after day? Well, it gives you the idea perhaps of just how it feels to be changeable. It's exhausting and tedious. Maybe what I have written makes you impatient with the book – but that's how I personally felt about it too! And now it was nearly time to leave Pluto.

Diary 3 July 2002 (written on the fifth)

Birthday girl!

Got up, had breakfast, did chores, Victor typing more changes, me packing ready to leave. Victor got me a lovely top and pair of matching pants for my birthday – they're gorgeous. We chose them together, but I wouldn't have even known the shop. In Charlotte Amalie I tend to keep my head fairly well out of shop windows – it could be dangerously expensive to do otherwise. There was no post on the third so I have received two physical cards and lots of e-cards. More proper cards may of course follow. My birthday turned out to be Emancipation Day holiday in St Thomas. So, there was a real festive feel in the air. In the street I ran into the owner of the Internet shop and found out that I share my birthday with his father – more celebrations! I spent some time too in meditation and writing items down to help me to leave Victor – they are in the back of my diary. We have a last dinner together going to the Pointe restaurant for a change – saves being maudlin and sentimental about the Mill. Best to go to a fresh place. A gourmet meal with just the right amount to eat – not overwhelming, just totally satisfying.

Back home we make love big time. He really is a dream of a lover. I fall away from him feeling dizzy. My head is on leaving and I have a numbness in my mind, just like I used to get as a child just before sitting an exam. A quietness of mind so that I might keep my energies intact. Now, I had the anticipation of leaving, but without wanting to think of it.

But I must go, follow my mission. Victor concerns me because he never seems to do much without a cigarette or booze break. The bottle of brandy I gave him lasted untouched for days, then a drop went and two days later the empty got tossed in the bin. What am I looking at? He laughs more, now that I am happy. He is happy with his progress on his book, but feels he needs to finish it before returning 'home'. This has been a window of opportunity for him. I have looked at keeping in touch via mobile phone, but what they use in the USA isn't compatible with South America so it wouldn't work. So much for one world!

My birthday feels a bit odd. We do finishing off chores and I don't swim. Now that is unusual. In Greece I always swim on my birthday. I swim most days anyway. Well, not swimming will keep my hair purple – sea water kills the purple. The purple is so dark it looks almost black, like a so-called black tulip. It's a bit of a shock to be dark haired.

Part of me felt a bit disappointed not to have 'done' more in the time I have been here, but another part says it was necessary to stop and restore my batteries before going on. A much-needed rest after getting 'beached out' down the Caribbean. The packing went slowly, torpid even.

Diary 4 July 2002

OK, this is it! The aromatherapy oils help me with the travel ahead: benzoin, on my wrists for the journey. I cry a little at breakfast. Victor then types, I quietly do things towards leaving. The agreements for the pictures are signed and the manuscript does read better for Victor's work. He tussles to get what he calls 'the messages' in the right place, though some of the changes are more profound in his eyes than mine.

I feel very calm: almost not thinking, not wanting to think. I have given Victor a Sanjeevini card about duplicating the vibrations of medications, but he now gives it back to me telling me he is way beyond that stage. He occasionally seems to want to vie with me on spiritual progress.

I've been here ten days and the bottle of Courvoisier lasted three days unopened and then disappeared a while ago. I have been counting the number of Guinness bottles and occasional rums Victor has in restaurants. Is it a lot? I don't know. Victor's Sagittarius moon could give rise to addictions.

At the airport I join a short queue, but have a long wait. We still have time for a coffee, but I fall into ill humour with the serving girl who won't give me hot water with a drop of milk in it (I don't drink coffee since having had a duodenal ulcer, and I still keep to that regime because I have a certain weakness in that area). Victor comes to my rescue with the waitress and I get what I want. We chat about this and that. He tells me we are only time and space away and I agree. From time to time I sniff the benzoin. It's a real comfort.

Then I go through customs, disappear, and look back for a moment. Victor is still there, then I go. That's it. The mundane takes over and I leave St Thomas and the long journey starts to unfold. I fall asleep directly I get on the plane. I suddenly feel weary. Obviously the emotions of leaving have all been there, just tied down.

I wake to see the clear, turquoise blue sea of the Bahamas. I muse for a moment about visiting them, but my desire is to press on with my 'mission', as I now seem to regard my travel. I have not left Victor in order to dilly-dally in the Bahamas, but to go and meet Jupiter in Rio. The fields are again black, burned and ready for planting.

★

So, what have I learnt? Money grows on trees: don't fear poverty: I live beyond my means.

Don't sleep around: have a period of innocence to allow intimacy to develop. This is a discipline for staying faithful, which any husband would seek in a wife (and vice versa).

Acknowledge my own womanhood, let go of the character of a stereotypic man. I now have the opportunity to see if I can be steadfast to Victor. Treat men like girl friends; I am their sister. Sexual relations are not power trips; they are the flowers of a period of growth: a period of innocence.

There are plans other than mine, relax and let them arise.

Humour myself; I am not responsible for everything. Nobody is to blame for my relationship with Dave ending; it has been an opportunity for growth, no need to kick myself.

Miracles happen; they are often the small things that feel like a little magic wand, keeping us safe or giving life an extra portion of fun – the twist of lemon on the top of a drink.

Death, loss, rejection and victim still remain words to be dealt with, but I'll get there – watch out Pluto I'll be back! Except that I had met the loneliness of death at Titou Gorge and confronted my own mortality.

Of Barbados – just don't let me go on honeymoon there, divorce would hang in the air.

Of Pluto: setting an agenda for change seems to work. So, if you want a quiet, stable 'normal' life, as I did on returning to St Thomas to stay with Victor – you'd be on the wrong planet. 'It can be more than the organism can bear,' the A★C★G book said.

In Miami, I went to the beach. It was busy: fourth of July – American Independence Day! So, I got free celebratory food in a bar, picking my way carefully between the meat dishes. Another thing I have learnt: never get anxious, because God's plan is always best.

In the evening I caught the plane and all went without a hiccup. There was no veggie food on board. I felt lonely: no one sat by me. From my window seat I looked down into the twilight. I left Miami in a blaze of patriotic fireworks all over the city. What a send-off!

Notes in the back of my diary, to help our parting:

Let me always feel my love for Victor and his for me like a fresh daisy and let my longing for him dissolve in that love. Let there be no sense of loss, knowing our hearts are linked. Amen.

I shall go to Rio tomorrow knowing that any day I can return. I stay by my own free will. God stands beside me and within me.

Let my love for Victor be restored and refreshed each day. I don't need to see God to love him/her more each day, so I don't need to see Victor either for my love to remain and grow, for he is a manifestation of God and God's love.

Let our parting have joy in the knowledge that only time and space separates us and the bond of love and joy remains, to be relinquished only if it is outside of our life paths.

May the time till we meet again flow beautifully for both of us so that our separation strengthens us. Amen.

★

But somewhere within me lurks a shadow: how deep is our love? With Dave it had affected every cell of my body, and somehow this felt just pore deep, but so, so intense. How could I turn and put my new lover behind me so easily? I knew more than ever that I was held on my journey and protected so that I could continue it; just a feeling of numbness reminded me of our love. I faced Jupiter in the morning.

Postscript

Well, are you ready to rock 'n' roll? Have I whetted your appetite to take an A★C★G trip or shall I hold your hand as we travel to Jupiter and beyond?

As you can see, taking the easy routes can be hard and taking the hard ones can be liberating, but as Maggie in San Diego would say 'The world's your stage – play on it!'

Appendix

Glossary

Astro★Carto★Graphy the means of my travel described by Equinox Astrology: www.astrocartography.co.uk. It allows you to know what it would feel like if you were born in another part of the world and therefore had a different astrological reading as an overlay on your original birth chart. For me, feeling rather stuck, it provided a means of experiencing change in my life so that I could move on.

Devas A deva can be described as a spiritual force that is part of nature and which can be drawn into being to help a physical aspect of nature – like a woodland or tree.

Gayatri Mantra A powerful Indian chant taught to me at Sai Baba's ashram. It is very good for endurance.

Herbalife Herbalife International Inc., supplements for healthy nutrition and weight control. www.herbalife.com.

Kinesiology A method of finding answers to questions about yourself by turning inward and asking your inner self for the answer to a question, then muscle testing to see what the answer is – yes or no. I used the Perelandra method of muscle testing as described in the literature produced by Michaelle Small Wright www.perelandra-ltd.com. I often refer to Kinesiology in the text as asking myself a question, rather than referring to it specifically by name.

Maggie Smith	Flower Essence Practitioner and producer, www.FlowerEssenceEnergy.com
Mary McFadyen	a Reiki master, one of only twenty-two masters initiated into Reiki by Mrs Takata who brought Reiki to the Western world.
Medicine Cards	produced by Jamie Sams and David Carson for everyday use, 1997 published by Bear & Company, Santa Fey, New Mexico. Copyright St Martin's Press.
Meditation to Planet	This was a method taught to me by Sue Parker, a Huber Method Astrologist in North Wales. The method for the meditation is to first of all become quiet, look at your birth chart, place it in the direction of the planet you want to visit. Relax. Imagine yourself in the centre of your birth chart and then, with your eyes closed, ask for a guide to appear. You take note of what the guide is like. Then you roll out a silver carpet in the direction of the planet and see what the planet looks like. You walk with the guide down the carpet and visit the planet. You feel the energy of the planet. You ask several questions and ask the guide for assistance if you don't understand the answers. So I asked what energies the planet wanted from me, whether the planet was getting enough of these energies from me already, what gift the planet has for me and what I do with the gift: where I carry it and what it is for. Then you say thank you to the planet, walk back up the silver carpet with your guide. Roll the carpet back up again and say thank you to your guide. Then open your eyes and write down how the guide was, what the planet looked like and the answers to the questions.
Nature Essences	These are a set of Nature Program Essences, each containing a balancing pattern which is

not found in any single element or combination of elements found on the planet. They can be used instead of antibiotics. Instead of killing the microbes in your body, they balance the energies between your body and microbes so you become symptom-free without upsetting the balance of nature. They have been developed by Michaelle Small Wright at Perelandra Centre for Nature Research in Virginia (USA), www.perelandra-ltd.com.

Reiki Tera Mai™   Tera Mai is the trademark of Kathleen Milner, who developed this particular branch of Reiki. It is a form of energy healing using symbols. The initiation that practitioners receive involves a 'calling in' of guides and people to help the practitioner to be a channel for healing energies.

Sanjeevini   This is a method of vibrational healing which can duplicate the vibration of pharmaceutical products. It is described in the book, *Sanathana Sai Sanjeevini... Healing Fragrances, A Healer's Guide* by Poornima Nagpal, published by Sthitapragnya, Mumbai, India. Available for free downloading at http://www.saisanjeevini.org.

Sathya Sai Baba   Usually described in the text as Sai Baba, this is a holy man in India whose ashram I had visited in New Year 2000 and again in September that year. I also visited the ashram in 2001. He is known as a man of miracles and for me he took away my bad temper on my first visit and made changes to me, at my request, on subsequent visits. I first came across his name in a Reiki call-in of guides when I was initiated into the Tera Mai™ system of Reiki, an energy healing system.

Seichem Tera Mai™	This is a form of energy healing using a wider range of energies than Reiki.
West Crete Holidays	A holiday business providing yoga and health holidays run by Juliet Green and David Lister in Crete, www.westcreteholidays.com.
Women Welcome Women World Wide (5W)	A women's international friendship organisation, more details from www.womenwelcomewomen.org.uk.

Bibliography

Doughty, Andrew and Harriett Friedman, *Hawaii The Big Island Revealed The Ultimate Guidebook*, second edition, Wizard Publications, 2001

Lewis, Jim, 'Astro★Carto★Graphy Explained. Analysis of three locations for Juliet Green. Interpretation by Jim Lewis', produced by Equinox Astrology.

——, *Astro★Carto★Graphy Explanatory Handbook*, produced by Equinox Astrology

Porter, Darwin and Danforth Price, *Frommer's Caribbean from $70 a Day*, 4th edition, Hungry Minds Inc., 2001

Walsch, Neale Donald, *Conversations with God Book One*, Hodder and Stoughton, 1997

Wright, Machaelle Small, *Perelandra Garden Workbook*, Perelandra Ltd., 1993

Yogananda, Paramahansa, *Autobiography of a Yogi*, Self Realization Fellowship, 2006

27493624R00199

Printed in Great Britain
by Amazon